UNLOCKING TRIATHLON

Training Plans and Coaching Support for a Confident Race Day

Alison Freeman

HUMAN KINETICS

Library of Congress Cataloging-in-Publication Data

Names: Freeman, Alison, 1971- author
Title: Unlocking triathlon : training plans and coaching support for a confident race day / Alison Freeman.
Description: Champaign, IL : Human Kinetics, [2027] | Includes bibliographical references.
Identifiers: LCCN 2026017951 (print) | LCCN 2026017952 (ebook) | ISBN 9781718245686 paperback | ISBN 9781718245693 epub | ISBN 9781718245709 pdf
Subjects: LCSH: Triathlon--Training | Coaching (Athletics) | Triathletes--Training of
Classification: LCC GV1060.73 .F732 2027 (print) | LCC GV1060.73 (ebook) | DDC 796.42/57--dc23/eng/20260715
LC record available at https://lccn.loc.gov/2026017951
LC ebook record available at https://lccn.loc.gov/2026017952

ISBN: 978-1-7182-4568-6 (print)

Acquisitions Editor: Kessa Kuyper
Senior Developmental Editor: Laura Pulliam
Publication Services Manager: Anna Lan Seaman
Senior Graphic Designer: Joe Buck
Cover Designer: Keri Evans
Cover Design Specialist: Susan Rothermel Allen
Photograph (cover): Patrick McDermott/Stringer/Getty Images Sport/Getty Images
Photographs (interior): © Human Kinetics, unless otherwise noted
Photo Manager: Taylor Canada
Photo Production Manager: Jason Allen
Senior Art Manager: Kelly Hendren
Illustrations: © Human Kinetics
Editorial and Composition Services: S4Carlisle Publishing Services
Printer: Sheridan Books

Human Kinetics books are available at special discounts for bulk purchase. Special editions or book excerpts can also be created to specification. For details, contact the Special Sales Manager at Human Kinetics.

Printed in the United States of America 10 9 8 7 6 5 4 3 2 1

The paper in this book is certified under a sustainable forestry program.

Human Kinetics
1607 N. Market Street
Champaign, IL 61820
USA

United States and International
Website: **US.HumanKinetics.com**
Email: info@hkusa.com
Phone: 1-800-747-4457

Human Kinetics' authorized representative for product safety in the EU is Mare Nostrum Group B.V., Doelen 72, 4831 GR Breda, The Netherlands.
Email: gpsr@mare-nostrum.co.uk

L1341

For all my athletes – especially my beginner triathletes and first-time finishers – who have allowed me to be a part of their journey and bear witness to their incredible accomplishments.

CONTENTS

ACKNOWLEDGMENTS

This book wouldn't be possible without the athletes I've coached and my incredible coaching colleagues. My athletes entrusted me with their dreams and, in doing so, gave me a platform to grow as a coach and educator. My fellow coaches have generously shared their knowledge and support throughout my years of coaching, and none more so than Julie Dunkle and Maria Simone.

My family's support is unbounded. My husband, Chris, patiently endured months and months of "don't talk to me, I'm writing," and still replies "as you wish" when I ask him to refill my water bottle. My three children, Gray, Colby, and Daisy, who will always be my greatest achievement, have actually bragged to their friends about *me*, and any parent will understand the significance of that statement. And my parents, Fran Freyman and Dana Lowry, are the biggest cheerleaders a kid could have.

The writing aspect of my career would never have gotten off the ground without my editors at *Triathlete Magazine*: Emma-Kate Lidbury, Susan Lacke, Chris Foster, and Rebekah Brately, who provided the space for me to find my voice and become the writer I am today.

Lastly, it has been a joy to work with the entire Human Kinetics team. I am indebted to Kessa Kuyper for initiating this entire adventure by sending the best email I have ever received. Laura Pulliam's gentle guidance refined and clarified many discussions in the manuscript, and Anna Lan Seaman patiently shepherded it into book form, helping to craft a finished product that I am immensely proud of.

INTRODUCTION

Completing a triathlon is an inspiring, sometimes big, often scary goal. I tell all my beginner triathletes – of which you are now one – that they are braver than most for even considering the goal. Where others will quickly rattle off why they could never complete a triathlon, you looked at the challenge and found it exciting. Maybe exciting and a little daunting, but that's what we triathletes call fun.

That daunting piece probably brought you here, because preparing for a triathlon can feel complicated. There's the gear, the training for three sports at once, maybe learning a new sport or two along the way, and then figuring out how to put all three sports together on the same day. That's why you've sought guidance, and that's where I come in. I have over a decade of experience working with beginner triathletes, and over the course of this book I will share all of my beginner triathlete guidance and conversations with you.

I realize you may not be a beginner athlete, but a beginner triathlete. Maybe you've even completed your first triathlon, but you still feel like you have a lot to learn. If so, your experience with swimming, biking, or running, or a background in sports or fitness, provides a solid foundation for your development as a triathlete. If not, that's okay, too – with time and focus, I believe that anyone can become a triathlete. No matter your background, this guide aims to meet you where you are and build from there. The information provided within this book will supplement the experience you already have and fill in the gaps across swimming, biking, and running. On top of that, we'll layer information designed to increase your athletic and triathlon-specific IQ to maximize your training, your fitness development, and your success on race day. You'll apply those skills and that knowledge to a training plan tailored just for you, using sport-specific training levels appropriate for your background and experience in each sport.

We will, however, start with the basics. I want to make sure that you know what you're signing up for, what you'll need to get across the finish line, and what it takes to get there before you commit to your race. I also want to ensure that you select your race with intention and clearly understand your "why," the driving force behind your motivation to complete a triathlon. (Already selected your race? No worries – not everything happens in order.)

With those basics in place, we'll turn to skill and fitness development. We'll cover the full range of swim, bike, and run skills necessary to support your fitness growth in each sport. You'll get up to speed (pun intended) on transitions – swim-to-bike and bike-to-run – so you can be quick without hurrying. And you'll learn the fundamentals of fueling and hydration, so that your body will be primed to take advantage of your hard-earned fitness come race day.

We'll also discuss training zones and when and why we train in each one. We'll talk about when and how we build both speed and endurance, and the role that strength training plays in overall fitness development. We'll walk through how we structure training weeks, cycles, and seasons to maximize fitness development and prepare you for race day.

To translate those skill and fitness development concepts into practice, I'll walk you through how to use the training plans provided in this book to build a tailored training plan for your season. We'll draw from three distinct types of plans to construct your season: preseason training plans, sprint- and Olympic-distance training plans, and the Olympic- to half-distance training plan. The preseason training plans are designed to provide a sport-specific or overall fitness boost before beginning a sprint- or Olympic-distance training plan. The sprint- and Olympic-distance training plans are built with flexibility, so they can be tailored to both your strengths and those areas where you'll need more support. The Olympic- to half-distance training plan is singularly focused on building the endurance necessary to cover 70.3 miles (113.1 km) with confidence. I will guide you through the process of selecting and sequencing the training plans to support your triathlon season, ensuring you've chosen the right plan (or plans) to best fit your chosen race (or races), your athletic background, and your current fitness level.

Once the training plans are loaded onto your calendar, we'll walk through the keys to successfully executing them: approaching workouts with intention and an open mind, layering execution and mental skill development onto fitness development, and incorporating race specificity into your training environments. Knowing that things never go exactly according to plan, you'll be given clear guidelines for handling the inevitable training disruptions caused by injury, illness, or just life.

And then – finally! – we get to race day. Actually, race weekend. We'll walk through the whole weekend, in extraordinary detail, so you know what to expect every step of the way. From writing a race plan to your race day packing list to your day-before meals, we'll cover every aspect of race weekend. We'll tackle race day itself, starting from the moment your alarm goes off, so you can envision every minute before the start and every mile of the race right up to your hard-earned finish line. And finally, we'll discuss what happens after your race. You'll have the chance to conduct a post-race reflection, capturing the experience and codifying what worked well and what you might want to improve upon if there's a next race. We'll also discuss how to choose your next adventure, triathlon or otherwise.

Across everything – the fitness and skill development, the training plans and their execution, and your race experience – my goal for you is to fall in love with the sport just like I did. For the structure and pattern of training weeks, the ebb and flow of training, racing, and recovering, to become a part of you. For you to be so enticed by the quest for a perfect race that you can't not come back to it, season after season.

I believe the key to loving the sport is to enjoy the process of training as much as you enjoy the experience of racing. And to enjoy either, let alone both, you need to feel like you are succeeding. Succeeding is built upon having the tools for success: Not just knowing what to do in training, but also how and why. Not just developing fitness, but also developing the skills that allow you to use that fitness wisely come race day.

You have already shown that you are brave enough to take the plunge into triathlon and wise enough to seek guidance along the way. By absorbing the information found within this book, you will understand how to develop fitness, increase your triathlon skillset, and know what to expect come race day. By applying that knowledge – and a bit of dedication – to the training plans, you will not just show up at the start line of your triathlon prepared and confident, you will finish with your head held high and a smile on your face. And I cannot wait to see that happen.

– Coach Alison

PART I

GETTING STARTED

> We [do these things], not because they are easy, but because they are hard.
>
> John F. Kennedy

It's part thrilling and part terrifying, but you're going to do it. You're going to complete a triathlon. You know it will take work to achieve this Big, Scary, Awesome Goal, and you are prepared to tackle that challenge head-on. But where do you start? At the beginning, of course – by making sure you know what you're signing up for, choosing the perfect triathlon for you, and ensuring that you're fully equipped to get the job done.

1

DEMYSTIFYING TRIATHLON

Yes! You're going to do it: You're going to complete a triathlon. Maybe it's a well-thought-out plan, maybe it's a completely spontaneous goal, or maybe it's on a dare. You might be able to articulate exactly why this challenge appeals to you, or it may be more of a vague feeling that you can't quite explain. No matter how you got here, let's make sure that you understand what you're signing up for and why you want to tackle this challenge.

So, what *are* you signing up for? You may think you are simply signing up to complete a triathlon. That's certainly a part of it, but whether you realize it or not, when you sign up for a triathlon, you are also signing up to become a triathlete and join the triathlon community. And you may or may not know instinctively *why* you are signing up for a triathlon, but your reason is surprisingly important – and we'll make sure to get to the bottom of that. But first, let's start at the beginning: by ensuring you understand the event you're signing up for and the community that you're joining.

Defining Triathlon

Simply speaking, a triathlon is swimming, biking, and running, in succession and in that order, without taking an extended break between sports. And while you typically don't have a picnic or take a nap between sports, you will spend a few minutes switching from swimming to biking and biking to running, so a triathlon also includes those swim-to-bike and bike-to-run transitions.

There are four standard triathlon distances: sprint-distance, Olympic-distance (the distance in which athletes compete at the Olympics, sometimes referred to as *international-distance*), half-distance (a.k.a. an *Ironman 70.3* or *Half-Ironman triathlon*), and full-distance (a.k.a. an *Ironman triathlon*). We typically refer to sprint- and Olympic-distance triathlons as short-course events and half- and full-distance triathlons as long-course events. Each of the four triathlon distances has corresponding standard distances for each of the three sports, as shown in table 1.1. Given the nature of roads and trails and the challenge of creating bike and run courses that are exactly a specific distance, it's not uncommon

TABLE 1.1 Standard Triathlon Distances

	Sprint	Olympic	Half	Full
Swim	750 meters (0.47 miles)	1,500 meters (0.93 miles)	1.2 miles (1,930 m)	2.4 miles (3,860 m)
Bike	20 kilometers (12.4 miles)	40 kilometers (24.9 miles)	56 miles (90 km)	112 miles (180 km)
Run	5 kilometers (3.1 miles)	10 kilometers (6.2 miles)	13.1 miles (21 km): half-marathon	26.2 miles (42 km): marathon

for a race to vary slightly – or sometimes more than slightly – from these distances.

These distances, while common now, evolved alongside the birth and development of the sport of triathlon. Triathlon originated in San Diego, California, in 1974, with 46 local athletes competing in a swim-run-bike multisport event. The Collins family participated in that inaugural event and enjoyed it so much that they spearheaded additional local triathlons in Southern California. Then in 1978, after relocating to O'ahu, Hawaii, John and Judy Collins pioneered the full-distance triathlon. They combined the courses from three existing events – the Waikiki Rough Water Swim, the Around O'ahu Bike Race, and the Honolulu Marathon – to create the "Hawaiian Iron Man Triathlon." Fifteen athletes participated in that original long-course triathlon, and by 1980, when ABC's "Wide World of Sports" first televised the event, it had grown to over 100 participants.

Peter Read Miller/Sports Illustrated via Getty Images

Then, in 1982, "Wide World of Sports" captured Julie Moss's iconic crawl to the finish line, and a movement was born.

At about that same time, Carl Thomas, a marketing executive at Speedo and former all-American swimmer at UCLA, conceived of a shorter triathlon event that would be more accessible to the everyday athlete and more attractive to the International Olympic Committee. In 1982, Thomas and Jim Curl, a California-based sports promoter, launched the United States Triathlon Series (USTS), featuring a new, shorter race distance. They drew from existing Olympic events – the 1,500-meter swim, the 40-kilometer bike, and the 10-kilometer run – to create the international standard distance triathlon. Over the next two decades, triathlon gained popularity, and the sport grew both in the United States and internationally. Finally, in 2000, triathlon was added to the Olympics as a medal sport.

The Ironman-distance and international, or Olympic-distance events, along with their halved partners, have cemented themselves as the standard distances for triathlon. While the allure of long-course triathlons may be what initially drew you to the sport, the short-course distances provide a more accessible and smarter entry point for first-time triathletes.

Defining the Triathlete Community

To understand triathletes and the triathlon community, you first need to understand type II fun. You are probably already familiar with type I fun, which is just . . . regular fun. Type I fun encompasses everything you normally think of as fun, like attending a game night with friends or seeing your favorite band in concert. Things that are fun while you're doing them and fun to remember afterward.

Type II fun is a little different. It is largely specific to physical activity and is not so much fun while you're doing it as it is challenging. It is fun – or more accurately speaking, it's rewarding – to remember it afterward. I know that doesn't exactly sound like the fun you're familiar with. But I'm guessing you can look back and remember something you did – a challenging hike or a long bike or run, for example – that was difficult in the moment but is kinda cool to think about now. That's type II fun.

Triathlon is chock full of type II fun, and for some crazy reason, that appeals to triathletes. We choose goals that we know present challenges, and we find that exciting. We're not looking for the easy route or the slam dunk, but rather something that will push us outside our comfort zone and beyond our current limits. The fact that success is not guaranteed draws us toward the challenge and drives us to do the work necessary to achieve our goals.

We know this journey will require us to get uncomfortable and even suffer a bit along the way. We aren't bothered by that; in fact, a piece of us seeks that out. That may sound a little nuts, but bear with me here. A good friend, licensed therapist, and overall insightful human once told me she never understood my enjoyment of extreme endurance events until she remembered the psychiatrist Victor Frankl. She explained to me that Frankl, a holocaust survivor who wrote *Man's Search for Meaning* in 1946, believed there are three ways people find meaning in life: through creating a work or doing a deed (think artists, crafters, gardeners, and volunteers); through experiencing and appreciating love, beauty, and goodness; and through the attitude we take toward suffering. She suggested, and I believe, that we triathletes – and endurance athletes in general – find some meaning in life through suffering, that we find personal fulfillment in pushing ourselves through grueling events and coming out the other side whole, with a deeper understanding of who we are and what we are made of.

Beyond that, I believe that we triathletes – and endurance athletes in general – find even deeper meaning in sharing these experiences and this suffering with fellow athletes. There is certainly personal satisfaction in getting through a tough workout or a long run on a cold, rainy day. But it is even more gratifying to finish a long run, soaking wet and shivering, and celebrate the shared triumph with your running partner. It's like a shared secret, an experience that only those who were there can truly understand and appreciate.

What Is a Triathlete?

A triathlete is any person who finishes a triathlon: who swims, then bikes, then runs, in that order and without taking an extended break between sports. Period, full stop.

To be a triathlete, you don't have to swim, bike, or run a certain pace. You don't have to look a certain way or be a certain age. You can be first or last or anywhere in between; you just have to swim, then bike, then run, in that order and without taking a break in between.

You also don't have to do a full-distance triathlon to be a triathlete. An individual who finishes a sprint-distance triathlon is just as much a triathlete as one who finishes a long-course triathlon. It's not about the distance; it's just about swimming, then biking, then running, in that order and without taking a break in between.

And once you're a triathlete, you're a triathlete for life.

Defining Your *Why*

The enjoyment of type II fun and the meaning we find in pushing ourselves to or even beyond our limits drives many triathletes to their 1st and 15th and even 50th finish lines. But that doesn't have to be why *you* have decided to complete a triathlon. You have your own reason for being drawn to this sport, and that's fine. Your reason – your "why" – doesn't have to make sense to anyone but you.

But let's back up for a second. What exactly do I mean when I talk about your "why"? I'm referring to the gravitational force that pulled you toward this Big, Scary, Awesome Goal of completing a triathlon. What you hope to find in the process of training, out on the race course, or as you cross the finish line. It's the voice in your head that can't be quieted or the feeling deep down in your gut that won't go away. You may already be able to define your "why," or it might take some time to surface, but I believe it's in there somewhere. Even if your "why" didn't immediately present itself when I teed up this conversation, *something* brought you here. If you give yourself some space and some quiet and remember to listen for it, your "why" will present itself. Maybe all at once, or maybe just in glimpses at first, but eventually it will rise to the surface.

Once you've found your "why," hold onto it. This "why" of yours matters. It matters because training for and completing a triathlon is not easy, and as exciting as the challenge is, it's still a challenge. There are going to be days when you really don't feel like lacing up your shoes and going for a run, or driving to the pool, or heading out on your bike. Mornings when that alarm comes way too early. Miles that feel like they stretch forever and moments when you question what the heck you were thinking getting yourself into this whole thing. Your "why" will carry you through those moments, get you out of bed, and get you started on your workout, even when your mind is screaming "no." Your "why" is how you will ultimately get the job done.

2

CHOOSING YOUR RACE

Choosing your triathlon is so exciting. It's the embodiment of your Big, Scary, Awesome Goal and your "no-turning-back-now" moment. I want you to be excited when you click "Sign Up" and officially commit to your race. I also want you to go in with eyes wide open, fully aware not only of what you will do between the start and finish lines but also of what it will take to arrive at the start line prepared and confident.

Because when you sign up for a triathlon, or any endurance event, you are committing to more than just the race. You are also committing to the training required to prepare for the race. The race is one day. One possibly arduous, challenging day, but one day and a discrete number of miles and minutes (or, more appropriately, hours). You do need to think about that day and whether the date and event distance and venue location and all the additional details will work for you. But you also need to think about all the weeks before the race, when you'll be training alongside all the other things you normally do in a week, and ensure that those weeks are compatible with the training necessary to prepare for your chosen race.

So, let's approach this race-choosing exercise with intention. We'll start by selecting your race distance, ensuring the required training fits into your life along with your other commitments and activities. Then we'll determine the optimal months in which to schedule that training. With that timing in mind, we'll find a race that meets these criteria while considering factors such as race location and course details. Before you officially sign up, we'll make sure you have buy-in from your people to pave the way for support instead of friction. And we'll wrap up the exercise by discussing goals for your training season and your race. (If you already selected your race, that's okay! This exercise will highlight where your chosen race aligns with your life and give you advance notice of possible challenges.)

Selecting Your Race Distance

I already said this, but it bears repeating: When choosing your race, what you are actually choosing is the training. If you love the idea of the accomplishment but cannot – or just don't want to – squeeze all the swim-bike-run hours into your week, then it becomes really hard to make the idea of that accomplishment a reality. As a coach, my primary goal is to set you up for success. I do that in part by ensuring that the training you commit to is training you can and want to do. So, let's make sure you understand the training required for each race distance, compare those hours to the hours you have available in your life, do a quick gut-check on the commitment, and then make your race distance selection official.

Understanding the Training Commitment

The number of workouts you'll complete each week and the number of hours those workouts will consume stem directly from your race distance. Race distance, number of workouts, and training hours are tied together for two distinct and important reasons. First, you'll need to individually prepare for the three sport-specific distances, achieving the fitness in each sport to cover – or often exceed – that sport's race distance in a single workout. For example, to cover a 25-mile (40-km) bike leg after you swim and before you run, you'll want to prepare so that you can cover 25 miles (40 km), and more typically 28 to 30 miles (45-50 km), in a single training session. Second, you'll want your overall peak, or maximum, weekly training volume to appropriately support the total time you'll be on the race course during your event. In other words, you want your peak weekly training volume to exceed, typically by an order of magnitude, the amount of time it'll take to complete your triathlon.

Table 2.1 shows the number of workouts and weekly training volume, and table 2.2 shows the longest swim, bike, and run workouts that the average triathlete will complete when preparing for each of the four standard triathlon race distances. A few factors can push an athlete's training schedule outside the ranges shown in table 2.1. For example, a faster athlete might complete their training in fewer hours, or a more competitive athlete might add workouts or increase their training volume to further enhance their fitness. Most athletes, though, along with the

TABLE 2.1 Weekly Training by Triathlon Distance

	Sprint	Olympic	Half	Full
Swim workouts	2	2	2-3	2-3
Bike workouts	2	2	3	3
Run workouts	2	2	3	3
Total workouts	6	6	8-9	8-9
Average volume	4-5 hours	6-7.5 hours	8.5-11 hours	10.5-14 hours
Peak volume	4.5-5.5 hours	7-8 hours	11-14 hours	14.5-17.5 hours

TABLE 2.2 Longest Workout Duration by Triathlon Distance

	Sprint	Olympic	Half	Full
Longest swim	1,000+ yd/m	2,000+ yd/m	2,500-3,000 yd/m	4,000-4,500 yd/m
Longest bike	15 miles (25 km)	30 miles (50 km)	55-60 miles (90-95 km)	100+ miles (160+ km)
Longest run	3+ miles (5+ km)	6+ miles (10+ km)	2-2.25 hours*	2.5-3 hours*

*For long-course triathlon training, we limit longest-run durations because of the increased training stress and fatigue resulting from extending these long runs even further.

training plans provided in part V of this book, will follow these training patterns and fall within these ranges.

As you wrap your head around these numbers, we also need to factor in time spent outside of swim-bike-run training. Most athletes will benefit from incorporating strength training sessions into their week, so that's another 0.75 to 1.5 hours. Then there's driving to and from the pool and possibly to the starting point of your bikes or runs, plus extra laundry and lots of snacks and recovery time on the couch during those bigger training weeks. Which is all to say: You need to round up, padding those weekly training volume ranges by at least 1.5 hours and potentially several times that.

Understanding Your Life

So, how do those hours and workouts listed in tables 2.1 and 2.2 mesh with your life, as it's currently structured? You may have looked at the numbers, hours, and distances in the tables and immediately gauged how much of that your life can accommodate. Or maybe you have a race distance in mind and assume that the training will fit into your life simply because you want it to. Maybe it had never occurred to you to think about how much time it takes to train for a triathlon. Whatever your initial thinking, let's take a minute to put an actual pencil to paper, mapping out your typical weekly commitments and activities, then filling in workouts and hours in the space remaining. I want you to really work through the details of when you're going to do all these workouts and how your life will be affected by adding them to your calendar. Go ahead and do it now; I'll wait.

Now that you've mapped out your weekly schedule, you have a clearer picture of what your life allows for in terms of workouts and training volume. And by "allows for," I specifically mean what fits within your week in a way that won't ruin your relationships or lead to a bad performance review at work. Setting yourself up for success starts with not putting more on your calendar than will actually fit. So be honest and realistic, not optimistic or expecting compromises or assuming that you'll suddenly become a morning person after 15 years of sleeping through your alarm. With all that in mind, note the race distances with corresponding training patterns and volumes that align with the time available on your weekly calendar.

Incorporating the X Factors

You did a great job determining how much training your life can accommodate, and now we have just a few more factors to evaluate before you lock in your final answer on race distance. First, consider not only how much training your life *can* accommodate but also how much training you *want* your life to accommodate. Maybe your weekly schedule does have room for 6 to 8 weekly hours of Olympic-distance training, but 6 to 8 hours of weekly exercise is more than you can get your head around, or you want to be sure to protect a sufficient amount of family time or time for other hobbies or even couch time. No problem. You don't have to pick the longest distance race that is compatible with your calendar, so scale back to the distance that feels best for you and your life and how you want triathlon to fit into it.

You also want to factor in your athletic background and current fitness level when looking at race distances. I believe anyone with any athletic background, from no fitness experience to varsity captain, can complete a triathlon of any distance . . . given enough time to prepare for it. But to get there, you have to start where you are and build slowly. So, unless you are currently training 6 to 8 hours per week, have experience with endurance events lasting 4 or more hours, or have previously completed an Olympic-distance triathlon, you'll be best served by selecting a sprint- or Olympic-distance event this season. If you do have a high volume of current training, or triathlon or endurance event experience, you could consider a half-distance triathlon. However, ideally, you'll still plan for a sprint- or Olympic-distance practice event before the half-distance race. I recommend that all athletes hold off on considering a full-distance triathlon until they have at least one season of experience training for and completing an Olympic- or half-distance triathlon.

Okay, that's everything you need to consider! You've got the training pattern and schedule required for each race distance, the training pattern and schedule that your life will accommodate, how much training you actually want to do, and your athletic background and current fitness. That Venn diagram will converge on the viable distance options, so we've finally arrived at the moment when you get to pick the race distance for your triathlon from that list. You got it? Yes! Big decision made.

Selecting Your Race

Now that you've selected your race distance, you're ready to select the triathlon itself. We'll look at your calendar to determine the best window for focused training and identify possible race weekends. We'll then find triathlon options at your race distance that are available on those weekends, evaluate the choices, and settle on the best available event for your triathlon.

Checking Your Calendar

Similar to how you looked at your weekly schedule to determine where the training sessions would fit within your days, you also want to step back and examine your annual calendar to determine where focused training weeks will best fit within your year. No one expects triathlon training to proceed for months on end without the occasional disruption from other aspects of your life, but ideally, you want to minimize disruption during the most important weeks of training.

Scan your calendar for a period of at least 5 weeks, and optimally 6 to 8 weeks, that is free of known training conflicts. By "known training conflicts," I'm referring to vacations, projects that extend your working hours, family commitments, and so on. And to be clear, you're looking for this block of conflict-free weeks to coincide with the months when triathlons are typically scheduled in your area. (Most regions schedule their triathlon season from late spring through early fall, but those living in tropical climates might find their triathlon seasons flipped from that schedule.) Once you find the ideal window for peak triathlon training, note the weekends at the end of that window as possible race weekends.

Checking the Race Calendar

You've decided on the race distance and identified some race weekends that will allow you to focus on training during those critical final weeks, so now it's time to find the actual race. If you have friends, family, colleagues, or acquaintances who've done triathlons, they are a great resource for getting to know the local scene. If not, the website for your country's governing body for triathlon – such as USA Triathlon, British Triathlon, or AusTriathlon – often provides a comprehensive, searchable listing of all sanctioned triathlons. Alternatively, an Internet search for "triathlon near me" will yield both websites that list events and websites for local races.

Once you've had conversations with local triathletes and have done the web searches, put together a list of possible race options on your selected weekends and at your chosen distance. Ideally, there's a local race of your

Getting Buy-In

Before you hit "Submit" on your registration, I recommend teeing up conversations with your people about the journey you're about to embark upon. By "your people," I'm specifically talking about the individuals who might feel impacted by your focus on something other than them. And you want their buy-in because they are probably the same people you are hoping will show up to support you throughout your training and on race day, despite the fact that they are getting less of your attention. Possibly they are already on board and excited for you, but if not, giving them a heads-up on your plans will do wonders to grease the wheels for the future.

chosen distance on the perfect weekend, but that's not always the case. You might need to expand your list of options to include less-than-local races, look at other weekends, or even consider other distances in order to have a few races to choose from. But if you end up with only one option, then that option will do.

Weighing Your Options

Whether a single race makes up your entire list or it's populated with a wealth of options, it's good practice to familiarize yourself with the features and characteristics of each event you're considering. Start with the race location and its proximity to your home, thinking through exactly how you plan to get yourself, your bike, and your gear to the race venue, as well as the timeline and cost of those travel logistics. Look at the race venue and course profile, which provide important clues about your potential race experience. Are you swimming in a pool, a lake or reservoir, a river, or an open body of water? Are you cycling on roads or trails, are they flat or hilly, and are they long and uninterrupted or requiring lots of turns and maybe even U-turns? Same for the run – road or trail, flat or hilly?

When considering race details, there is no "right" recipe for your triathlon, but there is the recipe that's right for you. If you have identified races of your chosen distance and on your selected weekend, but those races have deal-breakers – you don't want to drive more than two hours or have to stay overnight at a hotel, you don't want to swim in water with a current, you don't want to bike on trails – then those races should come off your list. If that eliminates all the races from your list, you may need to revisit the race distance or date to find one that avoids your deal-breakers. Choose a race that will set you up for success by finding the trade-offs that yield your best possible race option.

With that work behind you, you're finally here. You found race options that meet your criteria for race distance and date, evaluated the logistics and characteristics of those races, revised your criteria as needed, and considered your choices. And now . . . drum roll, please . . . it's time to officially decide on your triathlon. Have you picked it? Yes! Huge decision locked in.

Setting Training Season Goals

You did it! You went through an intentional process to select your triathlon, got buy-in from your people, clicked "Sign Up," and now you are ready to start dreaming about the finish line. You may even be tempted to start thinking about your race goals. And I did say that we'd wrap up by discussing race goals . . . but what I actually meant was that we'd discuss why you shouldn't yet define them. (Sneaky, right?) Because here's the thing: From where you sit today, you have no idea how your training will unfold, how your sport-specific fitness will develop, and how that individual sport fitness will hold up on a multisport day. If this is your first triathlon, you don't yet know how you will feel when you put all three sports together on race day, especially when you get to the second half of the run. You'll better understand your race-day potential as you move through your training, particularly when you complete your longest workouts and race simulation days. So, let's hold off on setting specific race goals until we get closer to race day, and for now just stick with the Big, Scary, Awesome Goal of completing your race.

You can, though, start thinking today about goals for your training season. Broadly speaking, your training goals outline what you plan to put into your training season – your training execution and skill development – and what you hope to get out of it – your fitness development. We'll take a deep dive into skill development, fitness development, and training execution across parts II and III, so for today, we'll start with big-picture training season goals, a blueprint you can build on as you move through the next two sections of the book.

We can look at our friend Alex's Season Goal-Setting Worksheet from their first triathlon season as an example of how to think about season goals. If you're a big fan of goal setting, you can create a document based on the worksheet to set your goals and track progress against them. If not, the worksheet can serve as a backdrop for this conversation. Either way, let's put pen to paper – literally or figuratively – as we walk through the development of your training season goals.

Start by listing the race (or races) you're training for and their date, distance, and course features and characteristics, since your training goals will be defined specifically to support your success on race day. Then go through each discipline – swim, bike, run, and triathlon – and

Alex's Season Goal-Setting Worksheet

Race Name, Date, Distance, and Course Attributes

- Sunset Triathlon, August 11th
- Olympic-distance (1,500 m swim + 27 mile bike + 10 km run)
- Lake swim + road bike (moderately hilly) + dirt run course (flat)

Season Goals

Swimming: Some experience

- Skill development: skills focus TBD, definitely need to learn open-water swimming skills
- Fitness development: swim 2,000m comfortably

Cycling: Brand new, weakest sport

- Skill development: starting from scratch, need to learn all the skills but focus on bike handling
- Fitness development: bike 30 miles

Running: Lots of experience, strongest sport

- Skill development: skills focus TBD
- Fitness development: run 7 miles; improve 10K pace

Triathlon: Brand new

- Skill development: need to figure out workout fueling
- Fitness development: feel comfortable training 6 days a week, improve strength

Training:

- Establish good training habits (finish every workout!)
- Don't skip the strength training

note your experience level; pinpointing your strongest and weakest disciplines identifies where you can capitalize on your strengths and where you have the greatest room for improvement.

Next, determine skill development and fitness development goals for each discipline. Make skill development a high-priority goal for any discipline where you lack confidence, especially when that's due to limited experience. If you don't yet know enough about a discipline to identify specific areas for skill development, you can leave those lines blank for now and fill in the details as you move through part II of the book. In terms of fitness development, having the endurance to complete the race distance for all three triathlon sports is – obviously – an important goal. If you have a solid base of fitness and experience in a sport, you can also consider adding a goal to improve your speed or pace in that sport. Triathlon fitness goals often address overall strength and fitness development, such as weekly training volume.

Finally, let's think about training execution goals. Consider your prior training habits, or even life habits, and reflect on how those habits could show up in triathlon training and, therefore, on race day. Create training goals based on either habits you want to reinforce, habits you'd like to change, or both. If you're struggling to come up with a training goal, workout consistency is a great place to start, and chapter 11 will provide plenty of additional options.

So there you have it. Your race has been selected, your season goals are in place, and you are primed and ready to step into your triathlon journey. Next, we'll make sure you are fully geared up for the task at hand, and then we'll take a deep dive into each of the three (actually five – trust me on this) triathlon disciplines.

3

SELECTING ESSENTIAL GEAR

I happen to be a person who loves gear. And when I commit to something, I am all in. So when I began training for my first triathlon season, I also began accumulating tri stuff. I bought a bike, of course, and I also ordered a triathlon top and shorts and a wetsuit and a transition bag, and probably a few other things. As the packages started piling up, my husband started to question exactly what was going on. I mean, it was February and therefore months before my first race. Plus, my husband is decidedly not a gear guy and figured I could have just made do with what I already had. It turns out we were both right, to some degree. I definitely did not need to purchase all of that gear before my first race. But I did use everything I bought, and enough times that all of my purchases ended up being completely worth it.

What's the lesson here? I guess that while you can purchase a seemingly never-ending list of gear to support your triathlon training and racing, you can also largely make do with what you already have. There are likely a few pieces of gear you'll need to add to your collection for training, racing, or both, but you can hold off on purchasing much of the rest until you know you'll be sticking with this triathlon thing for a while.

With that in mind, let's walk through the complete list of gear you could use for triathlon training and racing. There's a big difference between could use and absolutely will use, so as we move through the list, I'll be clear about what's required, what's recommended but not mandatory, and what's optional. It's also worth noting that you probably already have some of the gear you'll need, so the shopping list may not be quite as lengthy as it appears. To make the list feel more manageable, you might want to note the gear you already own or have access to, the gear you need to purchase now, and the gear you might need – or want – to purchase down the road.

Swim Gear

There's the swim gear you need for training, likely in a pool, and the swim gear you need for race day, assuming you'll swim in open water for your event. We'll go over the swim gear for pool training here and dive into what you need for open-water swims in the Race-Day Gear section.

Alison Freeman

Required

- *Swimsuit*. Specifically, a swimsuit designed for lap swimming rather than casual splashing around in a lake or the ocean.
- *Goggles*. Swim goggles come in lots of colors and subtly different styles. Look for practice goggles, which are more comfortable than competition goggles, and be sure to get a tinted pair if you swim outdoors. Pro tip: If the gasket forms a seal around your eye socket without using the head strap, the goggles fit (a proper fit minimizes leakage).

Recommended

- *Swim cap*. Anyone with hair on their head, especially long hair, will benefit from a latex or silicone swim cap. And everyone will need to wear one for their triathlon, so it's good to get accustomed to the feel before race day.
- *Swim paddles*. Swim paddles are to swimming what hills are to biking and running: They increase resistance and build power. Paddles also improve your feel for the water and so are often used in swim drills. Swim paddles should be sized so that they extend from the base of your palm to just beyond your fingertips; bigger, in this case, is not better.

Optional

- *Swim fins*. Swim fins can help improve body position and increase propulsion, making it easier to execute swim drills. Look for shorter, training swim fins rather than longer, floating fins.

- *Swim snorkel.* A swim snorkel, which features a center-positioned breathing tube instead of the side-mounted version used for snorkeling, allows you to focus on your stroke technique and isolate it from your breathing technique.

The Bike

A bike is, of course, required. Which bike, though, merits discussion. First off, any bike will get the job done, especially for your first triathlon and even more so if it is a sprint-distance event. You do not need a new bike, or a triathlon-specific bike, or even your own bike. You can use any bike with two wheels and no motor as long as you have ridden it at least a few times before race day. If you want – or need – to purchase a bike, there are two things to keep in mind as you search for your new steed. First, start with a road bike (rather than a triathlon, or time trial, bike) because it's more comfortable, easier to handle, and more applicable to different riding environments. If you fall in love with the sport, there will be ample time in the future to upgrade to a tri bike. Second, there are lots of great deals on used bikes and multiple tiers of bikes to choose from, so don't feel that you have to buy a new bike or the fanciest bike – new or used.

What you do want to prioritize, whether you're getting a new or new-to-you bike, entry-level or top-of-the-line, is ensuring the bike frame is the right size for you. How do you determine your bike size? I wish I could give you a straightforward formula, but unfortunately, it's not that simple. Your height and inseam, as well as your torso length, arm length, and hamstring flexibility, all influence your bike fit. Beyond that, bike frame sizes and the range of saddle height and handlebar positional adjustments differ by manufacturer, so "your bike size" isn't going to be the same for each manufacturer. Given that complexity, I recommend starting the process by consulting with a professional bike fitter. Your local bike shop often has a bike fitter on staff who can recommend bikes they sell that offer the frame size and adjustability best suited for your body geometry and preferred bike position.

Bike Components and Accessories

As if getting a bike wasn't enough, you also want to pay attention to the bike's components and accessories. By components, I mean all the parts of the bike except the frame, as they contribute to the comfort and functionality of the bike. Accessories are items that go with the bike but don't come with it when purchased.

Required

- *Saddle*. No, I did not think you would ride a bike without a saddle. But you certainly might ride a bike with a profoundly uncomfortable saddle. Saddle fit, which directly relates to comfort, is highly individual, so the saddle that comes with your bike may or may not be the most comfortable one for you. If you're not comfortable on your bike (you will know), then swapping saddles can do wonders for your overall enjoyment of cycling.
- *Tires*. Again, I'm not worried that you'll ride a bike without tires, but it's worth making sure you have tires that aren't worn out and that offer a good balance of puncture resistance and road grip – neither bulletproof-but-slow tires nor racing slicks. While you're looking into that, make sure you know the recommended tire pressure for your tires.
- *Bike tire pump*. Speaking of tire pressure, you'll need a bike tire pump to set your tire pressure, which you will do before every ride.
- *Bottle cages*. Carrying fluids while cycling is essential, so you'll want at least one bottle cage mounted on your bike frame. If you plan on doing an Olympic-distance or long-course triathlon, you'll benefit from mounting a second bottle cage on the frame (if possible) or behind your saddle.
- *Bike water bottles*. A bike-specific water bottle has two important characteristics: First, it fits securely in a bike bottle cage. Second, it has a sport-top lid so that you can drink from it using one hand while the other steers your bike. You'll want at least one or two to start, but don't be surprised if you end up with an entire collection.
- *Flat kit*. Getting a flat tire while biking is an inevitable part of the cycling experience, so as insurance, you'll want to carry a flat kit on every ride. A small bag secured under your saddle can be a great way to carry the flat kit components, which will differ depending on whether you are riding tubeless or tubed tires, along with a bike multitool.

Recommended

- *Bike safety lights*. Bike lights are a key safety element for anyone cycling on the road. High-powered lights with a steady beam or a blinking light pattern attached forward-facing to the handlebars and rear-facing to the saddle or seat post will make you more visible to cars from both directions.
- *Bike computer*. A bike computer attaches to your handlebars and provides real-time information on your speed, distance cycled,

elapsed time, and more. Entry-level bike computers will determine speed and distance based on your wheel rotations; higher-end models are GPS-based and include maps, grade, and elevation information, among other features.

- *Cadence sensor*. As you'll learn in chapter 5, your cycling cadence provides valuable information about your cycling efficiency. To measure your cycling cadence, you'll need a cadence sensor paired to a bike computer or a multisport watch (which we'll get to in the Etcetera section).

Optional

- *Top tube bag*. A top tube bag is a small zippered bag or pouch mounted on the top tube of your bike frame, directly behind the headset (where your handlebars connect to your bike frame). The top tube bag helps carry snacks, car keys, and so on.
- *Clipless pedals*. Your bike will likely come with flat pedals, which you can use with sneakers or running shoes. It may come with cages for the flat pedals, also called *clips*. For this reason (although I will always take issue with it), the pedals you clip into with compatible cleats mounted on cycling shoes are called *clipless pedals*. Clipless pedals allow you to take advantage of the full 360-degree pedal rotation, but they do require some getting used to. If you plan to make the leap to clipless pedals, give yourself plenty of time to practice with them before race day. Also, make sure you get road-specific clipless pedals, rather than those for mountain biking or gravel cycling. (As you consider pedal options, I believe that clipped – caged – pedals are actually more risky than clipless as they are harder to get out of quickly.)
- *Aero bars*. Aero bars are the straight, forward-facing bars that come standard on triathlon bikes and can be mounted onto the top, flat section of drop bars for road and gravel bikes. They offer a distinct aerodynamic advantage – as in, they make you faster – but they also require solid bike handling skills. As with clipless pedals, be sure to allow plenty of time to practice riding in the aero bars before race day.
- *Power meter*. While a power meter is one of the best tools to help you become a better cyclist, it is not something you need as a beginner cyclist. If you stick with the sport long-term, love data, and want to improve your cycling, then you can explore cycling with power. (If you have or purchase a power meter, it will also serve as your cadence sensor.)

Cycling Gear

Once you have the bike and it's properly equipped, you want to make sure *you* are properly equipped with the personal items that will keep you safe and comfortable. The following gear is designed to ensure exactly that.

Required

- *Helmet*. Absolutely, unequivocally required, for every ride, always. But it doesn't have to be fancy – any bike helmet under 5 years old will do just fine. (After 5 years, the materials start to break down, and the helmet will no longer protect your head.) I would, in fact, steer clear of the pointy-tailed aero helmets; unless you maintain sufficient speed and the correct head position for the vast majority of your ride, you won't get the promised aerodynamic benefit.

Recommended

- *Cycling shorts*. As the primary point of contact between you and your bike, the chamois – or padding – included in bike shorts will do wonders for your comfort and therefore your enjoyment of cycling. Cycling shorts have a wide range of price points; typically, the more expensive the shorts, the longer you'll stay comfortable.
- *Cycling jerseys*. Cycling jerseys differ from regular workout tops in that they include rear storage pockets. These pockets are great for holding car keys, snacks, and discarded layers, and can even hold a bike water bottle.
- *Cycling gloves*. Your hands are the second point of contact between you and your bike, so a pair of (fingerless) cycling gloves with a bit of padding is a staple element of the cycling wardrobe.
- *Chamois cream*. While cycling in clean bike shorts prevents most chafing, the occasional discomfort or saddle sore is somewhat inevitable. You'll be happy to have some chamois cream at the ready when the need arises. (Pro tip: To minimize chafing, nothing – as in, no underwear – is worn under cycling shorts.)
- *Cycling sunglasses*. Sunglasses will protect your eyes from anything kicked up from the road by passing cars or other cyclists. Cycling-specific sunglasses are additionally designed to reduce glare and prevent fogging, making them a worthwhile upgrade from your everyday pair.

Optional

- *Cycling layers*. Cycling shorts and a short-sleeved top or cycling jersey will typically suffice for cycling in temperatures from the mid-60s and up (18+ degrees Celsius), but below that you'll likely want to add some layers for warmth. Long-sleeve cycling jerseys

Your Local Bike and Run Shops

In the age of e-commerce, I feel compelled to point out the value of your local bike and run shops. Let's start with your local bike shop (a.k.a., your LBS). From cycling clothing to bike components and accessories, your LBS is your best and most accessible resource for anything on your shopping list. Their service center is also your go-to resource for bike maintenance and learning about your bike components, including how to change a flat tire. Additionally, the LBS personnel typically includes at least one bike-fitting expert who can help with your initial bike purchase and future adjustments as you get more comfortable on your bike. You'll benefit from forming a relationship with your LBS and turning to them for any bike-related needs you might have.

Similar to your LBS, your local running store serves as a key resource for your running gear needs. Most importantly, your local running store is the best place to purchase running shoes. Running shoes cannot be selected based on color or style, and they should not be purchased without trying them on. The staff at your local running store is knowledgeable about running shoe brands and models and have years of experience matching runners to the right shoes. Additionally, they often offer a generous return policy for shoes in any condition, allowing you to try them for a few weeks, knowing that you can return them if they don't work for you.

and jackets, like standard cycling jerseys, offer storage pockets and are often designed with wind protection for added warmth. For temperatures below the mid-50s (sub-13 degrees Celsius), full gloves, a thermal jacket, toe covers for your shoes, and even leg warmers can be helpful. Bonus points for layers that are "packable" and can be stored in jersey pockets if the temps warm up during your ride.

- *Cycling shoes*. Cycling shoes are necessary if you need to mount cleats for your clipless pedals. Entry-level shoes will get the job done, but if you want an upgrade, look for shoes with carbon fiber soles. Just be sure to get shoes compatible with your cleats, as the mounting hole placement varies by cleat type.
- *Cycling socks*. Cycling-specific socks will keep your feet warm, avoid blisters, and can even help with aerodynamics. Plus, they make a great fashion statement.

Not Recommended

- *Headphones*. I'm a firm believer that headphones have no place in cycling. Sure, music, audiobooks, and podcasts help make the time go by. But – especially, *especially* on the road – your full attention should be paid to your surroundings. Even on the trail, you'll benefit from hearing the calls from oncoming cyclists and fellow trail travelers.

Run Gear

Compared to cycling, running feels like a gear-light sport. But a few run-specific items can make your running experience that much more enjoyable.

Required

- *Run shoes*. The most important role running shoes play is that of injury prevention. Your feet and lower legs absorb an incredible amount of impact when running, and your shoes provide the support that helps your body handle that repeated impact stress. For that reason, you should only run in run-specific shoes that have been selected specifically for your foot structure and run mechanics. Additionally, running shoes should be replaced every 300 to 500 miles (500-800 km), or every 6 months, as wear does compromise their function.

Recommended

- *Run shorts, tees, and socks*. There is nothing more chafe- and blister-inducing than wet cotton. So do yourself a favor and invest in shorts, tees, and socks made from sport-specific fabrics designed to wick away sweat. (Pro tip: As with cycling, to minimize chafing, nothing is worn under the built-in briefs or shorties that come with running shorts.)

Optional

- *Run layers*. Similar to cycling, shorts and a short-sleeved tee will work well for running in temperatures at and above the mid-50s (13+ degrees Celsius). Below that, you'll benefit from adding long-sleeve layers and a hat, and as the temps drop further, adding a running jacket, running tights, and gloves. Wick-away fabrics for these layers help keep you warm, as damp and cold feels notably worse than just cold.
- *Running hydration vest or handheld running water bottle*. If your long runs last beyond an hour, especially in temperatures above 70 degrees Fahrenheit (21 degrees Celsius), carrying water becomes extremely helpful, if not a true safety concern.
- *Running sunglasses, hats, and visors*. All of these accessories protect you from sun glare during your run. Hats and visors additionally offer sun protection and keep sweat from dripping down your face. Be sure to go with wick-away fabrics, as with all running gear.

Training Environments

While not necessarily gear, training environments are also a key factor in successful workout execution. I recommend thinking through your use of or access to the following training environments in advance of when you will actually need them.

- *Outdoor cycling and running routes*. If you're not yet a cyclist or a runner, you likely don't yet have a mental catalog of routes of varying distances and profiles. Local athletes and the "popularity heat map" feature of workout tracking websites and apps are good route resources.
- *Gym or recreation center membership*. You'll likely need a gym for one or both of two important training resources: first, a pool for swim training, and second, indoor training options for cycling and running. For indoor bike training, look for a facility that provides access to spin bikes rather than fitness bikes, as they better mimic the experience of riding your own bike.
- *Access to an open-water swim venue*. You don't necessarily need access to open water throughout your entire training season, but practicing swimming in open water prior to race day improves both your open-water swimming skills and your confidence and comfort with open-water conditions.

Etcetera

In addition to swim, bike, and run gear, there are a few final, optional training items that you might find helpful throughout your training season.

- *Multisport watch*. A GPS-based multisport watch is a popular – maybe the most popular – accessory among triathletes. It can provide real-time data within your swim, bike, and run workouts and even more data to review afterward. Multisport watch models range from relatively cost-effective, entry-level options to very expensive, I-can't-name-even-half-the-features-this-includes models. The cost-effective ones will provide all the necessary swim, bike, run, and triathlon features, so there is no pressure to upgrade here.
- *Heart rate monitor*. Many multisport watches now include optical heart rate monitors, which can be somewhat accurate for some people and wildly inaccurate for others. A heart rate chest strap provides more accurate heart rate readings, but keep in mind that

"220 minus your age" is not, in fact, how you determine heart rate zones, and the heart rate data is useless if you don't know how to interpret it.

- *Indoor bike trainer*. There are several benefits to having your own indoor bike trainer rather than using a spin bike at the gym. First, an indoor bike trainer allows you to ride your own bike, so the bike fit and muscular demands are exactly what they will be when you ride outdoors. Second, using an indoor bike trainer allows you to train using a virtual cycling platform, which effectively mimics outdoor cycling and improves the quality of interval workouts. All that being said, a spin bike will absolutely get the job done.
- *Recovery equipment*. There are all kinds of fancy recovery tools on the market, but a basic foam roller is a great way to start building out your recovery toolbox.

Race-Day Gear

Keeping my story in mind, these items specific to race day don't need to be purchased today. I do recommend purchasing them at least a month before your race, though, so you can test out all your race-specific equipment before the big day.

Recommended

- *Triathlon shorts*. You can change your top in transition, but nudity is not allowed, and those port-o-potties are a bit cramped for a head-to-toe change. Which means you will need something you can wear for your entire race, or at least bottoms that will work from start to finish. Triathlon shorts, or tri shorts, are essentially bike shorts with a very minimal chamois and are designed to satisfy exactly this requirement. (Looking to limit your purchases? Your next best swim-, bike-, and run-compatible option is a swimsuit.)
- *Wetsuit*. Assuming that your triathlon includes an open-water swim and the expected water temperature is below the mid-70s (sub-23 degrees Celsius), you'll likely benefit from wearing a wetsuit for your triathlon swim. In addition to providing thermal insulation in cold water, a wetsuit aids in buoyancy and improves your hydrodynamics. In other words: You will typically swim faster in a wetsuit than without one. For your first wetsuit, a sleeveless (rather than full-sleeve) entry-level option is a good pick. Your local multisport shop may also offer wetsuit rentals, eliminating the need for an expensive purchase early in your triathlon career. Regardless of the source, make sure you select a wetsuit designed for swimming versus scuba diving or surfing, as the construction differs based on expected usage.

- *Body glide*. If you do wear a wetsuit, body glide helps avoid chafing on the back of your neck and, when applied to your wrists and ankles, makes it easier to get the wetsuit off when you're done swimming.
- *Backpack, duffel bag, or transition bag*. You'll need something to transport all your gear from your car to the race site and back, ideally in a single trip while also pushing your bike. Triathlon-specific transition bags are designed for that purpose, but any sufficiently large backpack or duffel bag will do.
- *Race belt*. A race belt is an adjustable belt that holds your race bib number, avoiding the need for safety pins and simplifying your transitions. (The race bib is not worn during the swim, may be required for the bike, and is always required for the run.) Many race belts also feature loops to hold gels or small zippered pockets for storage.

Optional

- *Triathlon top or one-piece triathlon kit*. A triathlon top, or tri top, is essentially a more aerodynamic, fitted bike jersey that pairs with tri shorts to create a complete tri kit, allowing you to wear a single outfit from top to bottom (well, except for shoes and socks) for swim, bike, and run. You can also opt for a one-piece tri kit instead of a tri top and short separates. In either case, a sleeved tri top or one-piece tri kit will be more aerodynamic and (surprisingly) cooler than a tank-style top.
- *Open-water goggles*. Open-water goggles offer a wider field of vision and typically come with tinted, polarized lenses to reduce sun glare. They are a relatively small addition to your gear locker that can make a noticeable difference on race day.
- *Speed laces*. Several varieties of elastic speed laces for running shoes are available, all designed with the same purpose: to eliminate the need to tie your running shoes. Tying your shoes mid-race may not seem like a big deal, but it feels surprisingly challenging when your heart is racing and you're rushing through transition. Plus, with speed laces, there's no concern that your laces will come untied mid-race. You may find that you never want to tie your shoes again.

And that's it. We made it. Yes, the list of everything you could purchase for your triathlon journey is extensive. But no, you really don't need everything on the list, and despite my first-season shopping spree, I can tell you with certainty that you don't need everything right away. Use what you have, purchase what's necessary as you need it, and by the time race day rolls around, you'll have a sufficiently equipped gear locker.

PART II

DEVELOPING TRIATHLON SKILLS

> Practice does not make perfect. Only perfect practice makes perfect.
>
> Vince Lombardi

During your triathlon training season, you will execute countless repetitions of swimming, biking, running, and triathlon skills: swim strokes and breaths, cycling pedal strokes and turns, running strides and hills, triathlon transitions and fueling. So let's make sure those repetitions reinforce productive and efficient movement patterns and habits. Part II will focus on the key swimming, biking, running, and triathlon skills that will support your success in training and racing.

You might be tempted to skip over a chapter that covers the sport where you already have some experience. And I get that – these skills chapters will naturally provide the greatest benefit for those sports where you are brand new. But the most successful athletes consistently work on their skills across all disciplines, from their strongest sport to those with a more obvious need for improvement. So I encourage you to read – or at least skim – each chapter in this section, because even if you have decades of experience in a sport, there is always more to learn and always ways to improve.

4

SWIMMING

Ahhhhh, swimming. By my estimate, roughly two-thirds of triathletes would list swimming as their weakest sport. Of those who don't, at least half have a swimming background. There's a logical reason why becoming a swimmer as an adult poses a bigger challenge than becoming a cyclist or runner: You likely learned to ride a bike as a child, running is a fundamental gait pattern that you don't even remember learning, . . . and then there's swimming. If you didn't learn to swim as a child, picking up the technique as an adult feels far from intuitive. And yet many say swimming is 90 percent technique and 10 percent fitness, so you can't just fake your way to swim proficiency. Becoming a swimmer as an adult requires focus, commitment, and attention to detail. And that focus doesn't end: Proficient swimmers still benefit from working on their technique during every swim session.

This chapter will provide an in-depth discussion of swim technique, specifically geared toward beginner swimmers – but even those with swim experience will find insights that can improve their swimming technique and efficiency in the water. We'll start with two big-picture thoughts that lay the foundation for how to approach swimming. Next, we will get you breathing smoothly, because with breath comes comfort. Then we'll discuss the three core principles of swimming, to maximize the effectiveness of your swim form. Finally, to translate our pool swimming to triathlon swim venues, we'll dive into the details of open-water swimming. Throughout this discussion, I will provide cues to help illustrate the techniques and that can be applied during your swim sessions to develop and refine your swim form. Because active focus on your technique during each and every swim session is what makes you a better swimmer.

And while this chapter focuses solely on freestyle swimming technique, let me clarify one point: There is no rule anywhere in triathlon that says you have to swim freestyle. Most people swim freestyle because it's the most efficient swim stroke, but it's not the only way to get from the swim start to the swim finish. You can choose to swim an alternate stroke for all or portions of the swim leg if you need to take a break or if *your* most efficient swim stroke is not freestyle. In fact, I recommend incorporating an alternate stroke, such as breaststroke or backstroke, into your swim warm-ups and cool-downs so you have an option in case you need to take a break on race day. But since freestyle typically *is* your most efficient swim option, let's get back to improving your freestyle technique.

Big-Picture Thoughts for the Beginner Swimmer

Before we get into the details of swim technique, let's review two big-picture concepts I discuss with all of my triathletes. These overarching ideas set the stage for the three core principles of swimming; think of them as the basis for your swimming mindset.

Pull, Don't Kick

Instinctively, many beginner swimmers rely on their kick to create forward propulsion in the water. I get it – you haven't yet established a strong pull, you know you need to move forward, and you really don't want to sink. Kicking, which is a more intuitive movement than the swim stroke, will get the job done and provide forward progress, but it does so at a cost.

Kicking actually serves three purposes within your swim: First, it provides propulsion (duh). Second, it keeps your legs closer to the surface of the water, which helps you maintain a level body position. Third, when timed correctly, it adds an extra bit of "oomph" to your pull. But here's the trade-off when you rely on your kick for propulsion: A strong kick requires rapid, powerful movement from the muscles in your hips and thighs. When those large muscles are used for rapid, powerful movement, they require a lot of oxygen. When your muscles' oxygen requirement increases, so does your heart rate and breathing rate, and all of that creates fatigue.

You may have seen competitive swim races where athletes kick like motorboats, generating incredible propulsion and moving like lightning across the pool. These sprint-distance swimmers compete in events lasting no more than a few minutes and can tolerate a bit of hypoxia, or oxygen deficiency, since they can rest and breathe after finishing their race. Endurance swimmers, including all triathletes and therefore you, compete in events with durations that exceed the body's capacity to manage hypoxia. Because of this, endurance athletes need to moderate the strength of their kick to properly manage their oxygen requirements, heart rate, breathing rate, and fatigue. In other words, if you kick hard, you'll get really tired, really quickly. So, to become an efficient endurance swimmer, you'll want to rely more on your swim pull for propulsion than on your kick.

Move Water With Your Arms

Knowing you need to create forward propulsion through your pull does not automatically translate to actually creating forward propulsion through your pull. We'll talk about the specific techniques that create forward propulsion in a minute, but for now, I want you to get your head around this: There is a profound difference between moving your arms through the water and moving water with your arms.

Bear with me while we briefly revisit high school physics (I promise, you will not be tested on this material). Let's think about Newton's third law of motion and equal and opposite forces. Distilling down the complexities, Newton and the laws of physics explain that if you – specifically your arm and hand, from your elbow to your fingertips – exert a force on the water directed toward your toes, the resulting force will create movement in the opposite direction. Creating forward propulsion, then, comes from your arm and hand actually pushing on the water rather than simply slipping through it – moving water with your arm, rather than moving your arm through the water.

Sergey Mironov/Moment/Getty Images

Breathing

We begin with breathing – and not stroke mechanics – because efficient swimming is comfortable swimming, and you won't be comfortable if you can't breathe. But before we discuss how to breathe while swimming, let's talk about how *often* to breathe. I'll start by stating the obvious: Oxygen is good – necessary, even. If I told you only to breathe every fourth step while running or every fifth pedal stroke while cycling, you would think I was crazy. So why limit your breathing to every third or fourth stroke while swimming? Again, we're not training for sprint-distance swim events where tolerating hypoxia is part of the program. Sure, bilateral breathing (breathing every third stroke, alternating breathing sides) makes you look super cool, but again, oxygen is good. So please, breathe when you need to, even if that's every stroke.

But don't take that to mean that you don't need to learn to breathe on both sides eventually. Breathing on both sides throughout a swim session, over a swim interval, and within a swim length balances out your swim stroke and helps maintain proper stroke mechanics. When you're ready, test out breathing patterns that allow for both sufficient oxygen and alternating breathing sides, such as 3 breaths-3 strokes-3 breaths or half a length breathing on one side and half a length on the other. The ability to breathe on either side becomes especially important when you move to open-water swimming, where the placement of buoys, the glare of the sun, and even the most modest of ripples can mean that breathing to one side is highly preferable over the other.

Timing

The breathing cycle begins with a long, slow, and complete underwater exhale through either your mouth or nose that finishes as the hand on your breathing side moves past your hip. (Fun fact: You should not hold your breath while swimming – to avoid that, lengthen your exhale to match the time between breaths.) That complete underwater exhale allows you to take a full, unrushed inhale when you turn your face out of the water, which you'll do as your pull finishes and your elbow lifts your arm out of the water. You'll return your face to the water as your elbow passes above it, as if your arm is nudging your head back to its original position.

Mechanics

The mechanics of breathing ultimately boil down to keeping the head turn to just that, a simple head turn. Be sure to turn your head directly to the side without first lifting your chin, since lifting your chin and therefore your head will cause your legs to sink. And be sure to turn just your head, without exaggerating the normal rotation of your shoulders and hips, so that you don't cause your legs to splay. Keeping your lower eye in the water helps limit your head turn, lessening the likelihood of both chin lift and over-rotation (figure 4.1).

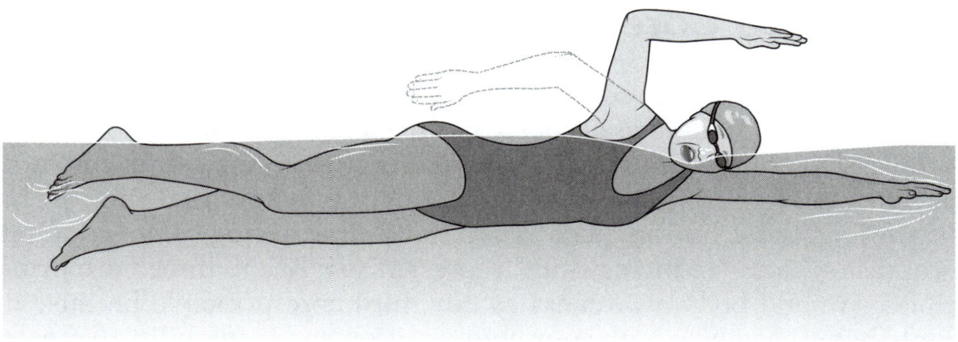

FIGURE 4.1 Head turn while breathing.

PILLOW CUE

Equipment: Swim paddles (optional), swim fins (optional)

Objective: Eliminate chin lift when turning your head to breathe.

Coaching Direction: When you are taking a breath, imagine that you are resting your head on a pillow. When your head turns, feel the water on the side of your face just as you would feel the pillow on your cheek.

CHIN PIN CUE

Equipment: Swim paddles (optional), swim fins (optional)

Objective: Eliminate chin lift when turning your head to breathe.

Coaching Direction: When you are taking a breath, imagine that your chin is pinned to your shoulder. Turn your head to breathe as your shoulder and arm on your breathing side rise out of the water, looking back toward your shoulder instead of ahead, and return it to the water as your shoulder drops and your hand re-enters the water.

UNDERWATER VIEW CUE

Equipment: None

Objective: Limit the degree of your head turn when breathing.

Coaching Direction: Each time you turn your head to breathe, keep your lower eye below the surface of the water. To help with that, maintain your gaze on something below the water, such as the lower half of the lane line or the side of the pool.

Three Core Principles of Swimming

With the two big-picture concepts and your breathing technique in place, let's turn to the fundamentals of swimming technique. Swimming, in its simplest form, is about efficiently creating that all-important forward propulsion while simultaneously reducing the factors that limit it. In swimming, those limiting factors are called *drag*, so logically, "creating propulsion" and "reducing drag" represent two of the three core principles. We add body awareness as our third core principle because it contributes heavily to both your body position and your ability to create forward propulsion *efficiently*.

Reducing Drag

We first focus on reducing drag so that your efforts to create forward propulsion actually go toward creating propulsion, instead of fighting against an impeding force. There are two primary ways athletes create drag in the water: with a sloped body position and with an oversized kick width.

Proper Body Position

For many athletes, the combination of a raised head position and lower-body muscle mass often causes the hips and legs to sink in the water. This sloped body position revolves (literally) around the chest, which has incredible buoyancy owing to all the air in your lungs. So your head is raised – especially when turning your head to breathe – and your chest floats, causing your hips and legs to sink and resulting in that sloped body position. To counteract this natural tendency and encourage your legs to float up toward the surface, tuck your chin to your chest and hold your head lower in the water, so that the water line falls right at the crown of your head (figure 4.2).

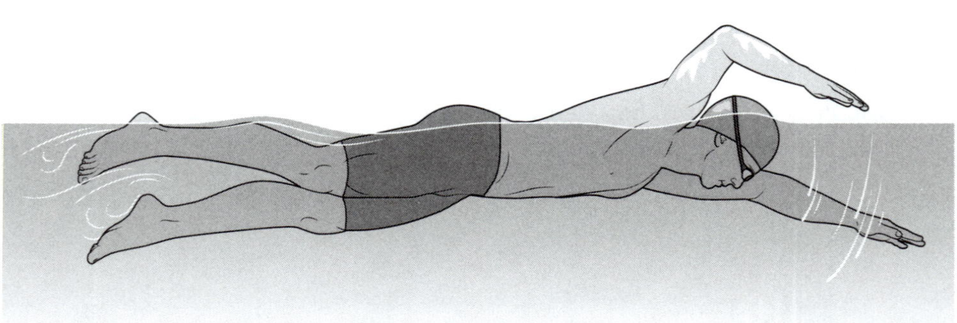

FIGURE 4.2 Proper body position.

STRETCH AND REACH CUE

Equipment: None

Objective: To gain the feel for a flat body position in the water.

Coaching Direction: Push off the wall at the end of the pool lane and glide forward for a few seconds, keeping your chin tucked to your chest, holding your thumbs together, and reaching your hands toward the other side of the pool, so that your body is stretched from your fingertips to your toes. Feel how this position helps your body stay flat in the water.

HEAD POSITION CUE

Equipment: Swim snorkel (optional)

Objective: Adjust your head position to elevate your hips, and therefore your legs, improving your body position in the water.

Coaching Direction: Swim with your chin tucked to your chest, resulting in a head position where the water level is at the top of your head.

SEESAW CUE

Equipment: Swim snorkel (optional)

Objective: Achieve an improved, flattened body position.

Coaching Direction: Think of your body as a seesaw, with your lungs as the fulcrum. Press your chest and shoulders downward on one side of the seesaw, and feel how that lifts your hips and legs on the other end.

The Flutter Kick

As for the kick, let's start with what it's not: The swim kick is *not* a knee-driven, lower-leg, big-range-of-motion movement (figure 4.3). A proper flutter kick originates in your hips, is executed with straight legs bent gently at the knee, and involves only a limited range of motion, as if your

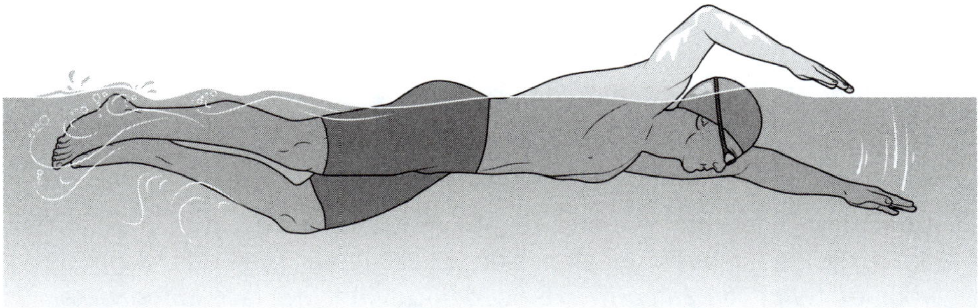

FIGURE 4.3 Incorrect flutter kick form.

hips are fluttering two wet noodles instead of your legs (see figure 4.2). Transforming your kick from a knee-driven motion to a hip-driven motion will reduce its width and therefore reduce or even eliminate persistent kick-related drag. Maintaining that small range of motion when you rotate to breathe, rather than letting the legs splay to help with balance, eliminates the second source of kick-related drag.

SMALL KICK CUE

Equipment: None

Objective: Reduce drag by reducing the width of your kick.

Coaching Direction: Kick with your big toes pointed slightly inward and held close enough together that they brush each other during the kick. Picture your feet trapped in a bucket while you are kicking, forcing your big toes to stay within 6 inches (15 cm) of each other at all times.

Body Awareness

We turn to body awareness as our second core principle because the subtleties of muscle engagement – and lack thereof – aid in maintaining body position, leverage more than just your arms and shoulders to create force behind your pull, and allow you to use your energy efficiently when swimming.

Engage Your Core

Engaging your core – the network of muscles that stabilize your torso – benefits your swim form in three different ways: First, it helps maintain a straight, unwavering body position that reduces drag. Second, it allows your obliques (your side abdominal muscles) to contribute to your pull. Finally, it connects your hips to your upper body, so that your lower-body rotation also adds to the force behind your pull. (Do you feel your upper body bobbing during your swim? That's a key indication that your core isn't engaged, and your best reminder to turn those muscles back on.)

KICK ON YOUR SIDE CUE

Equipment: Swim fins (recommended)

Objective: Learn to engage your core and hold a long, straight body position.

Coaching Direction: Kick one length on your right side, with your right arm extended underwater alongside your right ear, then one length on your left, with your left arm extended. Kick with your face in the water, turning it to breathe, and focus on engaging your core.

HIP DRIVE CUE

Equipment: Swim paddles (optional), swim snorkel (optional)

Objective: Learn to rotate your hips along with your upper body during the entry phase of your stroke.

Coaching Direction: Swim one length concentrating on driving each hip down simultaneously with hand entry on that same side. Swim the next length concentrating on lifting each hip up simultaneously with the pull on that same side.

Relax During Recovery

Until now, I've barely mentioned the recovery phase, or the portion of your swim stroke that happens above the water. Beginner swimmers often focus a great deal of energy on how their arms move out of the water, holding tension through a deliberate above-water movement pattern. What happens above the water, though, doesn't contribute at all to creating forward propulsion. So release that tension and relax your arms during the aptly named *recovery phase*. Give them a rest and allow for some fluidity of movement, reserving your energy for the work to be done underwater.

MARIONETTE CUE

Equipment: Swim snorkel (optional)

Objective: Initiate the recovery phase with your elbow and hold a relaxed arm through the entire phase.

Coaching Direction: Imagine that you are a marionette (e.g., Pinocchio) and that someone controls the movement of your arm during the recovery phase using strings attached to your elbows. Allow your arm to be lifted from the elbow, keeping it relaxed as you move it forward above the water.

ARM SHAKE CUE

Equipment: Swim fins (optional), swim snorkel (optional)

Objective: Emphasize a relaxed arm during the recovery phase.

Coaching Direction: When your arm is out of the water during the recovery phase of each stroke, shake out your arm and hand a few times to confirm that it's loose and relaxed.

Swimming With Sporks

Your hand position can have a surprising impact on how much water you move with your pull. Many people think that a tightly held, semi-cupped hand position – a spoon, if you will – moves the greatest amount of water. And while that hand position effectively grabs the water, it doesn't move the *most* water. If you flatten your palm and your fingers – like a fork – you increase the area covered by your hand, but you also allow water to slip through your fingers. The in-between position, with fingers just barely splayed and your hand slightly cupped – like a spork! – widens the area of the hand without allowing water to slip through your fingers, maximizing the amount of water pushed (figure 4.4). Don't believe me? Play around with it next time you're in the pool and see for yourself. Stand at the end of the lane and move your hand from front to back in the fork, spoon, and spork positions – you'll feel the difference.

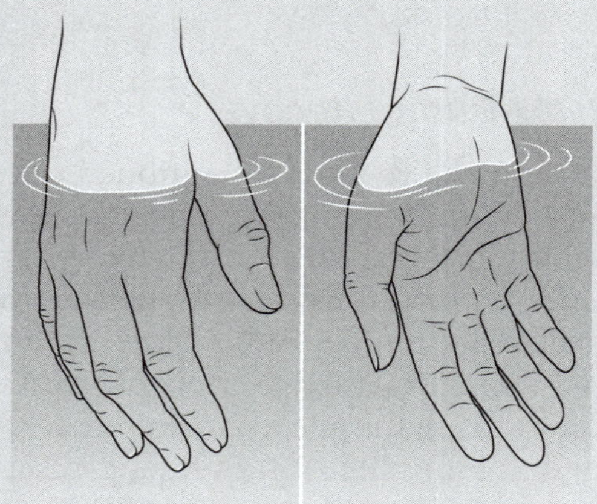

FIGURE 4.4 Ideal hand position.

Creating Propulsion: The Four Phases of the Pull

Finally – finally! – it's time to discuss swim stroke mechanics, and specifically the underwater pull. As an endurance swimmer, you predominantly create forward propulsion through your pull. To do that, you want to maximize the amount of water you're moving, the speed at which you're moving it, and the distance you're moving it with each pull, because that directly translates to how fast and far each pull moves you forward. And let's clarify that *the pull*, a term often used to represent the entire underwater portion of your swim stroke, actually has four distinct phases: the entry, the catch, the pull, and the finish. Each phase serves a distinct purpose in creating forward propulsion.

Phase I: The Entry

The entry phase, when your hand enters the water, sets up the remainder of your pull. You'll want a flat hand to enter the water directly above your shoulder and a few inches in front of your head (figure 4.5).

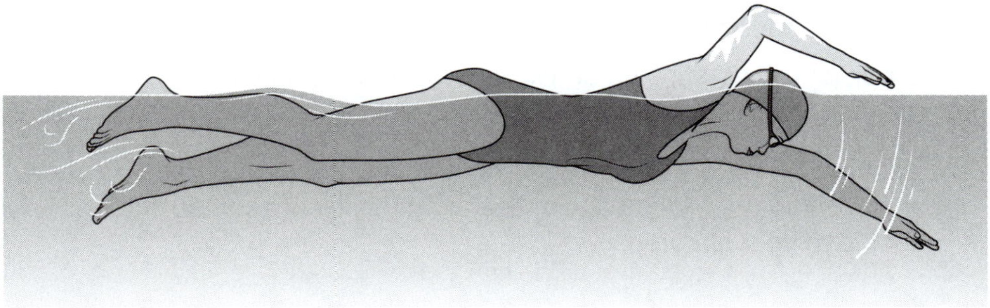

FIGURE 4.5 Hand entry.

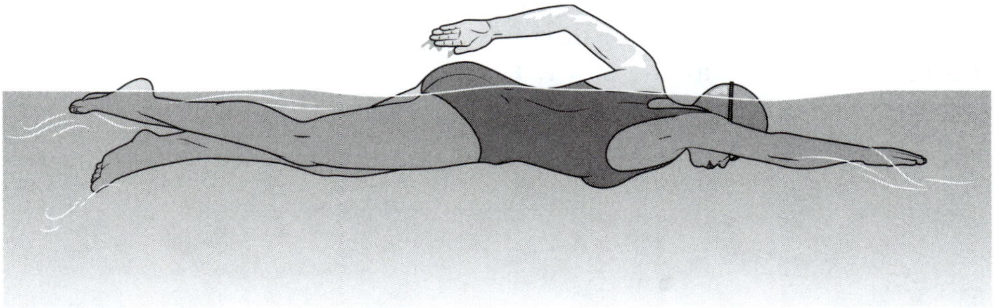

FIGURE 4.6 The glide position.

With a dropped and extended shoulder driving body rotation, that hand then reaches forward, stretching directly above your shoulder to your maximum reach and descending a few inches below the water's surface (figure 4.6). Holding that full-reach position for a beat after hand entry and before initiating your catch is known as the *glide*.

POINTER FINGER CUE

Equipment: Swim fins (optional), swim snorkel (optional)

Objective: Ensure proper hand position relative to your body as you execute your entry.

Coaching Direction: Focus on your pointer fingers, directing them toward a hand entry position directly above your shoulder and a few inches past the crown of your head, and continuing after entry in a strong, straight motion to the glide position.

MIDDLE FINGER CUE

Equipment: Swim fins (optional), swim snorkel (optional)

Objective: Increase rotation during your entry and glide.

Coaching Direction: Drive your middle finger forward in a rapid, straight, and strong motion from the point of hand entry through to the glide position, as if you are stabbing your finger forward to full reach.

ARMPIT DRIVE CUE

Equipment: Swim fins (optional), swim snorkel (optional)

Objective: Increase rotation and achieve full reach for the glide position.

Coaching Direction: Drive your armpit downward as you transition from hand entry to the glide position. Feel how this elongates the line from your hip to your fingertips.

Phase II: The Catch

After your glide, you initiate your catch. Your hand and forearm "catch" the water that you will move during your swim pull, and hold onto it as you bend your arm at the elbow to transition your hand and forearm from a horizontal position to a vertical position (figure 4.7).

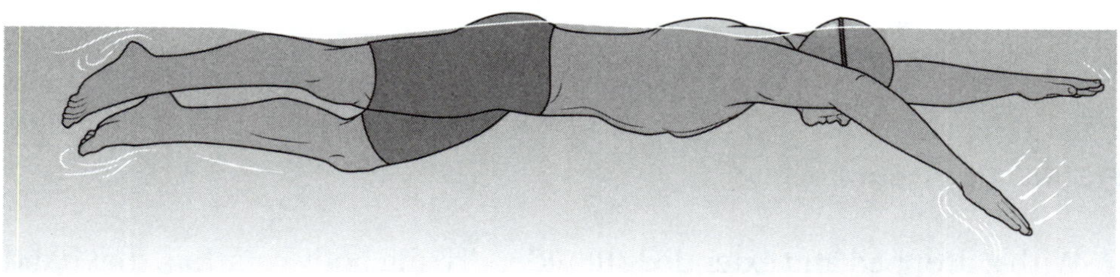

FIGURE 4.7 The catch.

OVER THE BARREL CUE

Equipment: Swim paddles (optional), swim snorkel (optional)

Objective: Increase the effectiveness of your catch and improve your transition from the catch phase to the pull phase of the stroke.

Coaching Direction: Imagine that your swim lane contains a row of barrels, lying on their sides and perpendicular to your swim direction. Initiate your catch as if you are swimming over these barrels, their shape requiring your elbow to stay high near the surface of the water.

Phase III: The Pull

The pull phase of your swim stroke begins when you transition your hand and forearm from a horizontal to a vertical position and continues as your arm moves past your body. During this phase, keep your elbow bent and high in the water to maintain the vertical position of your hand and forearm, a position known as the *high-elbow pull* (figure 4.8). Keeping your arm just wide of your body, pull your hand and forearm straight back alongside your torso toward your hip.

FIGURE 4.8 The high-elbow pull.

STRING CUE

Equipment: Swim paddles (optional), swim snorkel (optional)

Objective: Prompt a high elbow during the pull phase.

Coaching Direction: As you are swimming, picture a string held taut between your wrist and your armpit. Keep your elbow bent and held above that string from the moment you begin your catch and through your pull.

SURFBOARD PADDLE CUE

Equipment: Swim paddles (optional), swim snorkel (optional)

Objective: Ensure that your pull is wide, straight, and with a high elbow.

Coaching Direction: Swim as if you are lying on a surfboard and paddling out to a wave: The width of the board forces your entry and pull outside of it and holds your elbow in a high, bent position.

PAINTBRUSH CUE

Equipment: Swim paddles (optional), swim snorkel (optional)

Objective: Reinforce a vertical forearm and high-elbow pull position.

Coaching Direction: Imagine your forearm and hand form a paintbrush; keep your elbow – the end of the paintbrush's handle – high in the water, and hold your lower arm and hand – or paintbrush – vertically while painting straight lines on the bottom of the pool with your fingertips.

FIST CUE

Equipment: Swim fins (recommended), swim snorkel (optional)

Objective: Emphasize the use of the forearm during the pull.

Coaching Direction: Swim with your hands balled into fists, forcing you to move water with your forearms during your pull. This cue will be very challenging initially, but stick with it; the rewards are worth it. (If you are using swim fins, be sure not to be overly reliant on them to maintain forward propulsion or you will defeat the purpose of the cue.)

SHOULDER BLADE CUE

Equipment: Swim paddles (optional), swim snorkel (optional)

Objective: Engage the large back muscles during the pull.

Coaching Direction: Initiate your pull by drawing the inside tip of your shoulder blade toward your spine. Notice how this action engages your latissimus dorsi (a.k.a. *lats*) and takes pressure off your shoulders.

Phase IV: The Finish

The swim stroke finish involves transitioning from a bent elbow, vertical forearm position to a horizontal arm position with your hand by your hip (figure 4.9). Think of it as the icing on your swim stroke cake. A strong and complete finish maximizes the distance and duration of your pull – and therefore how much water you move – and initiates the recovery, or above-water, phase of your swim stroke.

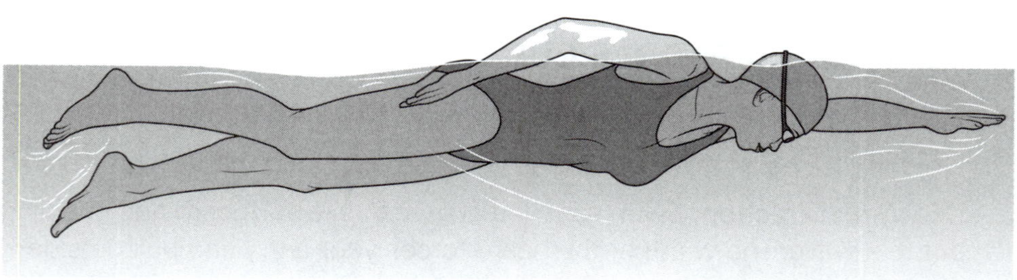

FIGURE 4.9 The finish.

EMPTY THE POOL CUE

Equipment: Swim paddles (optional), swim snorkel (optional)

Objective: Overemphasize the final portion of your pull in order to extend the length and improve the strength of your finish.

Coaching Direction: Finish your pull by flinging the water past your hip so hard that your hand comes out of the water, as if you are trying to throw the water out of the pool.

The Complete Pull

While understanding and improving each distinct phase of the pull is important, you ultimately will put these phases together into a complete, fluid swim stroke: entry, catch, pull, finish, above-water recovery, repeat.

And you'll execute this pattern with both arms, concurrently but with alternating timing. By alternating, I don't mean exactly opposite – you actually want to align the timing of your pull on one side with the entry and reach on the other.

Let's break that timing down step by step. First, you initiate your catch, say on the right, as your left arm passes by your head (figure 4.10*a*). As your left hand enters the water and reaches to full extension, your right arm will execute your catch, pull, and finish (figure 4.10*b*). Your left arm will then hold the glide position – it will glide! – until your right arm passes by your head, at which point your left hand will initiate its stroke, and the cycle will continue (figure 4.10*c*).

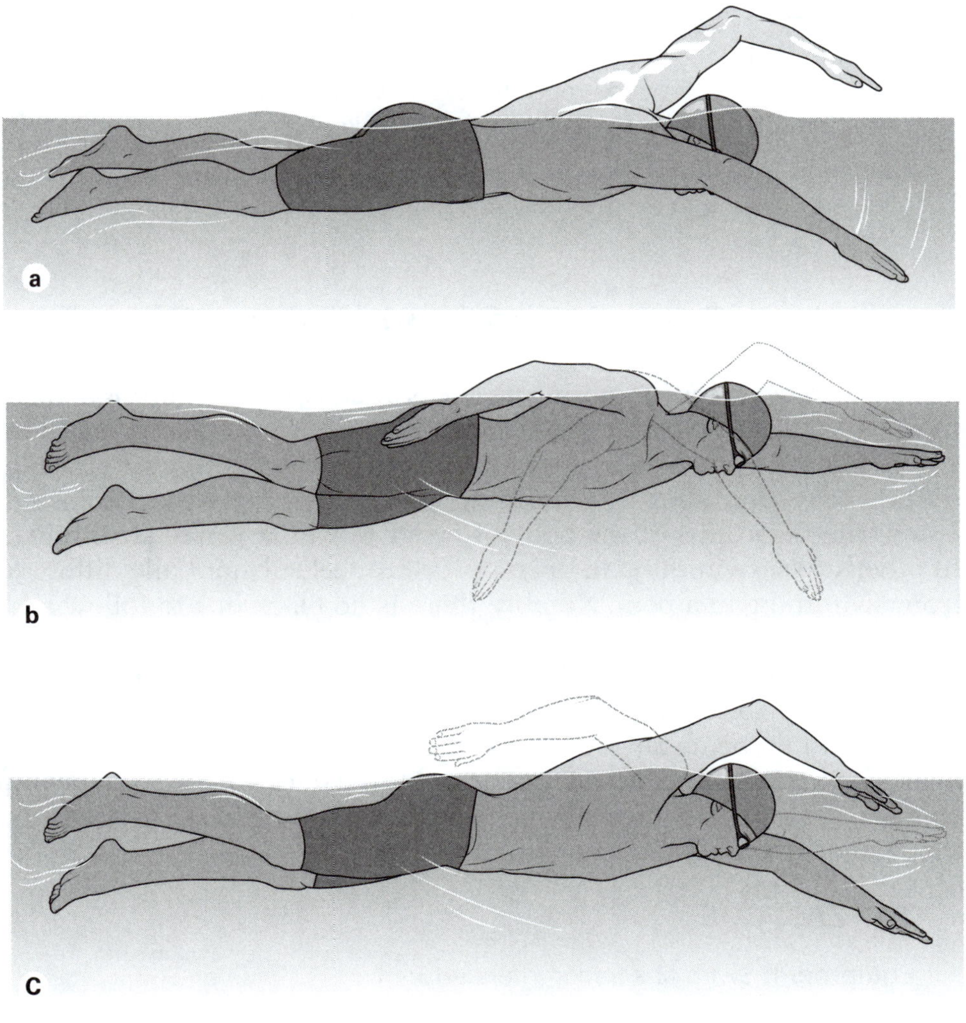

FIGURE 4.10 The complete swim stroke and its timing: *(a)* the entry start (L) and catch (R), *(b)* the entry finish (L) and the pull and finish (R), *(c)* the glide (L) and recovery (R).

L = left arm; R = right arm.

PHASES CUE

Equipment: Swim paddles (optional), swim snorkel (optional)

Objective: Isolate and focus on each phase of the swim pull.

Coaching Direction: For the first half of the first pool length, focus on your hand entry and glide. Focus on initiating a strong catch for the second half of the first length. Focus on a forceful high-elbow pull for the first half of the second pool length. For the second half of the second length, focus on a strong push past your hips to finish your stroke.

LATE START CUE

Equipment: Swim paddles (optional), swim fins (optional), swim snorkel (optional)

Objective: Move toward proper timing for your swim stroke by overemphasizing the glide before initiating each stroke.

Coaching Direction: Begin each stroke on a delayed basis, extending the glide and waiting to initiate the catch until the opposite hand enters the water.

Open-Water Swimming

The final piece of our swimming puzzle is open-water swimming. While most of your swim training will take place in a pool, your triathlon will likely take place in open water. In some ways, there's not a big difference – swimming is swimming, and everything we've discussed holds true regardless of the body of water in which you're swimming. In other ways, swimming in open water can feel substantially different from swimming in a pool. Notably, there is no black line to follow and no lane lines keeping you on track. In fact, unless you are swimming in a remarkably clear lake or a spectacular ocean venue, you probably won't even be able to see the bottom of the lake, reservoir, river, bay, or ocean. Without being able to see a black line or lane lines, you will have to lift your head out of the water and "sight" the buoys marking the swim course or a landmark toward which you're swimming in order to ensure that you're swimming in the right direction.

TARZAN CUE

Equipment: Swim fins (recommended)

Objective: Swim with your head held out of the water so that you can see in what direction you're swimming.

Coaching Direction: Using a wider-than-normal hand entry and a slightly elevated stroke and kick rate, swim with your head (or at least your eyes) held out of the water for 4 to 6 strokes, maintaining a head position and gaze focused directly ahead, rather than turning your head side to side. (Note that this is significantly easier when wearing a wetsuit, which aids in buoyancy.)

SIGHT BREATHING CUE

Equipment: Swim fins (optional)

Objective: Incorporate a quick sighting action within a single stroke and breath.

Coaching Direction: During the catch phase of your stroke, press down on the water to elevate your upper body and increase the strength of your kick to maintain momentum. Use one of two options to sight: (1) Turn your head to the side for a breath, and then lift your chin as you inhale to look directly forward and quickly "sight" buoys or landmarks before returning your face to the water in time with your hand entry or (2) lift your chin and sight first, then turn your head to the side and breathe. Try both options and see which feels more comfortable, then practice until it feels natural.

Now that you understand the principles and techniques that lead to strong and efficient swimming, it's time to reshape your swim form to incorporate what we've discussed. You can apply the cues found throughout this chapter during your swim sessions, concentrating on just one cue within a pool length, only two during any single workout, and no more than three at a time as your overall focus. Prioritize those cues that address your greatest deficits, which side- and front-view videos can help you identify. As you work your way through the different cues, some will provide a near-instantaneous feeling of improvement, while others might feel a bit awkward and unproductive. Don't give up on them, though, as you may find that on the second or third or fifth try, they suddenly click.

Above all, try not to get discouraged! Your hard work and dedication will pay off, even if you don't see immediate results. Swimming progress is measured in seconds per hundred, and those seconds come at an agonizingly slow pace – but they do come. While you're waiting for the clock to validate your efforts, focus on improvements in how swimming *feels*. Even without changes in swim pace, achieving those paces with less effort or simply feeling more comfortable and fluid while doing so is a victory.

5

BIKING

Biking is just *fun*. The wind on your face, the road flying by beneath your wheels – it brings back memories of childhood and summer adventures and freedom. And yes, you've probably been riding a bike for decades, so we're not going to dive into the basics of cycling the way we started with the fundamentals of swimming. Instead, we'll focus on making you a *better* cyclist. A cyclist with an effective pedal stroke, who uses cadence and gearing to manage their effort level, who can fuel and hydrate while cycling, and who descends and corners like a pro. As with swimming, I'll sprinkle in cues along the way to illustrate the techniques and help you integrate these skills into your cycling form. But in contrast to swimming, where technique is an ongoing work in progress, you can typically integrate all of these skills into your cycling form within a single season of training.

Starting and Stopping

Bear with me, because I did just say we weren't going to start with the basics, and then I immediately started with the basics. But cyclists starting inefficiently is one of my biggest pet peeves, and also starting and stopping seem really simple right up until you do your first ride with clipless pedals. So we're going to take just a minute to quickly review starting and stopping techniques, which apply no matter what type of pedals you're using.

First off: Starting. My pet peeve is when a cyclist pushes off the ground 2 or 3 or 4 times on one foot to gain momentum so they can start cycling. The more efficient way to start cycling from a stop is as follows:

1. Be sure you are in a gear that will provide sufficient counter-resistance when you push on the pedal, but not so much resistance that you can't start with a sufficiently quick pedal stroke (you will learn this with practice). It's best to have shifted into this gear as you approached the stop sign, traffic light, or whatever prompted your stop.
2. Stand straddling your bike with foot one on the ground, and bring foot two and its pedal up to the top of the pedal stroke.

3. When you're ready to start, push down *hard* on the pedal with foot two, then place foot one on its pedal and take several strong pedal strokes on each side to build momentum – even if one or both feet haven't yet clipped in. Once you've got sufficient momentum to coast, you can clip into the pedals.

Next: Stopping. Yes, I'm sure you know how to stop your bike. Stopping takes virtually no thought or skill when you are riding a bike with flat pedals. But having the forethought to shift into the correct gear for when it's time to restart your bike is a skill worth adding to your repertoire. And, if you are cycling with clipless pedals, remembering to unclip one foot before stopping takes a bit of diligence (it's best to keep the other foot clipped in until you're fully stopped). In addition, paying attention to your weighting when stopped with one foot still clipped in will help you avoid the ubiquitous slow-motion tip-over: You'll want to shift your weight over the foot placed on the ground, rather than being center-weighted. I learned that the hard way.

The Slow-Motion Tip-Over

Every cyclist who rides with clipless pedals has stories about tipping over on their bike. That's because every cyclist, and I do mean *every* cyclist, has fallen over. At least once. There's the requisite fall within your first two or three rides, when you're still getting used to everything. Then there's the requisite fall a bit later, once you've gotten comfortable and have stopped thinking so much about falling over, but before muscle memory for the starting and stopping movement patterns has set in, and you can actually do that without thinking.

My first tip-over was on my first day with my first road bike, when I had difficulty clipping in to get started. My second tip-over was a few months later with a new cycling buddy who was fitter and more experienced than I was. As we approached a stop sign, I unclipped on the right and put my foot down, but then my weight shifted slightly left, and I executed a brilliant slo-mo tip-over. My calf was slashed and bleeding from my cassette, as if I'd gotten in a fight with a bear, and my ego was severely bruised. But, like everyone who has had a very public and very embarrassing tip-over (which, again, is every cyclist), I popped up in a flash, said I was absolutely fine, and let the adrenaline fuel the next several miles of my ride.

Pedaling

Before you turn the page to jump ahead, thinking that I'm once again launching into a basic skill I promised not to spend time on, hear me out: I agree that pedaling a bike with flat pedals is a basic skill and one that we don't need to review. But pedaling a bike with clipless pedals does, in fact, involve technique. Clipless pedals can transform the pedal stroke from one where you push down for only a portion of the pedal stroke, as you do with flat pedals, to one where you exert force on the pedal for the entire 360-degree rotation. But simply putting clipless pedals on your bike won't change how you pedal. Unless you've practiced full-circle pedaling, you're likely clipped in but still pedaling exactly as you did when you first learned to ride a bike using flat pedals, just pushing down for a portion of the pedal stroke. So let's walk through full-circle pedaling step by step – actually, quadrant by quadrant – so you can learn to exert a continuous force on the pedals for the entire 360-degree rotation.

We break the pedal circle into four quadrants corresponding to four distinct phases of the pedal stroke (figure 5.1). The front quadrant, the first phase, is the one you've known your entire cycling career and is the strongest power phase of the pedal stroke. It involves a strong, quadriceps- (a.k.a. *quad-*) dominant downward push on the pedal, but can be enhanced by activating and engaging your gluteus maximus (the largest of your three gluteus muscles, a.k.a. your *glutes*) as you initiate the downstroke. As you leave the front quadrant and enter the bottom quadrant, the second phase, the workload transitions to your hamstring and calf as they pull your foot back through the bottom portion of the pedal stroke. During the back quadrant, the third phase, your calf and tibialis anterior (a small muscle in your shin) engage as your hamstring releases and you pull up on the pedal. Finally, your quad and glute reengage during the top quadrant, the fourth phase, as you propel your

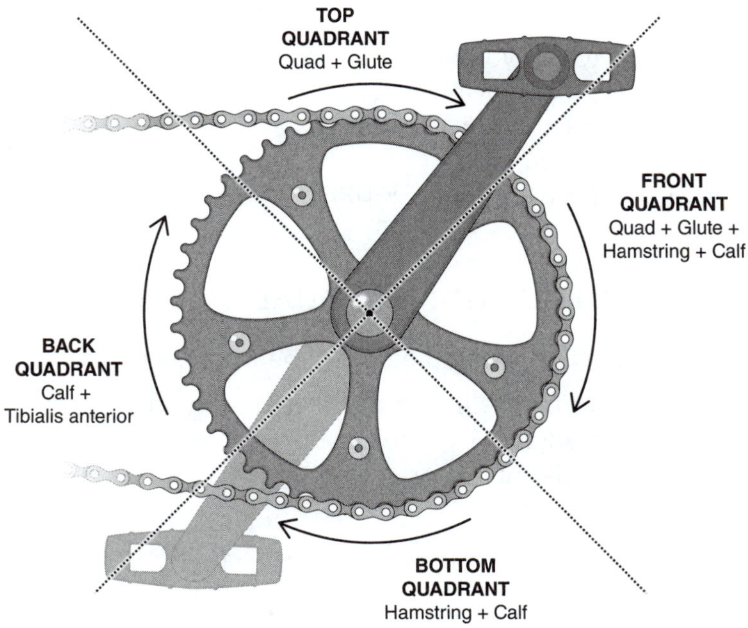

FIGURE 5.1 The four quadrants of the pedal stroke.

foot over the top of the pedal stroke and create momentum for the next pedal rotation.

To practice full-circle pedaling, first incorporate the four quadrant cues that follow into your warm-up or when pedaling comfortably on a flat, uninterrupted stretch of road. Spend time focusing on each cue in sequence, working your way around the four quadrants. After a round of cues – 30 seconds to 1 minute of focus for each quadrant – put all four together into a complete, balanced pedal stroke. Notice how both legs working continuously and simultaneously creates a more fluid movement pattern and lessens the force required to generate speed on the bike; how the leg pushing down is aided by the opposite leg pulling up, and the leg pulling back is aided by the opposing leg kicking forward. Once you've gotten comfortable with full-circle pedaling, add the single-leg pedaling cue to further develop your pedaling technique; this one will be challenging at first, but if you stick with it, you'll feel the improvement in your pedal stroke.

As you work on your pedaling technique, also pay attention to your feet and your knees. Focus on pedaling with flat feet rather than on your toes, to shift power-production responsibilities from your calves to your quads, hamstrings, and glutes. At the same time, think about pedaling from your knees rather than your feet, as if the lower halves of your legs are pistons driven by the force created by your upper legs – your upper legs do the work, while your lower legs are just along for the ride (figure 5.2). The overall effect should feel almost like your feet are floating in your bike shoes.

FIGURE 5.2 Pedaling with piston legs and flat feet.

HEELS DOWN CUE (FRONT QUADRANT)

Objective: To activate your glute during the front quadrant phase.

Coaching Direction: Initiate your downward push on the pedals at the top of the front quadrant by dropping your heel as you add pressure on the pedal with the ball of your foot. Feel your glute engage as you do so.

SCRAPE IT OFF CUE (BOTTOM QUADRANT)

Objective: To actively engage your hamstrings and calves as you move through the bottom quadrant.

Coaching Direction: Keeping your heel down, pull your foot back through the bottom quadrant as if you're scraping gum or mud off the bottom of your shoe.

PULL UP CUE (BACK QUADRANT)

Objective: To connect the hamstring-dominant phase that precedes and the quads-dominant phase that follows the back quadrant of your pedal stroke.

Coaching Direction: Actively pull the foot up from 7 o'clock to 11 o'clock along the back quadrant of the pedal stroke.

KICK FORWARD CUE (TOP QUADRANT)

Objective: Create rotational momentum within the top quadrant that will enhance the power generated in the front quadrant.

Coaching Direction: Kick your toes forward as you come over the top of your pedal stroke.

SINGLE-LEG PEDALING CUE

Objective: To isolate the movement patterns of each leg, allowing you to focus on generating smooth, continuous circles where all four quadrants are connected, and to identify and improve deficiencies in your pedal stroke.

Coaching Direction: Unclip one foot and pedal solely with the other. You'll likely notice a "dead spot" or clunk at the top of your pedal stroke; to reduce or eliminate it, work on actively engaging during the bottom and back quadrants to smooth the transition into the top quadrant. Start with 30 seconds per side, and work your way up to a minute.

Cadence

Now that you have perfected your pedaling form (or are actively working to improve it), let's talk about your pedaling rate, or cadence. We talk about cadence in terms of rotations per minute (rpm), counting rotations on one leg to determine that number. Indoor spin bikes, indoor bike trainers, cadence monitors, and power meters will all provide this metric for you, or you can calculate it by counting how many times one knee hits the top of your pedal stroke during a 6-second window and multiplying that number by 10.

Your cycling cadence combined with the force that you deliver to the pedals – how fast and how hard you are pedaling – produces your cycling power, which translates to your cycling speed. That combination of factors also dictates how quickly you will fatigue when cycling, so you want to be intentional about not just how much power you produce when cycling but also whether you derive that power predominantly from pedaling hard or from pedaling fast. I'll spare you the physics lesson (you're welcome), but trust me when I tell you that your pedaling speed – your cadence – and your pedaling force have an inverse relationship. In other words, you can produce the same power, and therefore speed, by pushing harder on the pedals with a slower cadence as you do when pushing more gently on the pedals but with a quicker cadence. So which combo will serve you better: big force, low turnover or less force, quick turnover?

The answer to that question ties into our use of energy systems. We'll talk more about energy systems in chapter 8, but for now, we'll use an analogy to illustrate the optimal balance of cadence and force for cyclists (yes, you are a cyclist): Imagine that we are going to take the stairs up to the top of the Eiffel Tower. I give you two choices: You can make the whole trip either by taking the stairs three at a time or one at a time, no breaks allowed. You picture how quickly you'll go at first if you take the stairs three at a time – using a lower cadence – but you can also practically feel how your legs will be screaming for a break before you get even halfway to the top. That's your power-based energy system, generating strong leaps up the stairs but tiring quickly. Then you picture

Meg Oliphant/Getty Images for IRONMAN

taking the stairs one at a time, using less powerful but quicker steps – a higher cadence – and relying more heavily on your cardiorespiratory-based (cardiovascular plus respiratory) energy system. You know your heart rate and breathing rate will increase, you will certainly break a sweat, and your pace might slow down after a while, but you will have a much better chance of making it to the top without needing a break. Translating this analogy to cycling: Your cardio-based energy system – and a lower force, higher cadence pedaling technique – best supports your long, endurance efforts.

So we agree, then, that using a higher cadence and lower force per pedal stroke will be an excellent way to cycle for miles and miles at a time while minimizing fatigue. In practice, this translates to a cadence target of 80 to 90 rpm whenever your gearing and the terrain allow it, which should be most of the time. But because variations in terrain will occasionally push you outside this target range, every cyclist should be comfortable cycling with cadences as low as 60 rpm and up to at least 100 rpm. And while you want to maintain your well-practiced, full-circle pedaling at any cadence, the back and top quadrants drive high cadences, while the front quadrant is unsurprisingly dominant at lower cadences.

HIGH CADENCE SPIN-UP CUE

Objective: Gain comfort pedaling at high cadences (100-120 rpm).

Coaching Direction: On flat terrain and in an easy gear outdoors or with light resistance on an indoor trainer, bring your cadence up to 100 to 120 rpm for 30 to 60 seconds. Focus on the back and top quadrants, thinking about driving the pedals from your knees, not your feet, and engaging your adductors (your inner thighs) to maintain stability in your pedaling motion.

LOW CADENCE CUE

Objective: Gain comfort pedaling at low cadences (60-70 rpm).

Coaching Direction: On a hill outdoors or with moderate to strong resistance on an indoor trainer, cycle with a cadence of 60 to 70 rpm for 2 to 5 minutes, or as long as it takes to get to the top of the hill. Focus on engaging both legs through the entire pedaling circle, using the bottom and back quadrants to provide a counterforce to the work done in the top and front quadrants.

Gearing

Knowing when to ride in which gear – and when to change gears – plays a crucial role in managing your effort level on the bike. You want to use your gears to establish an appropriate effort level and then to maintain it

Understanding Your Gears

When we talk about the gears on your bike, we are actually talking about two different gearing options in combination: the front chainrings and the rear cassette. The front chainrings are part of your crankset, which also includes the crank arms that the pedals attach to. Many bikes have two chainrings, but yours could have one or three. The biggest, outer chainring corresponds to the hardest gearing; the smallest, inner chainring corresponds to the easiest gearing. The gearing difference between chainrings is dramatic, so chainrings are typically only switched when going up or down hills. The cassette is mounted on the rear wheel and provides much more nuanced gearing changes. Opposite to the chainring, the easiest gear on the cassette is the biggest sprocket and is closest to the wheel, and the hardest gear is the smallest sprocket and is furthest away.

Your total gearing range is defined by your biggest and smallest chainrings and your biggest and smallest sprocket. If you have multiple chainrings, the gear ratios of the gearing combinations overlap, so you will typically switch chainrings before you get to either end of the cassette. A few quick tips on the mechanics of gear changes:

1. Never change your chainring and cassette simultaneously, as that often leads to "dropping" your chain. (Dropping your chain happens when the chain drops off the chainring. As a result, your pedaling will no longer rotate the gears on the cassette, so you will no longer provide power to the rear wheel, which generally means you will no longer move forward. The solution is to stop and manually place the chain back onto the teeth of the chainring, which is a messy and annoying task and one you want to avoid.)
2. Immediately before or after changing chainrings, offset that move with a few counterchanges of the cassette (e.g., if you are switching to an easier chainring, first move the cassette one or two sprockets harder).
3. Never ride with a "cross-chain" in the hardest chainring and easiest sprocket, as that gear combination stretches the limit of your chain length.

regardless of varying terrain, rather than allowing the terrain to dictate your effort level and unintentionally creating a high-intensity workout. Because high-intensity workouts are tiring, and you definitely don't want to be high-intensity-workout tired when it's time to ditch the bike and start running.

Start by determining your "Goldilocks" gear for riding on flat roads. Your Goldilocks gear matches your ideal cadence with just the right force in the pedals to produce your endurance effort level (which we'll define in chapter 8). One gear harder, and maintaining your ideal cadence requires more force, increasing your effort level. One gear easier, and that ideal cadence requires so little force that your effort level is too easy. The Goldilocks gear will be your baseline, your go-to gear for flat roads, and your starting point for determining gearing on all other terrain. From there, you'll maintain your effort level by changing gears as frequently as necessary to maintain that perfect balance of cadence and force despite the changing grade of the road, always returning to your Goldilocks gear when you're back on level terrain. Your gear changes will maintain steady force in the pedals and effectively flatten out the road, making uphills feel easier and earning "free speed" downhill.

Hills

The proper approach to riding hills translates the concepts of our gearing conversation to the practice of shifting your gears in conjunction with the changing grade of the road. Let's assume you approach the hill in your Goldilocks gear. As the grade of the road increases, you start shifting to easier gears – one by one, maintaining your cadence and pedaling force as you do so (figure 5.3). You'll use all your gears, including switching to your littlest chainring, but eventually you'll run out of gears to change. At that point, you'll let your cadence drop and your effort level increase as you climb in your easiest gear combination up the hill.

As you approach the top of the hill, the road will start to flatten. Because you used proper gearing and didn't exhaust yourself getting up the hill, as the terrain levels and the force you're exerting on the pedals drops, you'll be able to slowly switch to harder and harder gears. You'll gain momentum, continuing to change gears, and launch yourself over the top of the hill. But you won't stop there. You'll switch back to your biggest chainring and continue to use harder and harder gears as the

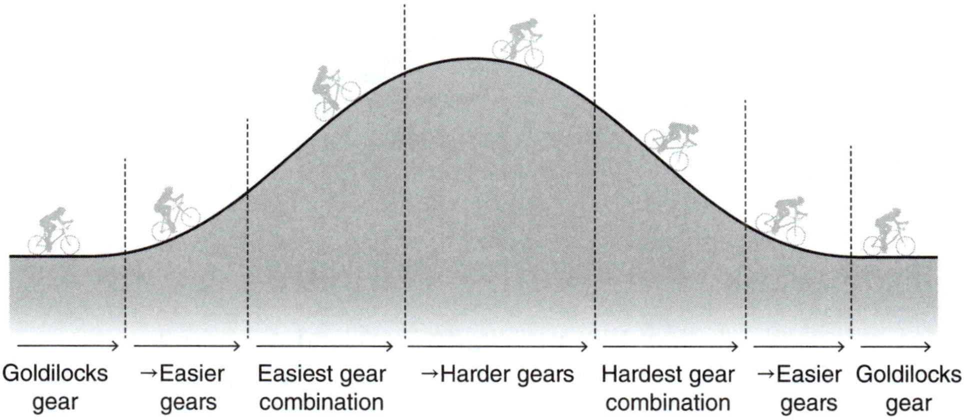

FIGURE 5.3 Gearing for hills.

road turns downhill, maintaining force in the pedals until you run out of gears and there's little to no resistance when pedaling.

At that point, you'll coast – or rather, fly – down the hill in your hardest gear combination, knowing that the road will soon level out again. As the road flattens, you'll resume pedaling once you can again apply force to the pedals, reversing the prior changes by switching back to more moderate gears. You'll soon find yourself on a flat road, in your Goldilocks gear, having left your competition far behind but holding onto the speed that you earned by riding that hill like a pro.

Descending

Your brilliant hill cycling skills can result in some pretty impressive downhill speed. And that speed can feel a bit unnerving if you aren't used to it. Moving into a bike position that maximizes stability will help you feel more secure on the bike and more comfortable reaching your top speed. Start by holding the pedals at 3 o'clock and 9 o'clock (it doesn't matter which foot is in front). Then, transfer most of your weight to the pedals, lift your rear up an inch (2.5 cm), and shift your hips back an inch or two (2.5-5 cm) so you're positioned over the back of the saddle (steeper hills will require a bigger shift). This stable bike position for descending (figure 5.4) lowers your center of gravity and shifts it uphill, increasing the traction and reducing the wobbliness of your rear wheel. (Pro tip: A similar position – without shifting your hips back and rising a bit further off the saddle – provides stability when going over any bumps you encounter on the road.)

FIGURE 5.4 Stable bike position when descending.

Eating and Drinking

We'll talk through why it's important to eat and drink (a.k.a. *fuel and hydrate*) in chapter 7, but for now, just trust me that you need to be able to eat and drink while cycling. And taking a sip from a water bottle or grabbing a granola bar while riding your bike may or may not come

Quick Primer: The Rules of the Road

Every cyclist should follow the traffic laws and rules of the road, both for their own safety and to help foster a positive relationship between cars and cyclists. Be sure to check local rules and traffic laws because they may differ from the following:

- Ride in the shoulder or bike lane in the direction of traffic (move to the center of the driving lane before executing a turn across traffic).
- When in a group, ride single-file.
- Signal before turning or merging.
- Stop at all stop signs and obey all traffic signals.
- Utilize front and rear lights when riding after dusk or before dawn. (They are also recommended to improve your visibility for cars and trucks during the day.)
- Provide an audible warning ("on your left!") before passing pedestrians or other cyclists.
- Always wear a helmet, whether it is required by law or not.

naturally to you. So if you're no longer – or maybe never were – the kid who shouts, "Look, mom, no hands!" then it'll take some practice to get comfortable managing the bike with one hand while grabbing a snack or bottle with the other.

BIKE YOGA CUE

Objective: To maintain your cycling speed and direction while cycling with one hand despite your shifting body position.

Coaching Direction: While cycling at low speeds on flat terrain, practice holding a straight path with one hand while moving through a range of motions with the opposite hand and arm: First, reach your hand over your head and across your midline, bending at the torso while you do so; second, rotate your torso while you reach behind your back; and third, rotate your torso while you reach across your front to your opposite shoulder. Be sure to practice on both sides.

BOTTLE GRAB PROGRESSION CUE

Objective: To develop the muscle memory that allows you to reach for a bottle without taking your eyes off the road for more than a quick second.

Coaching Direction: Execute the following while keeping your eyes on the road ahead of you; repeat each step until you're comfortable, then move on to the next.

1. Reach down and touch your water bottle, then return your hand to your handlebars.
2. Reach down and slide the bottle halfway out of the bottle cage, then return the bottle to the cage and your hand to the handlebars.
3. Reach down and remove the bottle from the bottle cage, then return the bottle to the cage and your hand to the handlebars.
4. Reach down, remove the bottle from the cage, take a sip from the bottle, then return it to the cage and return your hand to the handlebars.

Note: If you have a top tube bag or other storage on your bike for snacks, or keep them in a jersey pocket, practice a similar progression for grabbing and eating those snacks.

Steering and Cornering

I know, I know, you think we're back to basic skills because I want to talk about steering. Of course you know how to steer a bike, and I know that you know. But I want to point out something that you likely do intuitively, because it's a piece of the cornering puzzle: When you steer a bike, you are (of course) turning the front wheel, but you are also – maybe without knowing it – shifting your weight into the hand of the direction that you're turning. In fact, shifting the weight in your hands influences the direction of your bike so well that you can actually change the bike's direction by simply doing that, no wheel turn required.

FIGURE 5.5 Proper weighting when cornering.

The cornering puzzle, the pieces that we'll put together so you can take turns like you're in the Tour de France (okay, maybe not quite like that, but you get the idea), uses this hand weighting but starts with your foot position. As you approach a turn – the 90-degree corner of an intersection or any prominent bend in the road – position your outside foot at 6 o'clock and your inside foot at 12 o'clock (figure 5.5). Once your feet are at 6 and 12, place maximum weight on your outside (6 o'clock) foot, shifting weight off your inside foot and your saddle. That outside weighting provides counterpressure for our final piece of the puzzle: putting weight on your inside hand, to guide you through the turn without having to turn the wheel.

Even with that pro-level cornering technique, there's still a limit to the speed you'll be comfortable carrying through a turn. By combining proper weighting with taking the widest possible arc when executing your turn, you will maximize the speed you can safely carry through it (figure 5.6). Optimally, you will move outside the bike lane or shoulder and into the road in order to start your turn wide, then graze the tightest point of the corner at the midpoint of your turn, and finish wide once again in the road. Road and traffic conditions will dictate the width of your arc – you may or may not be able to start or end your turn in the road, and gravel or other hazards will affect how tightly you can hug the corner. Finally, if you do need to moderate your speed for the turn, avoid braking *during* your turn. Instead, brake as you approach the turn, coast through the corner, and then accelerate as you exit the turn.

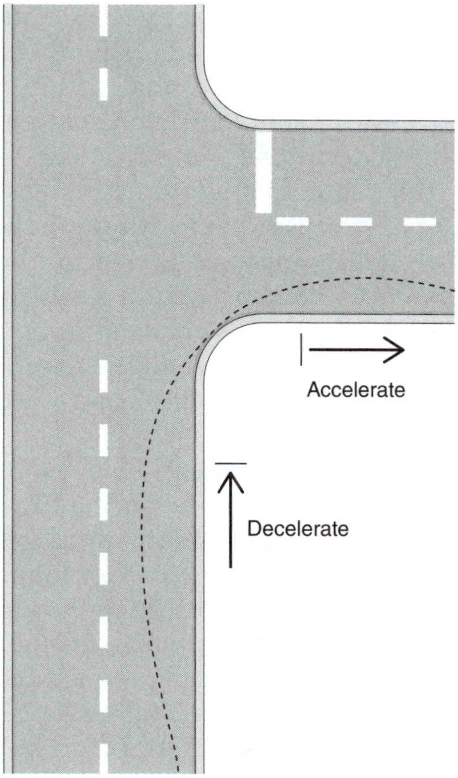

FIGURE 5.6 Bike path for corners.

Rain and Wind

Cycling in rainy or windy conditions requires some additional skills to stay "rubber-side down" on your bike. Rainy days and wet roads pose challenges as the moisture reduces tire traction, and your tires don't have much contact with the road to begin with. In wet weather, drop your tire pressure by about 10 percent to increase the amount of tire in contact with the road and improve traction. Additionally, allow for a greater stopping distance, reduce your speed through curves and around corners, and avoid the painted lines on the road as they are particularly slippery when wet.

Wind is fun (and I'm saying that with dripping sarcasm) because it comes in many forms: headwinds, tailwinds (okay, those actually are fun), crosswinds, and the ever-enjoyable wind gusts. Headwinds and tailwinds act like hills, making cycling either harder or easier; just like with hills, you will manage them by adjusting your gearing and maintaining a consistent force in the pedals. You can also adopt a slightly lower cadence into a headwind and a slightly higher cadence with a tailwind, but try to keep that differential within 5 to 10 rpm of your normal cadence. Crosswinds and gusts present particularly difficult conditions. Using a harder gear and a lower cadence puts more force in the pedals, lowering your center of gravity and increasing your stability. Additionally, bracing against crosswinds with the hand, arm, and shoulder facing the gusts while keeping the other arm loose allows you to counteract the wind force without becoming a stiff board that can be blown over. Finally, remember that as challenging as the wind conditions may be, eventually your path will turn and the relative wind direction will shift – or you will reach your final miles – and the ordeal will come to an end.

Incorporating these skills – from full-circle pedaling and ideal cadence to riding hills and cornering like a pro – will make you a more efficient and effective cyclist. And by more efficient and effective, I mean that you will be able to ride faster for longer with less expended effort. So make a point of regularly running through the pedaling cues during warm-ups and focusing on cadence throughout every ride. Think of each outdoor ride as an opportunity to practice your gearing; get comfortable eating and drinking while cycling; and improve your hill riding, descending, and cornering skills. And don't be such a fair-weather cyclist that the first time you experience rain or wind on your bike is on race day.

6

RUNNING

And then there's running. Running is a fundamental gait pattern – a foundational sequence of movements that is pre-programmed into your nervous system – and does not need to be taught. Running *well*, however, and specifically developing a durable running gait, takes practice and intention. So we are going to ensure that your run form supports your run durability – your ability to maintain your run pace and form on tired legs. Our conversation and the cues that support it will have the singular goal of building that durability, because the second half of the run in a triathlon relies on it.

Developing a running technique that supports durability translates to maximizing the efficiency, or economy, of your running form. An efficient, or economic, run stride is one in which the majority of the force from your foot striking the ground is returned and redirected as forward motion. (Yep, it's Newton's third law of motion and those reaction forces coming into play again.) In contrast, in an inefficient run stride, much of the ground reaction force is absorbed by your muscles, leaving less reaction force to generate forward motion. A durable running form maximizes energy return from your foot strike and minimizes fatigue caused by absorbing the ground reaction force, allowing you to run farther, at a stronger pace, and with less effort. And who doesn't want that? So we'll focus our discussion on two key elements of running form – your run posture and cadence – which will increase energy return and decrease fatigue, increasing your overall run durability.

Run Posture

Your run posture plays a critical role in determining whether your body acts as a cushion, absorbing the ground reaction force from your foot strike, or like a spring, returning that reaction force as forward motion. When your body acts as a cushion (figure 6.1*a*), your hip and knee bend as your foot strikes the ground, causing you to sink into your stride and directing a substantial portion of the ground reaction force to your muscles. Your muscles absorb that reaction force (tiring) and then contract to spring back up from your collapsed stance and push off the ground, contributing the vast majority of the force that moves

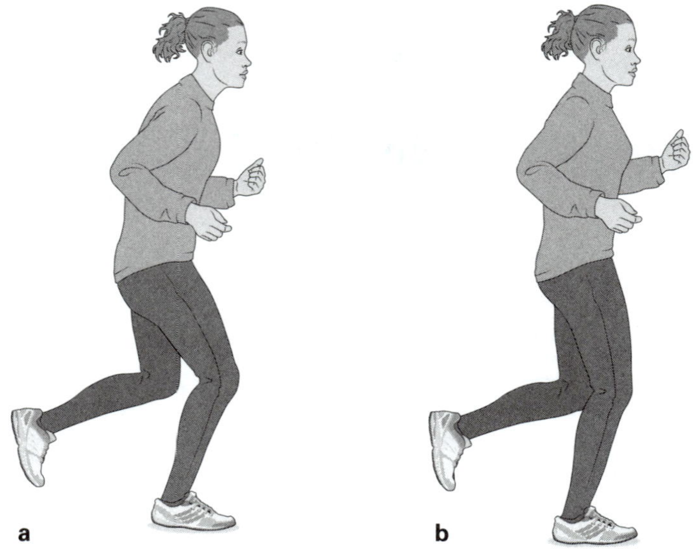

FIGURE 6.1 Run posture: *(a)* cushion versus *(b)* spring.

you forward (also tiring). In contrast, when your body acts like a spring (figure 6.1*b*), it stays solid and upright upon foot strike. The foot strike force is momentarily stored in your Achilles tendon; plantar fascia; and other tendons in your ankle, knee, and hip joints, and then released as a reaction force propelling you forward.

You might notice we didn't mention your muscles in the body-as-spring description. They are playing a role here, giving a helpful boost to the elastic recoil from your Achilles tendon, plantar fascia, and other tendons. But they aren't the main players driving you forward like they

Movement Prep

Running is a fundamental gait pattern established in early childhood and generally requires no conscious thought. However, the complex series of muscle activations that produce your running gait is not always as automatic as we'd like it to be. Those of us who spend the vast majority of our days sitting often have underactivated gluteal muscles, which can mean that our glutes don't always "turn on" when we head out for a run. Doing a quick 3- to 5-minute activation routine just before your run prepares your body for the movement of running by helping to "turn on" or activate your glutes and other muscles and by priming the neuromuscular connections that are used during running. What does a pre-run activation routine look like? It looks a lot like the lower-body mobility exercises outlined in appendix B – try a few before your next run, I bet you'll feel the improvement.

are in the body-as-cushion scenario. An efficient running stride utilizing the ground reaction force as elastic recoil relies on your muscles for only half the force propelling you forward, sometimes even less. This reduces the demand on your muscles, allowing you to maintain your running form and pace much longer. In other words, setting your body up to act as a spring while running is how we build the durability that allows you to run strong during the final miles of your triathlon.

So we agree, then, that body-as-spring is preferable to body-as-cushion. It's an easy concept to get on board with in principle, but a bit more complex to implement in practice. Simply deciding to become a spring doesn't magically make it so (unfortunately), but three targeted modifications to your run posture can allow you to put a cushion in a hat, wave a magic wand, and pull out a spring.

Hip Position

Your hip position lays the foundation for your running posture. The easiest way to find the proper hip position is to stand up straight and tall, then shift your hips slightly forward. As you move your hips into the correct position, you'll feel your glute muscles engage and notice a solidity in your stance as the support of your body weight transitions from your muscles to your skeletal frame. You want to find that ideal hip position where your hips aren't thrust too far forward, which can cause your torso to lean backward, and your hips aren't seated back, resulting in a subtle fold at and forward lean from your hips.

Proper hip position will result in "stacked joints," with your shoulders positioned above your hips, your hips positioned above your knees, and your knees positioned above your ankles. In this "stacked joint" posture, if you bounce up and down on your toes, your skeleton, tendons, and ligaments – not your muscles – will absorb the majority of the impact of your heels hitting the ground. (Play with the opposite: Sit your hips further back, noticing that this hip position causes your knees to shift forward. Feel how your muscles now support your body weight rather than your skeleton, and how they now must absorb the impact when you bounce on your toes.)

SUPERMAN RUNNING CUE

Objective: Achieve correct hip position.

Coaching Direction: Run with your chest forward and your shoulders slightly back, similar to when Superman stands with his hands on his hips; notice how the Superman posture prompts your hips to shift into their correct position.

WEAR YOUR CROWN CUE

Objective: Achieve correct body position.

Coaching Direction: Run standing tall, as if there's a crown just barely above and just barely in front of your head, and you want to wear it. Feel how this shifts your body into a stacked joint posture.

Foot Strike Position

In addition to your hip position, your foot strike position helps ensure a "stacked joint" posture at the point that your foot strikes the ground during your run stride (see figure 6.1*b*). By foot strike position, I'm not talking about what part of your foot strikes the ground first – there are plenty of examples of elite runners who are midfoot strikers, heel strikers, and forefoot strikers, so stick with whatever works for you in terms of foot strike mechanics. I am talking about whether your foot strikes the ground beneath your hip or in front of it.

Not sure where your foot lands relative to your hip when you run? Have someone record a side-view video of you while running (or record one of yourself running on a treadmill) and watch it in slow motion, pausing it when your foot first strikes the ground. A foot strike position in front of your hip – referred to as *overstriding* – is counterproductive to the idea of a "stacked joint" posture, because your hips can't be over your ankle if your ankle is in front of your hips. This can be a tricky element of your run biomechanics to modify, so aim to overcorrect – try to have your foot land *behind* your hip – when working to adjust your foot strike position. If you feel like you're falling forward, then you're doing it right (and I promise you won't actually fall).

HEAD, SHOULDERS, KNEES, AND TOES CUE

Objective: Ensure a foot strike position directly beneath your hip.

Coaching Direction: Focus on shifting your upper body so that your head and shoulders are positioned above your knee at the point of foot strike. Keep your hips in their proper position when shifting your upper body, resulting in a slight forward lean from your ankles, rather than a forward fold at your waist.

Leg Stiffness

Once your hips and foot strike are correctly positioned, you've set yourself up to land with stiff legs during your run stride. Now, by stiff, I don't mean rigid or unbending, like a metal pole. I'm referring more to the stiffness of a tightly coiled spring, which is exactly how we want your legs

Julio Aguilar/Getty Images for IRONMAN

to behave. Correctly positioned hips and stacked joints translate to legs that retain the stiffness of a coiled spring upon foot strike – that absorb the foot strike force into the skeleton (supported by your tendons and ligaments) and return a reaction force that moves you forward. Which has been our entire goal all along.

POGO STICKS FOR LEGS CUE

Objective: Improve leg stiffness.

Coaching Direction: Run as if you have pogo sticks for legs, stiff but springy. (Note that your pogo sticks aren't perfectly straight, but rather have a slight bend at the knee.)

Cadence

Run posture goes a long way toward increasing run durability, but doesn't fully maximize the economy of your run stride. Coupling that proper run posture with optimal run cadence, though, allows you to tap into the full potential of your run durability. We care about run cadence because we care about ground contact time – the amount of time that your foot is in contact with the ground during a single run stride. And we care about ground contact time because it correlates (actually, it inversely, or negatively, correlates) with the amount of ground reaction force that translates into forward motion.

Let me explain: Start by thinking of a single, single-leg hop as a scenario with infinite ground contact time. In this scenario, you land on the ground with a certain amount of foot strike force, and your leg absorbs all of the ground reaction force. As you transition to hopping repeatedly on that one leg, you decrease your ground contact time and a portion of the ground reaction force now becomes energy return – some of the foot strike force gets stored in your Achilles tendon; plantar fascia; and other tendons in your ankle, knee, and hip joints as you land, then released as a reaction force that propels you upward for the next hop. The quicker you hop, the shorter your ground contact time, the greater the portion of ground reaction force that becomes energy return, and the less it's absorbed by your leg.

Those hopping scenarios are just like running. A quicker cadence reduces ground contact time, reduces ground reaction force absorption and the resulting fatigue, and increases the amount of the ground reaction force that becomes forward motion. So let's talk about what we mean by "quicker cadence" and how to modify yours, if needed.

We talk about run cadence in terms of steps per minute (spm), counting total steps or run strides – left plus right – to arrive at that number.

Cadence Fun Facts

I've got a few additional tidbits for you – fun facts, if you will – on the topic of cadence:

- Height plays into optimal cadence: Runners with longer legs (typically taller runners) can be economical at cadences below 170 spm, and runners with shorter legs (typically shorter runners) may be comfortable at cadences above 180 spm.
- Quicker cadences are associated with a lower risk of running injuries. Given the prevalence of running injuries, anything you can do to reduce that risk warrants your attention.
- Cadence is not the only factor affecting ground contact time – it is also influenced by where your foot strikes the ground relative to your hips. A foot strike position directly beneath your hips allows for a quick and immediate push-off, increasing energy return and decreasing ground contact time. Overstriding, on the other hand, delays push-off and reduces energy return due to extended ground contact time. Heel strikers are the most common overstriders, but midfoot and forefoot strikers aren't immune.

Many smart and multisport watches can provide this metric for you, or you can calculate it by counting your run strides during a 6-second window and multiplying that number by 10. Like cycling, an "ideal" run cadence falls around 170 to 180 spm for most runners (if you run, you are a runner, so yes, that includes you).

Modifying your cadence for running typically presents a greater challenge than for cycling because your run movement patterns and timing are often deeply ingrained in your muscle memory. To make any modifications, you'll need to see your cadence in real time while running, so you'll need a data screen on your smart or multisport watch configured to display that metric. These watches also often have a built-in metronome, which may annoy your running buddies but provides immediate feedback when working to increase your run cadence. Set the metronome for 4 spm faster than your current average cadence, and run at that cadence for about 2 weeks – or as long as it takes for the slightly faster cadence to feel natural. Repeat this process until your cadence is in the mid-170s, any further increase feels unnatural, or you simply cannot increase your cadence further.

When you increase your cadence, you may find that your pace increases, resulting in a higher effort level that's harder to sustain. And that increased pace makes sense: Run speed is a direct product of your stride rate, or cadence, and your stride length. If you increase your stride rate and maintain your stride length, your pace will inevitably increase as well. So when you increase your stride rate, you need to decrease your stride length – take shorter steps – in order to maintain your normal run pace and effort level.

USE YOUR ARMS CUE

Objective: To match the cadence target from the metronome.

Coaching Direction: When running with a metronome, focus on matching your arm swing rate to the metronome beat as much or more than you focus on matching your leg turnover. Your leg turnover must match your arm swing rate, and arm swing rate often feels easier to increase.

RUNNING WITH GRANDMA CUE

Objective: To reduce your stride length while maintaining a high cadence.

Coaching Direction: Picture yourself running with your grandma. You want to maintain your high cadence target, but you can't leave grandma behind, so you need to take short, little steps to ensure that you stay at her pace.

EASING INTO RUNNING CUE

Objective: To find an appropriate stride length while running at a high cadence.

Coaching Direction: Begin your run (or return to running after a pause) by jogging in place at your target cadence. After 30 seconds of jogging in place, lean forward just slightly from your ankles and ease into a slow jog, maintaining your target cadence without opening up your stride. Let your stride lengthen gradually until you reach your normal run pace.

Modifying your run form takes consistent work, as your current biomechanics are deeply rooted in your nervous system and muscle memory, but with diligence and patience, you *can* improve your run economy and durability. Focus on a single modification for 2 or more weeks at a time before moving on to the next modification, to provide yourself with ample time to solidify the change in movement patterns. Return to each cue periodically to reinforce the change to your run mechanics and ensure its permanence. As you work to incorporate each element of your new run form, pause your run if you feel yourself losing grasp of the change, reset, and restart with the modification firmly in place.

7

TRIATHLON SKILLS

Triathlon involves swimming, biking, and running, so logically, we've spent time discussing how to develop your skills in these three disciplines. But triathlon also involves putting those three sports together within a single, multihour event, which brings us to transitions and fueling. Transitions and fueling are often regarded as triathlon's fourth and fifth disciplines. Which is fourth, and which is fifth? That depends on who you ask; different athletes and coaches have varying opinions on the matter. I believe it depends on your race distance: In short-course triathlons, quick transitions take priority, while in long-course triathlons, fueling properly and staying hydrated are critical to success. But regardless of your race distance, both are essential skills to learn and master.

Transitions

Triathlon includes two transitions, which are the portions of the race when you switch sports: the swim-to-bike transition (a.k.a. *Transition 1*, or *T1*) and the bike-to-run transition (a.k.a. *Transition 2*, or *T2*). For each transition, you'll need to manage both the logistics of switching from one sport to another, usually requiring some gear changes, and the physiology of quickly transitioning from the demands of one sport to the next. We'll cover how to set up your transition area and the race-specific logistics of transitions in chapter 13. For now, let's focus on the physiology and the big-picture logistical goal of transitions: to swap out your gear efficiently and with intention, so you move through transition quickly without forgetting to take off, put on, or grab a key piece of gear.

T1: The Swim-to-Bike Transition

Physiologically, the swim-to-bike transition involves moving from exercising in the horizontal plane to exercising in the vertical plane as well as shifting from an upper-body sport emphasis to a lower-body sport emphasis. This transition occasionally causes athletes to feel lightheaded when they stand up and start jogging or running after completing the swim, and it always requires the legs to start cycling without a proper warm-up. Both of these challenges can be addressed by increasing

Putting On and Taking Off Your Wetsuit

Putting on a wetsuit takes skill, but with sufficient time (usually 5-10 minutes), you can get the job done. Before getting started, clip your fingernails nice and short so you don't inadvertently puncture the neoprene when putting on the wetsuit. To put it on, first turn both legs inside out to about 6 inches (15 cm) above the ankle opening. Then, grab the inside lining and pull the remaining right-side out portion of each leg on and above your ankle. Next, still grabbing the inside lining, rather than the outer neoprene, roll the legs all the way up and pull the wetsuit over your hips. The suit should fit snugly at your crotch – if not, pull the wetsuit back down below your hips, roll down the legs to below your knees, pull the leg openings higher above your ankles, and try again. Once it's over your hips and fitting properly at the crotch, pull each arm on using a similar inside-out roll-up strategy. Then pull up the zipper strap (or have your friend do it for you), and you're ready to go!

Taking off a wetsuit is no easier, but it is a lot quicker. Once you're unzipped (easy to do yourself using the zipper strap), pull each sleeve down to your wrist, grab each rolled-off sleeve just below your hand, and swiftly yank it off. Then you'll pull the wetsuit down below your knees, use foot one to step on the opposite wetsuit leg (leg two), and swiftly yank leg two up to pull the wetsuit leg off – or at least further down toward the ankle. It may take a few rounds on each side, but you'll get the wetsuit off quicker this way than if you sit down and try to pull it off gently.

your kick rate during the final 50 to 100 yards (or meters) of the swim. Increasing your kick rate will raise your heart rate, which helps combat the potential to feel lightheaded. Additionally, increasing your kick rate increases the blood flow to your legs, which prepares them for the work they're about to do on the bike.

Logistically, the swim-to-bike transition involves ditching your swim-specific gear and putting on your bike-specific gear – while you're dripping wet. Ditching your swim gear doesn't require a lot of thought because you'll be excited to tear off your cap and goggles and rid yourself of your wetsuit. Your bike-specific gear list could be as short as helmet, shoes, and sunglasses but may also include a bike jersey (if you're not wearing a tri top), socks, gloves, or a race belt if your race bib is required on the bike. (You'll be wearing swim-bike-run compatible bottoms, so no need to change those.) You can practice the routine of donning your bike gear any time you head out for a ride: Set your bike gear next to your bike, put it on quickly and efficiently, and recite a T1 mantra to keep yourself on task: shoes-helmet-sunglasses. Practicing this while dripping wet can be accomplished on the race simulation days provided in the training plans in part V. Or, if you want extra practice, you can hop in the shower wearing your race-day outfit, just barely toweling off before you put on your bike gear and start your ride. (Yes, this sounds a little crazy, but it's effective.)

T2: The Bike-to-Run Transition

The bike-to-run transition presents a greater challenge than the swim-to-bike transition, but also offers more opportunities for practice. Physiologically, the transition is both nuanced and profound. The switch from one lower-body, 80 to 90 rpm (per side), repetitive cyclical motion to another lower-body, 170 to 180 spm (across both sides), repetitive cyclical motion seems like it should be straightforward, but it turns out that the biomechanics of cycling and running have more differences than might appear at first glance. The cycling movement pattern incorporates a series of concentric contractions (where the muscle shortens while contracting), while the running movement pattern utilizes both concentric and eccentric contractions (where the muscle lengthens under tension). These differences mean that when you finish the bike, your legs are both tired from the muscle contractions that supported pedaling and also fresh and rested for the muscular work that will support your run stride.

When you first ask your brain to switch the demand on those tired-but-rested legs from the neuromuscular activation that drives pedaling to the similar-but-different-and-certainly-more-complex neuromuscular activation that coordinates your run stride, it will be confused. Really, really confused. Which is why we incorporate so many bricks, or bike workouts followed immediately by runs, in training. Those bricks allow your body and brain to get accustomed to the physiology of the transition, so it's less and less confused each time you ask it to switch from biking to running. (The exact origin of the term *brick* is uncertain. It could be an abbreviation for a bike-run-in-combination workout, it could be that Dr Matt Brick coined the term, or it could refer to how your legs feel during those first minutes running off the bike.)

Brick sessions also provide an opportunity to practice the logistics of the bike-to-run transition. Similar to the swim-to-bike transition, you'll first ditch your bike-specific gear – your helmet, shoes (if they are bike-specific), and bike gloves (if you wore them), and sometimes your bike jersey and sunglasses (if you don't choose to keep them on for the run). You'll then put on any run-specific gear that can't be dealt with while running – typically run shoes (if different from your bike shoes), socks (if you didn't wear them on the bike), and a run top (if you're not wearing a tri top or sticking with your bike jersey for the run). Finally, you'll grab your remaining run items – usually your race belt with your race bib (if your race bib wasn't required on the bike), a hat or visor if you want one, and some fueling for the run – and don don or stash those once you're moving. You can treat each brick workout as transition practice

The Bike-to-Run Transition: A Reality Distortion Field

While the exact physiological explanation for this phenomenon is unclear, it's nearly universal: The bike-to-run transition creates a reality distortion field, often during brick sessions in training and almost always when moving through T2 on race day. Within this reality distortion field, your perception of your pace when running off the bike (how the effort level feels for a certain pace) is wholly divorced from the reality of your pace when running off the bike (how much fatigue that pace is producing).

It goes like this: You finish your bike, you're tired, but you pull on your shoes and start running. You feel like you're running a very easy, comfortable run pace – then you glance at your watch and see that you're running 30 to 60 seconds per mile (20-40 seconds per kilometer) *faster* than you think you're running. You feel good, so you think you're a rock star (I'm so fit! I'm so fast!) and you keep running at that pace. About 20 minutes later, you realize the pace actually *was* way too fast; you hit the wall and are forced to a slow jog or even a walk.

Knowing that this reality distortion field exists and extends about 20 minutes outside of T2 allows you to counteract its influence. Spend those 20 minutes practically staring at your watch, trusting the reality of the pace it's displaying more than you trust your body's feedback, and shortening your stride until you're running the pace you normally run. (The Running with Grandma Cue from chapter 6 can be very helpful here.) At some point around that 20-minute mark, you'll realize that the pace you *think* you're running and the pace you *are* running are more or less the same. At that point, you've escaped the reality distortion field, and you can once again trust your body's feedback and stop staring at your watch.

by laying out your run gear before starting your bike, returning from your bike ride and quickly swapping gear, then heading out on your run. Final tip: To prepare your legs for the transition from cycling to running, increase your cadence by 5 rpm and decrease your effort level just slightly during the final few minutes of your bike workout.

REALITY DISTORTION FIELD CUE

Objective: To appropriately manage your run pace for the first 20 minutes after exiting T2.

Coaching Direction: Set a pace target for your run off-the-bike, consistent with your zone 2 or endurance pace (which is discussed in chapter 8), and use your watch and the Running with Grandma Cue to adhere to that pace target for your run.

TRANSITIONS CUE

Objective: To simulate and practice the swim-to-bike and bike-to-run transitions.

Coaching Direction: Use the race simulation workouts to practice your transitions. Coordinate the workouts so they can be executed consecutively without interruption (for example, bike and run from the swim venue parking lot), organize your gear ahead of time, and treat each transition as if it were taking place on race day.

Fueling (and Hydration)

No matter how much fitness you've built in training and how well you've developed your swim, bike, run, and transition skills, you cannot take advantage of any of it if your body cannot function at its best. And in order to function, your body needs adequate fuel to power your muscles, fluids to stay hydrated, and electrolytes – namely sodium – to maintain your body's cellular-level fluid balance and support neuromuscular functionality. So let's walk through your body's specific fuel, fluid, and electrolyte needs for before, during, and after activity, and how to translate those needs to fueling and hydration plans for training and racing.

Fueling: Carbohydrates

Carbohydrates (a.k.a. *carbs*) are the primary fuel that drives your engine. While your body does use fat as fuel during low-intensity activity, carbs must be present in order to metabolize fat. (We often say that "fat burns in a carbohydrate flame.") Plus carbs, which convert to fuel faster and more efficiently than fat, are a critical fueling source for moderate- and high-intensity activity. So we talk about fueling exclusively in terms of consuming carbs, namely glucose and fructose. Glucose is our primary fuel source, and current studies show that our bodies can absorb up to 60 grams/hour of glucose through our sodium-glucose cotransporter 1 (SGLT1). If we need more fuel than our SGLT1 can provide, we turn to fructose. Our fructose transporter (GLUT5) can absorb up to 30 grams/hour of fructose, bringing our total possible fueling intake up to 90 grams/hour of carbs. But that doesn't mean you should plan to consume 90 grams/hour of carbs during your next workout – it takes your gut some time to get used to digesting that quantity of carbs during activity, and depending on the duration of your training session, you may not need that quantity of carbs anyway.

Your body stores a limited amount of carbohydrates, specifically glucose, in your muscles and liver as glycogen. Each muscle's glycogen stores fuel its own needs, while liver glycogen maintains your blood sugar levels, which are critical for brain function. The stored glycogen in your muscles can fuel up to an hour or so of moderate-intensity exercise, assuming that your normal daily nutrition sufficiently maintains those glycogen stores. If you go too far beyond an hour without an external carbohydrate source, your muscles run low on glycogen stores, causing your body to limit performance so it can preserve your crucial liver glycogen stores. The entire goal of fueling, then, is to top off (before), maintain (during), and replenish (after) those glycogen stores so you can perform to the best of your ability in training and on race day.

Fueling Requirements: Before

Aim to eat a pre-workout or pre-race meal 1 to 2 hours before your training session or 2 to 3 hours before your race start time. For workouts or events lasting up to 2 hours, consume 20 to 30 grams of carbs in the meal; for workouts or events lasting 2 to 4 hours, consume 30 to 60 grams of carbs; and for workouts or events lasting 4+ hours, consume at least 60 grams of carbs. Before runs and on race day, limit protein, fat, fiber, dairy, and acidic foods in your pre-workout or pre-race meal to reduce gastrointestinal (GI) distress during your workout or event. And on race day (in addition to breakfast), or for early morning training sessions where fueling 1 to 2 hours in advance isn't possible, use sport-specific fueling sources to deliver 25 to 30 grams of carbs 15 to 30 minutes before your race or workout.

Longer training days and race days can also benefit from additional carbs over several meals beforehand to ensure that your glycogen storage tanks are full (a.k.a. *carb loading*). Plan to increase your intake of high-density carbohydrates, such as bread or pasta, at one or two meals the day before a 3+ hour training day or short-course triathlon event, and increase your carb intake over three to four meals across the 2 days before a long-course triathlon event. Plan for your biggest meal to be breakfast or lunch the day before your event, then taper your food intake later in the day.

Fueling Requirements: During

Moderate-intensity biking or running typically burns 300 to 600 calories per hour, or the equivalent of 75 to 150 grams of carbs each hour. Given that your SGLT1 and GLUT5 combined can absorb a maximum of 90 grams/hour of carbs, your intake will typically not match your expenditure during exercise. Your goal for in-workout and in-race fueling, then, is to limit the depth of the carbohydrate hole that you are digging.

The bike presents an excellent opportunity for fueling, as the relatively stable bike position allows your GI system to work effectively. For training sessions and races lasting 1 to 2.5 hours, aim to consume

30 to 60 grams/hour of carbs, primarily glucose. For training sessions and races lasting more than 2.5 hours, aim to consume 60 to 90 grams/hour of carbs, combining glucose and fructose. (As you read food and fueling product nutrition labels, it's helpful to know that dextrose and maltodextrin are both forms of glucose, and sucrose [a.k.a. *table sugar* or *cane sugar*] is a combination of glucose and fructose.)

We downsize our carbohydrate targets on the run because the increased intensity and jostling of your gut pose a challenge to your GI system. For training sessions and races lasting 1 to 2.5 hours, aim to consume 30 to 50 grams/hour of carbs, primarily glucose. For training sessions and races lasting more than 2.5 hours, aim to consume 50 to 70 grams/hour of carbs, mainly glucose if you're consuming 50 to 60 grams/hour and combining glucose and fructose above that. As with your pre-workout meal, limit protein, fat, and fiber in run fueling sources to steer clear of GI distress – and in your bike fueling sources if you're running immediately afterward.

Fueling Requirements: After

Post-workout and post-race fueling promote recovery by replenishing depleted glycogen stores, topping off your tank in preparation for tomorrow's training. Post-workout fueling is only necessary when you have dug deep into your glycogen stores, typically for workouts lasting 90 minutes or longer – no need to grab a recovery shake after a 30-minute swim, bike, or run. Aim to consume 60 to 100 grams of carbs (0.5 grams per pound [1 g/kg] of bodyweight) within 30 to 60 minutes of finishing your workout or race. To aid muscle repair and further boost recovery, add 15 to 25 grams of protein to your post-workout fueling with a targeted carbs-to-protein ratio of 4:1. And if your workout or race was really long (4+ hours), additional carbs at your next meal will help truly top off those glycogen stores, which is especially important if you have a big training day again tomorrow.

Hydration: Fluids and Electrolytes

When we talk about hydration during activity, we're specifically talking about replacing the fluids your body loses during exercise due to sweat. Even more specifically, we're talking not just about consuming fluids but also ensuring that your body absorbs them. That's where electrolytes come in. Sodium, a critical electrolyte, draws the fluids you've consumed out of your gut and aids in moving them into your bloodstream, where the fluid loss originated.

So how much fluid and sodium do you need in order to replace what you lose through sweat while training and racing? Well, it depends. It depends on your individual physiology – your sweat rate and your sweat sodium concentration – and individual sweat profiles vary widely, so there's no universal answer. Which isn't to say there's no answer: A simple at-home sweat rate test can easily determine your sweat rate, and we can use your taste buds to target your sweat sodium concentration. Understanding your individual sweat profile allows us to define your fluid and sodium needs for training and racing.

Additionally, it's worth noting that besides helping with fluid absorption, sodium is also necessary for carbohydrate absorption. Remember SGLT1 from our carbohydrate discussion? To refresh your memory, it's the sodium-glucose *co*transporter – sodium and glucose move together from your gut to your bloodstream, where the glucose is then delivered to your muscles and converted into fuel. So while we're discussing fluids and electrolytes primarily in the context of hydration, they also play a critical role in fueling: Without proper hydration, all those carbs you're consuming will sit in your gut and cause GI distress.

Determining Your Fluid Loss Rate

Fluid loss rates typically range from 16 to 70 ounces/hour (~500-2,000 mL/hr) – it's quite a big range! You can determine your individual sweat rate by weighing yourself before and after a 1-hour (or so) bike or run workout. Any weight lost during that workout (net of anything consumed) comes from sweat, so your net weight loss translates to your hourly sweat rate. The specific at-home sweat rate test instructions are as follows:

1. Weigh yourself (naked) immediately before your workout (e.g., 165 pounds [74.85 kg]).
2. Complete a 1-hour (ish) bike or run (e.g., 1.25 hours).
3. Track your fluid intake during the workout; to be extra precise, you can pre-measure your planned fluid intake and consume it all during the workout (e.g., 24 ounces [710 mL]). Because it's difficult to account for the impact of food intake, it's best not to consume anything other than fluids.
4. Towel off and weigh yourself (again naked) immediately after your workout (e.g., 164 pounds [74.38 kg]).
5. Determine your measured weight loss during your workout (e.g., 165 pounds − 164 pounds = 1 pound [74.85 kg − 74.38 kg = 0.47 kg]). Depending on your sweat rate and the amount of fluid consumed, this number can be notable, minimal, zero, or even negative.
6. Convert your weight loss to match the units for your fluid intake (e.g., 1 pound × 16 ounces per pound = 16 ounces [0.47 kg × 1,000 mL/kg = 470 mL]).

7. Add the fluid consumed to your weight loss to determine your total fluid loss due to sweat (e.g., 16 ounces + 24 ounces = 40 ounces [470 mL + 710 mL = 1180 mL]).
8. Your hourly sweat rate is your fluid loss divided by your workout duration (e.g., 40 ounces/1.25 hours = 32 ounces/hour [1180 mL/1.25 hr = 944 mL/hr]).

Your sweat rate, or fluid loss rate, can vary across bike and run and with the weather, so it doesn't hurt to conduct this at-home sweat rate test several times under varying conditions.

Determining Your Sweat Sodium Concentration

Your sweat sodium concentration represents the ratio of sodium to fluid in your sweat. Like fluid loss rates, sweat sodium concentrations span a wide range, typically anywhere from 300 to 1,500 milligrams or more of sodium per bike bottle. (A typical bike bottle holds 24 ounces [710 mL] of fluid, and I consider it to be a standard unit of measurement.) While there is no equivalent to the at-home sweat rate test to determine your individual sweat sodium concentration, your body can give us some clues as to where you might fall within that range: If you routinely notice crusty, white salt marks on your face, hat, or clothing after exercise, or if you regularly reach for the salt shaker at meals, you are likely on the higher end of the range, requiring 1,000 to 1,500 milligrams of sodium per bike bottle. On the other hand, if you shy away from added salt or very salty foods, you may be on the lower end of the range, needing only 300 to 450 milligrams per bike bottle. If neither is the case, or if you're just unsure, aim for the median value of 600 to 800 milligrams per bike bottle.

Defining Your Individual Sweat Profile

Your individual sweat profile reflects both your sweat rate and sweat sodium concentration, combining a rate and a ratio. This often leads to some confusion, so let's talk through that distinction and how the two are related. Your sweat rate tells you how many bottles, ounces, or milliliters of fluid you need to consume each hour during activity. Your sweat sodium concentration, or sodium-to-fluid ratio, tells you how much sodium you need to put in each bottle or consume alongside every 24 ounces (710 mL) of fluid. Do not think about sodium on a per-hour basis; instead, scale your sodium intake with your fluid intake to maintain a consistent sodium-to-fluid ratio. Understanding your individual sweat profile is crucial for determining your before, during, and after hydration requirements.

Hydration Requirements: Before

Pre-hydrating leading into race day ensures that you show up to the start line hydrated rather than in a state of slight dehydration. Start pre-hydrating 3 to 7 days (or more) before race day, drinking an extra one to two bike bottles of noncaffeinated, noncarbonated fluids each day. Add 300 to 1,000 milligrams of sodium to that increased daily fluid intake to avoid diluting your sodium levels.

Athletes competing in long-course races, racing in hot and humid conditions, or with high sweat sodium concentrations can also benefit from preloading their fluids and sodium in advance of race day. Pre-hydrate the night before, the morning of the event, or both, by consuming a bike bottle of water with 1,500 milligrams of sodium. The extra sodium in your bloodstream will cause your body to retain the extra fluid, boosting your hydration status and increasing the volume of fluid loss that can occur before you become dehydrated.

(Note that I didn't mention prehydrating for training sessions. Because you are training daily, you want to be good about hydrating every single day, with the occasional added electrolyte supplement if you have a high sweat sodium concentration. A pale yellow urine color indicates proper hydration; darker and you're underhydrated, clear and you're overhydrated.)

Hydration Requirements: During

During training or on race day, you want to limit fluid loss to 2 percent of your body weight to stave off dehydration. But since it's challenging, if not impossible, to track and measure your fluid loss in real time, you'll aim to replace 100 percent of your fluid loss on the bike and a minimum of 70 percent on the run (it's harder and less comfortable to consume fluids on the run). In practice, this means that your hourly fluid requirement on the bike equals your hourly sweat rate; on the run, cut that requirement down to three-quarters of your hourly sweat rate. And always make sure your sodium intake is proportional to your fluid intake, based on your sweat sodium concentration (your sodium-to-fluid ratio). You know you're adequately hydrated if you need to urinate approximately once every 3 hours.

Hydration Requirements: After

Post-workout and post-race hydration corrects any dehydration that develops during the training session or event. Even if your in-workout or in-race hydration was perfect, it's good practice to get in the habit of consuming a bike bottle of fluid with sodium per your sweat sodium concentration shortly after all races, as well as after particularly hard training sessions, training sessions lasting 90 minutes or more, or training sessions done in temperatures above 75 degrees Fahrenheit (20 degrees Celsius). For races and training sessions that meet several of those criteria, such as a 3-hour race in 85 degrees Fahrenheit (25 degrees Fahrenheit) temps, or if your sweat rate exceeds 36 ounces/hour (1,000 mL/hr), you may benefit from a second bottle.

Developing Your Fueling and Hydration Plan

A fueling and hydration plan translates your fueling and hydration requirements from abstract details to practical application. A comprehensive plan will define the what, when, and how of fueling and hydrating for your training session or event: What you are consuming; when you are consuming it; and how you are carrying or acquiring the fueling and hydration that you will consume. It can be a bit of a process to take the fueling and hydrating requirements that we just defined and convert them to a full-blown before, during, and after fueling and hydration plan, so let's walk through the process used to create Alex's Fueling and Hydration Plan for their Olympic-distance triathlon.

> Alex starts by noting the race and its anticipated total duration. Alex then thinks through the what and when of their pre-race, or before, fueling and hydration. For a short-course triathlon, Alex's pre-race hydration begins several days before the race, and their pre-race fueling begins the day before the race. Alex also wants to pre-plan their race-day breakfast and be mindful of their race-week food choices to minimize GI distress. Based on that information, Alex develops their fueling and hydration plan for before the race.
>
> Alex then turns to the what, when, and how of their in-race, or during, fueling and hydration. They note the sports included in the race and the expected duration for each sport. Based on that information and their individual sweat profile, Alex lists their fueling and hydration requirements for during the race by sport. You can't fuel during the swim leg of a triathlon, so Alex's plan focuses on their fueling and hydration during the bike and run legs. Alex defines the what, when, and how of each fueling and hydration source for the bike and the run, and calculates the combined hourly fueling and hydration provided across all sources by sport.
>
> Alex then compares their planned hourly fueling and hydration on the bike and run to their original fueling and hydration requirements and confirms that their plan provides all of their required carbohydrates, fluid, and sodium. They feel really

confident about their in-race fueling and hydration after having thought this through in such detail! But there's one last piece of the plan still to complete. Alex rounds out their fueling and hydration plan by noting what they will consume after the race to help with recovery.

Alex's Fueling and Hydration Plan

Race or Workout and Expected Total Duration: Olympic-distance triathlon, about 3 hours

Pre-Race Fueling and Hydration (Before)

Notes: Limit dairy and acidic foods all of race week, low fiber the day before the race

The Week Before the Race

Hydration: 4, 3, and 2 days before race day: 1 additional bike bottle of water with 300-mg electrolyte tablet

The Day Before the Race

Fueling: Breakfast: pancakes with syrup
Lunch: sandwich, no tomato or lettuce, bag of chips
Dinner: moderate serving of rice, small serving of tofu, fish, or chicken

Hydration: Morning: 1 additional bike bottle of water with 300-mg electrolyte tablet
Afternoon: 1 bike bottle of water with 5 × 300-mg electrolyte tablets (1,500 mg total sodium)

The Morning of the Race

Fueling: 3 hours pre-race: bagel with peanut butter and honey (~60 g carbs)
15 minutes before race start: gel with 25 g carbs

Hydration: Sip pre-race: 1 bike bottle of water with 5 × 300-mg electrolyte tablets (1,500 mg total sodium)

In-Race Fueling and Hydration (During)

Sports and durations: Swim (~30 minutes), bike (85-90 minutes), run (~55 minutes)

Fueling and hydration requirements during the bike: 60 to 70 g/hr carbs, 32 oz/hr (950 mL/hr) fluids with 600 to 800 mg sodium per bike bottle

Fueling and hydration requirements during the run: 50 g/hr carbs, 24 oz/hr (710 mL/hr) fluids with 600 to 800 mg sodium per 24 oz (710 mL)

Bike

Source #1: 24-oz (710-mL) bottle of drink mix with 60 g carbs and 500 mg sodium

- 1/3 drink mix bottle every 30 minutes (bottle will last 90 min)
- In front bottle cage on frame

Source #2: 24-oz (710-mL) bottle of water with 3 X 300-mg electrolyte tablets (900 mg total sodium)

- 1/3 water bottle every 30 minutes (bottle will last 90 min)
- In second bottle cage on frame

Source #3: 1 package of 6 chews with 8 g carbs each

- 1 chew every 20 minutes (chews will last 2 hr)
- In top tube bag or bike jersey pocket

Total Hourly Bike Fueling and Hydration by Source

Source #1: 1/3 drink mix bottle every 30 minutes = 2/3 bottle per hour

- 2/3 bottle/hr X 60 g/bottle = 40 g/hr carbs
- 2/3 bottle/hr X 24 oz/bottle (710 mL/bottle) = 16 oz/hr (475 mL/hr) fluids
- 2/3 bottle/hr X 500 mg/bottle = 333 mg sodium with 16 oz (475 mL) fluid each hour

Source #2: 1/3 water bottle every 30 minutes = 2/3 bottle per hour

- 2/3 bottle/hr X 24 oz/bottle (710 mL/bottle) = 16 oz/hr (475 mL/hr) fluids
- 2/3 bottle/hr X 900 mg/bottle = 600 mg sodium with 16 oz (475 mL) fluid each hour

Source #3: 1 chew every 20 minutes = 3 chews per hour

- 3 chews/hr X 8 g/chew = 24 g/hr carbs

Total Hourly Bike Fueling and Hydration by Type

Carbs: 40 g/hr from drink mix + 24 g/hr from chews = 64 g/hr carbs

Fluid: 16 oz/hr from drink mix bottle + 16 oz/hr from water bottle = 32 oz/hr (475 mL/hr + 475 mL/hr = 950 mL/hr) fluids

Sodium: 333 mg and 16 oz (475 mL) from drink mix bottle each hour + 600 mg and 16 oz (475 mL) from water bottle each hour = 933 mg per 32 oz (950 mL) = 700 mg per 24 oz (710 mL) sodium concentration

(continued)

Alex's Fueling and Hydration Plan *(continued)*

Run

Source #1: 2 gels with 25 g carbs each

- 1 gel every 30 minutes (gels will last 1 hour)
- In loops on race belt

Source #2: Water, approximately 4 oz (120 mL) per cup

- Approximately every 10 minutes
- From aid stations

Source #3: 10 100-mg chewable salt tablets

- With every aid station water cup (tablets will last about 1 hour 40 minutes)
- In plastic bag in pocket of race belt

Total Hourly Run Fueling and Hydration by Source

Source #1: 1 gel every 30 minutes = 2 gels per hour; 2 gels/hr × 25 g/gel = 50 g/hr carbs

Source #2: 1 4-oz (120-mL) cup of water approximately every 10 minutes = roughly 6 cups per hour; 6 cups/hr × 4 oz/cup (120 mL/cup) = 24 oz/hr (720 mL/hr) fluids

Source #3: 1 salt tablet per 4-oz (120-mL) cup = 6 tablets per 6 cups = (6 × 100 mg) per (6 × 4 oz) = 600 mg per 24 oz ([6 × 100 mg]/(6 × 120 mL) = 600 mg/720 mL) sodium concentration

Total Hourly Run Fueling and Hydration By Type

Carbs: 50 g/hr carbs - see source #1 (gels)

Fluid: 24 oz/hr (720 mL/hr) fluids – see source #2 (cups of water)

Sodium: 600 mg per 24 oz (600 mg/720 mL) – see source #3 (electrolyte tablets)

Post-Race Fueling and Hydration (After)

Fueling: Within 60 minutes of finishing the race: 1 bike bottle of a recovery shake with 60 g carbs + 15 g protein

Hydration: Post-race: fluids from recovery shake
Race day afternoon: 1 bike bottle with 2 × 300-mg electrolyte tablets

Alex put together a great fueling and hydration plan for their Olympic-distance triathlon, providing appropriate pre-race and recovery fueling and hydration, covering in-race fueling requirements based on the duration of the event, meeting their individual hydration needs, and ensuring sufficient sources for in-race fueling and hydration. It was no coincidence that Alex did such a great job – they've been honing their fueling and hydration plan throughout their training season.

And that's exactly what you'll do across your training season. Developing your fueling and hydration plan is often a trial-and-error process, using your long training days – and brick sessions in particular – to test different foods and sport-specific fueling products along with various approaches for the timing and logistics of using those fueling and hydration sources. Creating fueling and hydration plans for those long training days throughout your season allows you to document and fine-tune the different strategies you test out, so that by race day your fueling and hydration formula is as tight as Alex's.

FUELING AND HYDRATING CUE

Objective: To test and practice fueling and hydration plans during long training days.

Coaching Direction: Before your long training session, develop an in-workout fueling and hydration plan. Execute the plan as best you can during the workout. After the workout, note what went well and what needs adjustment for your next long training session or race day.

Testing fueling and hydration strategies in training provides a range of benefits beyond perfecting your race-day fueling and hydration plan. Implementing pre-workout fueling guidelines and fueling and hydrating properly during workouts allows your body to perform at its best on training days, because that's just as important in training as it is on race day. And staying on top of post-workout fueling and hydration ensures adequate recovery from today's workout, so your body is ready for tomorrow's. In addition, practicing fueling and hydrating during training sessions acclimates your gut to eating and drinking while biking and running, and testing out race-morning breakfasts and day-before meals ensures they won't cause GI distress on race day. Finally, making fueling and hydrating so routine that you can do it without thinking allows you to focus on every other aspect of your execution on race day.

PART III

TRAINING FOR TRIATHLON

Stress + Rest = Growth

Steve Magness

At this point, you have a fabulous set of tools to help you develop your swimming, biking, running, and triathlon skills. But you also – of course – need to develop the fitness to cross the finish line of your triathlon feeling strong and with your head held high. So now we'll focus on how we transform you from the athlete you are today into a triathlete who is fit and prepared for their triathlon.

We'll start by defining triathlon fitness and discussing the building blocks we use to develop that fitness. Then we'll discuss how we use those building blocks to structure training weeks, cycles, and seasons. With that excellent understanding of how we build triathlon fitness in general, we'll structure the training for your triathlon season using the training plans in part V, ensuring that your training starts where you are today and culminates with the fitness you need to complete your event. And finally, we'll outline all the tools you need to navigate that season training plan successfully – everything from how to approach your individual workouts to how to address motivation challenges to how to handle (the inevitable) disruptions to the plan.

8

DEVELOPING YOUR TRIATHLON FITNESS

What exactly is fitness? And what does it mean to be "fit"? Fitness is generally defined as being fit (not a terribly helpful definition), and fit generally refers to being healthy or able to perform activity (also not super helpful). In practice, how we define fitness varies by sport: run-your-fastest-mile fitness differs from lift-your-greatest-weight fitness, which differs from climb-your-highest-peak fitness. And while developing fitness of any type taps into a fairly universal set of fitness building blocks, the way you utilize those building blocks differs from sport to sport.

Specifically, then, what does it mean to be "triathlon fit"? Triathlon fitness typically reflects your ability to comfortably cover your race distance at a speed appropriate for that distance. To develop that fitness, we primarily rely on the building blocks of endurance and speed, with support from strength and mobility. So, let's talk about those building blocks and how they contribute to fitness development. We'll take a deep dive into the endurance and speed building blocks, gaining a solid understanding of what they are, when and in what proportion we use them, and how we target them. Then we'll discuss the role that the strength and mobility building block plays in developing our largely cardiorespiratory-based triathlon fitness. And finally, we'll talk about what fitness development looks like in practice for each of our three triathlon sports.

Endurance and Speed Building Blocks

The endurance and speed building blocks align with the two main energy systems we use to fuel our muscles during activity: our aerobic and anaerobic energy systems. Our aerobic energy system relies on an oxygen-based fueling mechanism within our muscles, hence the "aerobic" designation. This aerobic fueling mechanism powers our slow-twitch muscle fibers, which are highly fatigue-resistant in a well-trained athlete and support continuous, low- to moderate-intensity activity. Since long bouts of low- to moderate-intensity activity translate perfectly to endurance work, the endurance building block develops our aerobic engine. Our anaerobic energy system, on the other hand, relies on a muscle-fueling mechanism that doesn't require oxygen, hence the "anaerobic"

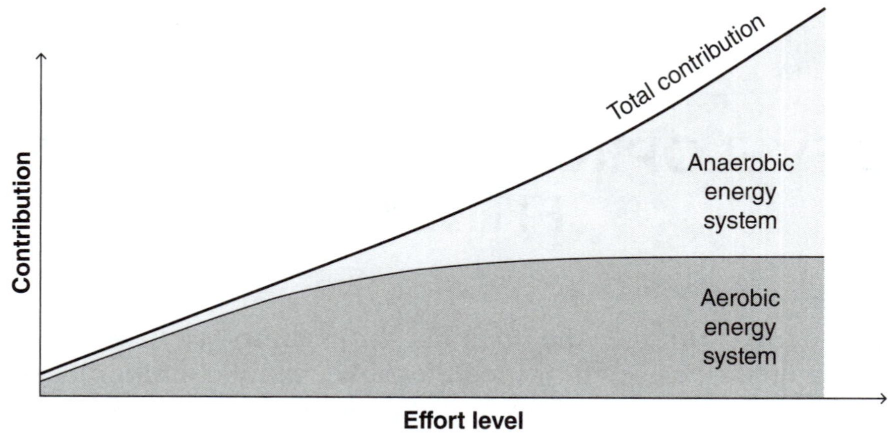

FIGURE 8.1 Aerobic and anaerobic energy system contribution to muscle fueling (illustrative only).

designation. This anaerobic fueling mechanism powers our fast-twitch muscle fibers, which fatigue after seconds of maximum output or minutes of near-maximum output during high-intensity activity, even in a well-trained athlete. Brief stints of high-intensity work allow for speed, so we use the speed building block to develop our anaerobic engine.

These two energy systems don't work in isolation. During endurance activity, where your aerobic energy system provides the vast majority of the fuel for your muscles, the anaerobic energy system still hums in the background. And while high-intensity efforts rely heavily on your anaerobic energy system, you combine that anaerobic fueling contribution with your maximum aerobic fueling contribution to meet the total fueling demand of your muscles (figure 8.1). Since these two energy systems work in combination, developing each individually benefits both the endurance and speed building blocks. Increasing the size of your aerobic engine through your endurance building block also improves your speed due to the boosted maximum aerobic contribution at higher intensities. Improving your anaerobic engine through your speed building block also increases your speed at endurance, or low- to moderate-intensity, efforts due to more efficient fuel production from the relatively small anaerobic contribution.

Using Your Endurance and Speed Building Blocks to Develop Fitness

A large aerobic engine and a well-developed anaerobic engine form the foundation of triathlon fitness, and we utilize the endurance and speed building blocks in a specific order and proportion to build this fitness. Because low-, moderate-, and high-intensity efforts all rely on your aerobic energy system, we always begin by focusing exclusively on your endurance building block. We continue to heavily emphasize the endurance building block throughout training because it develops the crucial element of fitness needed to comfortably cover your race distance, supports your ability to work on your anaerobic engine, and generates a relatively low fatigue burden compared to the fitness gained from any given workout. Once we have your aerobic engine sufficiently in place, we incorporate the speed building block to establish your anaerobic engine and acclimate your body to high-intensity work. We use the speed building block somewhat sparingly because it creates a significant fatigue burden and contributes less to overall triathlon fitness than the endurance building block.

Using Training Zones to Target Your Endurance and Speed Building Blocks

Training zones allow us to accurately target the intended building block and energy system within a training session. Table 8.1 defines the five zones commonly used within triathlon training (and cardiorespiratory training in general). Zones 1 and 2 are our low- to moderate-intensity zones; we primarily target our endurance building block and develop our aerobic energy system by training in zone 2. Zones 4 and 5 are our high-intensity zones, which are included in our speed building block and develop our anaerobic energy system; zone 5 includes our true anaerobic training zone, while zone 4 incorporates a balance of our aerobic and anaerobic systems that allows us to stretch the otherwise short spurts of anaerobic contribution to up to anywhere from 10 to 60 minutes.

TABLE 8.1 **Training Zones**

Zone (RPE)	Name	Description	Maximum duration	How it feels
Zone 1 (3/10)	Easy	Easy	All day	You barely break a sweat
Zone 2 (4/10)	Endurance	Moderate	All day	You are sweating but can sustain the effort level for a long time
Zone 3 (5/10)	Tempo	Strong	Several hours	You are working but can still maintain the effort for a while
Zone 4 (6-7/10)	Threshold	Hard	Up to an hour	It is hard to sustain the effort level, but you could still work harder
Zone 5 (8-9/10)	Anaerobic	Fast	Seconds to minutes	You are at an effort level that you can only sustain for up to a few minutes

RPE = rate of perceived exertion.

Fitness Development Versus Fatigue Burden

Fitness development requires a delicate balance. To develop fitness, you train – you stress your energy systems to produce adaptations that increase your fitness. But that training stress also creates fatigue; the more the training stresses your body, the more fatigue it creates. The ideal training level will stress the body enough to produce fitness adaptations while only generating a *manageable* amount of fatigue.

Along those lines, you may have noticed that I did not mention zone 3 when we discussed using training zones to target fitness building blocks. That omission was intentional. We often refer to zone 3 as the "black hole of training" because it doesn't effectively develop your anaerobic energy system, and the aerobic system adaptations it does produce result in an overly high fatigue burden. Dr. Stephen Seiler, an exercise physiologist who popularized the polarized training approach that emphasizes training in zones 1, 2, 4, and 5 while sidelining zone 3, believes that "we do not train at medium-hard intensity – it's too much pain for too little gain."

Note that I do make one exception to the "no training in zone 3" rule: When your intended race effort aligns with zone 3, we incorporate zone 3 intervals into long workouts so that you can acclimate to race effort.

Many athletes use metrics like heart rate, pace, or power to quantitatively define the range of each training zone. These numerical boundaries can be beneficial – if they are defined properly based on anaerobic or lactate threshold testing (note that the terms *anaerobic threshold* and *lactate threshold* are often used interchangeably; while they technically represent different physiological thresholds, the two thresholds occur at the same intensity level). Your multisport watch, indoor training software, training calendar app, and the big poster on the wall of your gym may claim to know your anaerobic threshold and training zones – but they don't! Those default or assumed values are often (almost always) incorrect. You're better off gaining an intuitive feel for each training zone and trusting your rate of perceived exertion (RPE). In fact, even if you do have a defined anaerobic or lactate threshold and training zones from lab or field testing, developing the skill to train and race by RPE is highly valuable. Measured rates of effort should confirm how you feel, not dictate it.

The Strength and Mobility Building Block

While your endurance and speed building blocks form the foundation of your triathlon fitness, your strength and mobility block ensures that your body functions well enough to develop that fitness in training and unleash it on race day.

Fitness Development and Strength Training

The role of strength-building work differs from the role of endurance- and speed-building work. Endurance and speed provide the cardiorespiratory fitness needed to succeed at your triathlon. Strength delivers muscles that can execute the swim-bike-run movement patterns for as many miles as we want and as hard as we want, even if we're tired. Developing that type of strength looks different than developing strength for strength's sake. We do more repetitions at lower weights, and never max out our muscles during a session. Because swim-bike-run is our main focus, not pure strength, we never want the work we do within our strength building block to impede our ability to do our swim-bike-run workouts.

We use functional strength training to build the strength that supports our swim-bike-run movement patterns. Functional strength training uses strength exercises that mimic the movement patterns and muscular demands of swimming, biking, and running, reflecting the functions our muscles perform in triathlon training and racing. These functional strength exercises are all compound movements that involve multiple joints and muscle groups working together, including squats, deadlifts, lunges, lat pulldowns, and rows. Because biking and running involve movement patterns where each leg works individually, we often incorporate single-sided versions of these exercises; this type of lower-body work also enhances lateral stabilization, which helps reduce the risk of injury. And finally, we can't neglect our core, which stabilizes our posture across all three sports and provides energy transfer across the body. Just remember that your core extends well beyond those six-pack abs – all the muscles from your ribs through your hips, including your glutes, are part of your core.

Fitness Development and Mobility

While strength builds muscles that can support the movement of swim-bike-run, mobility provides the range of motion that allows those movements to happen. Swimming, biking, and running all lean heavily on spine mobility. Swimming additionally requires shoulder mobility, and hip mobility is key for biking and running. Incorporating short, 10-minute mobility sessions into your weekly routine will help establish a sufficient range of motion at the beginning of your training and maintain it as your muscles become stressed and tight. Mobility work doesn't have to be limited to a few scheduled weekly sessions, though. It can also serve as an excellent warm-up for training sessions, a calm transition to your day each morning, or a peaceful way to wind down at night.

Sport-Specific Application of Fitness Development

While the fitness building blocks, energy systems, and training zones are consistent across all three triathlon sports, the fitness development goals and the nuanced feel of the training zones can differ from swim to bike to run. So let's take the sports one by one and outline how fitness development plays out in practice for each.

Fitness Development and Swimming

As we discussed in chapter 4, swim technique plays a larger role than fitness in swimming success, so swim fitness development also prioritizes technique development. To accomplish this, we structure swim workouts as a series of short swim distances accompanied by frequent rest. These short swim intervals allow you to swim only as long as you can maintain your form, and the subsequent rest period – even a very brief one – provides a reset, allowing you to begin the next swim interval with good form. As you build fitness, your interval distances will increase and your rest periods decrease, but the interval structure for workouts will remain.

Another distinction of swim fitness development is the larger emphasis on high-intensity training. Swimming is a low-impact (really, no-impact) and non-weight-bearing activity, which means that higher intensity efforts in swimming don't create the same fatigue burden as they do for biking and running. Additionally, once you achieve sufficient fitness and solid form, swim technique becomes more efficient and self-reinforcing at higher intensities. Given the interval structure for swim workouts, emphasis on high-intensity training, and focus on swim technique, a pool provides the best environment for developing your swim fitness. Open-water swimming plays a role in triathlon training – it gets you used to swimming in open water – but it doesn't allow for the short intervals and rest that support harder work intervals and form resets.

Practical Application of Training Zones

When it comes to swimming, start by ignoring the table of training zones and instead focus simply on developing your "gears" in the pool. At first, you will have just one gear: swimming. As you build fitness, you'll develop two swimming gears: easy and swimming, or swimming and swimming harder. And eventually you'll have three gears: easy, moderate (swimming), and strong, which align with zones 1, 2, and 3. Finally, you'll add hard, or zone 4, and fast, or zone 5. When you do move into those high-intensity training zones, remember to focus on swimming stronger (moving more water) and not just swimming faster (simply speeding up your arms).

Fitness Development Goal

From a fitness development standpoint, your primary goal is to develop the fitness to comfortably swim farther than your race distance. Specifically, for events up to half-distance triathlons you want to be able to comfortably swim 1.25 to 2+ times your race distance, with shorter race distances allowing for a greater multiplier. And sure, it's great to improve your swim speed too, but those improvements are measured in seconds per hundred yards or meters and may barely translate to minutes of time saved on race day. So, before concerning yourself with developing your swim speed, focus on improving your comfort in the water. While comfort doesn't necessarily translate to a quicker swim split, it does reduce your energy expenditure at your normal swim pace, which means you'll have more energy left for the bike and run.

Fitness Development and Biking

Many athletes who haven't received guidance on fitness development – virtually all beginner athletes, but also many athletes with years of experience – will bike at too easy an effort level. With biking, athletes often feel like they're working at an appropriate effort level on a bike ride simply because they're moving pretty quickly, or at least significantly quicker than they do on foot. So, if we want to develop bike fitness and put forward your best effort on race day, we need to transform how you think about cycling effort levels.

Practical Application of Training Zones

Your feel for working at higher intensities on a bike – in zones 4 and 5 – can be effectively developed in training by incorporating intervals of appropriate durations for the intensity. Those intervals will quickly teach you whether you can hold a particular effort level for 30 seconds, a minute, or five. But targeting the correct effort level at lower intensities can take some prompting. So I want you to think of zone 1 as your "picnic ride" effort level: It's enjoyable, light, and easy. Zone 2, your effort level when using your endurance building block, feels like work – but not hard work. You want to break a sweat, notice your breathing rate increase, and require just a little bit of focus to maintain your effort level. When you finish a zone 2 training ride, you want to simultaneously know that you've done something and that you could've kept going for a while longer.

Fitness Development Goal

Triathlon success is built off of bike fitness. Let me repeat that, because I want you to really absorb it: *Triathlon success is built off of bike fitness.* To that end, you want bike fitness to spare on race day – enough bike fitness to comfortably complete the race distance and still have plenty of endurance left in your legs for the run. That means you'll devote more hours each week to biking than to swimming or running. It also means you want to develop fitness that allows you to comfortably bike several miles beyond race distance (5 to 10+ miles [8-16+ km] farther than race distance), which is built primarily using your endurance building block. The speed building block comes into play for races where hilly terrain requires higher intensities or where your goals and the race distance point toward racing in zone 3 or 4.

Fitness Development and Running

In contrast to cycling, most athletes run too hard during their endurance run workouts. And I get it: Everyone wants to be a faster runner. So when an athlete goes out for a run, they'll naturally find an effort level that allows them to complete the distance without getting too exhausted, but also lets them feel like they ran strong and at a "fast" pace. Unfortunately, that natural pace is nearly always in zone 3, resulting in training that creates fatigue (I worked! I'm tired!) and negatively affects their performance in subsequent workouts. So while zone 3 runs make you feel like a faster runner, they don't actually make you a faster runner. Running slowly to eventually run faster may sound counterintuitive, but it is the most effective way to improve your run paces at every effort level.

Practical Application of Training Zones

Successful use of your endurance building block requires that you actually run in zone 2. But it will take more than a vague and subjective effort-level description to deprogram a natural gravitation toward running in zone 3. So allow me to introduce the conversational threshold: The conversational threshold reflects the top boundary of zone 2 and provides an objective way to monitor your effort level. If you are running below the conversational threshold, and therefore in zone 2, you can hold a conversation, comfortably speaking in full sentences. Once the effort level wanders above the conversational threshold and into zone 3, those full sentences become short phrases, just three to five words between breaths. So, to ensure that you're accurately targeting zone 2 and your endurance building block during your endurance runs, periodically chat with your running partner (real or imagined) using full, even elaborate, sentences.

Training Zones and Standard Running Race Distances

For athletes with experience running races of various distances, we can translate the effort levels used for standard running race distances to the training zones shown in table 8.1.

- Marathon effort level is typically equivalent to the upper end of zone 2 or the lower end of zone 3
- Half-marathon effort level is typically equivalent to the middle or upper end of zone 3
- 10 kilometer (6.2 mile) effort level is typically equivalent to the lower end of zone 4
- 5 kilometer (3.1 mile) effort level is typically equivalent to the middle of zone 4
- 1 mile (1,600 m) effort level is typically equivalent to the upper end of zone 4

Fitness Development Goal

Triathlon is, almost by definition, running on tired legs. So in addition to developing the fitness to run the race distance, you also want to cultivate the knowledge that you *can* run on tired legs. This translates to using your endurance building block on days when you are intentionally carrying fatigue from prior workouts, forcing you to run distances at or near (for long-course racing) or at or beyond (for short-course racing) your race distance on grumpy, tired legs. And this is also exactly why we emphasize run durability when developing your running skills.

To be triathlon fit – to comfortably cover your race distance at a speed appropriate for that distance – you want to develop endurance and speed, support the movement that drives endurance and speed with strength and mobility, and ensure the sport-specific fitness that will carry you the distance on race day. Next up: We'll talk through how we intentionally use those building blocks over the course of a training week, cycle, and season to effectively progress your fitness from where you are today to where you want to be on race day.

9

STRUCTURING YOUR TRIATHLON TRAINING

We've discussed in concept how to utilize the building blocks of endurance, speed, and strength and mobility to develop the necessary fitness to complete a triathlon. And concepts are great and all, but as they say, the devil is in the details. So let's talk in detail about how we use those fitness building blocks to structure training weeks, cycles, and seasons. How we specifically place those blocks within weeks, combine those weeks into cycles, and then cycles into seasons, to prompt the fitness adaptations that produce the endurance to comfortably cover the race distance at a speed appropriate for that distance. How we build triathlon fitness in practice, not just in concept.

In the fitness development world, when we talk about structuring training weeks, cycles, and seasons, we call that *periodization*. We can define periodization as a long-term training plan structured by shorter training cycles, each having a specific purpose, designed to achieve desired fitness adaptations while managing fatigue. To develop a periodized training plan, you structure workouts within microcycles, which are often – but not always – one week in duration. You use the microcycles to build mesocycles, which are often – but not always – four microcycles, or weeks, in duration. And those mesocycles combine to span your training season, or macrocycle. Structuring your triathlon training using periodization provides focus and progression across mesocycles while maximizing fitness development within mesocycles, and is the gold standard for fitness development (figure 9.1).

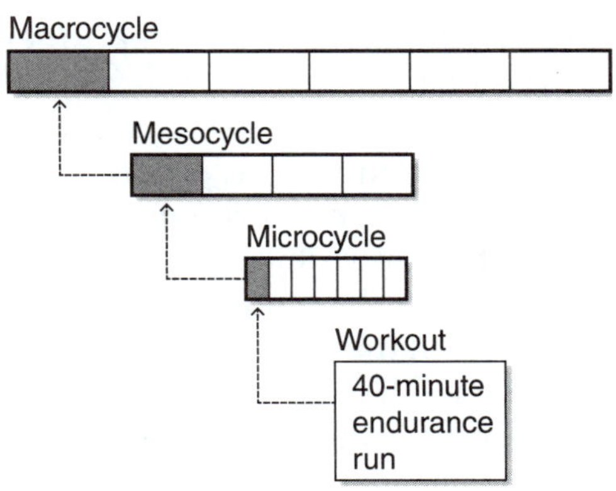

FIGURE 9.1 Training periodization.

Training Weeks (Microcycles)

Training weeks (a.k.a. *microcycles*) are the shortest repeated cycle in a training plan. A training week typically includes a defined set of workouts designed to cover the full range of fitness stimuli needed to prompt the fitness adaptations we are targeting. For triathlon, weekly workouts typically include two (short-course) or three (long-course) training sessions for each sport – swim, bike, and run. Given the importance of and foundational fitness provided through our endurance building block, we always, *always*, devote many of these training sessions to working in our endurance training zone. We typically use one or more training sessions to target the speed building block, depending on your starting fitness level, your athletic background, and where you are in your fitness development trajectory. And we usually designate one swim, one bike, and one run workout – often an endurance training session – as our "long" workout for that sport, focused on developing the specific endurance needed to cover the sport's distance in your triathlon. Finally, we layer on a couple of strength sessions and a mobility session or two to ensure that we regularly include that building block in our training.

We take all those swim, bike, run, strength, and mobility sessions and structure them in a specific way throughout the week to balance "harder" workouts and "easier" workouts. We think about "hard" and "easy" in terms of which workouts put the greatest training stress on your body and therefore produce the most fatigue. Hard workouts generate enough training stress that the resulting fatigue carries over to the next day, creating a cumulative fatigue burden. Easy workouts are not necessarily *easy*; they just usually don't add to your cumulative fatigue for the week. Hard workouts are typically the bike and run workouts that leverage your speed building block as well as your long weekly bike and run sessions. Because swimming doesn't create significant fatigue (relatively speaking), even speed-focused or long swim sessions aren't typically considered "hard" workouts. And because we use a low-weight, high-rep approach to strength training, those sessions don't often contribute to your cumulative fatigue for the week either. Mobility work is restorative, so those sessions are definitely classified as easy.

So here's where this gets interesting: If we count up our total possible hard workouts – a speed-focused bike, a speed-focused run, a long bike, and a long run – we're at four hard workouts. And given that there are only 7 days in a week, it's impossible to structure a week where you always have an easy day or a day completely off training before and after each hard day. Given that, we often place two hard workouts on back-to-back days, balancing those back-to-back hard days with an easy day or a day completely off training before and after. And we typically place the hard bike day before the hard run day because bike training, being only partially weight bearing, produces slightly less training stress and fatigue than run training. Also, triathlon is, almost by definition, running on tired legs, and training serves as a good opportunity to learn how to do that.

Using those four hard workouts as anchors for the week – often (but not always) scheduled on Tuesday, Wednesday, Saturday, and Sunday – we can then place the remaining workouts around them on the calendar. For short-course training, we typically schedule one swim, bike, or run workout per day and add the strength and mobility sessions as a second workout on some days. For long-course training, where there are more workouts than there are days in the week, we're forced to schedule "doubles" – days with two workouts – nearly every day. The most important principle when scheduling your training week, though, is to establish a routine that you can consistently follow. There's the typical way of scheduling, and there's what actually works for your life, and what actually works always wins.

Training Cycles (Mesocycles)

We take these carefully designed training weeks, or microcycles, and combine them to form structured training cycles (a.k.a. *mesocycles*). We use two formal guiding principles when stacking training weeks to form cycles: progressive overload and supercompensation. Progressive overload refers to the practice of gradually increasing training volume, intensity, or both, in order to stimulate fitness adaptations. That's the formal definition, but in more colloquial terms, I think of progressive overload like boiling a frog. If this is a new concept for you, allow me to explain: If you put a frog in a pot of boiling water, the frog will logically jump right out. However, if you put a frog in a pot of room-temperature water, the frog will feel comfortable and will sit and hang out in your pot. Then, if you turn the heat on very low, the water temperature will gradually increase, and the frog will barely notice the change. Next thing you know, your frog is sitting in a pot of boiling water without having realized what has happened.

This is how we want to use progressive overload within your training cycles. You never want to jump into a pot of boiling water, asking yourself to complete a week of training with volume or intensity that dramatically exceeds that of your current training. Instead, at the beginning of each cycle, your training should feel room temperature, at a volume and intensity similar to your current training load. Each week, the temperature of your training heats up just a little – a slight increase in training volume, intensity, or both, resulting in a slight overall increase in weekly

A Few Notes on Recovery Weeks

Supercompensation offers a compelling reason to incorporate recovery weeks at the end of each training (meso)cycle, but recovery weeks provide several benefits beyond just supercompensation. Recovery weeks also help alleviate the cumulative fatigue burden created through repeated weeks of progressive overload. When you take the cumulative fatigue produced by back-to-back hard workouts and then layer that onto itself over several weeks of increased training volume, intensity, or both, you'll find that you become pretty darn tired. A recovery week dials back that training stress, giving you a whole string of days that don't add to the cumulative fatigue burden, allowing that burden to actually lift.

The thing to remember, though, is that you won't feel rested just because you've entered a recovery week. In fact, athletes often find they feel worse during the first few days of a recovery week rather than better. Those first few days are when the cumulative fatigue burden feels the heaviest. By the end of the week, once you've had several days where the fatigue burden has gotten a little lighter, you'll finally feel ready to tackle another harder training week. But don't expect to feel *completely* rested and recovered – we save that special feeling for race week.

training stress. And then the next thing you know, you've developed the fitness you need to complete your triathlon.

The real magic, though, happens when you combine progressive overload with supercompensation. Supercompensation has two parts: First, you execute a period of training, usually lasting 3 weeks, where the training stress exceeds your current fitness level – in other words, multiple weeks of progressive overload. Then you follow those weeks with a recovery week that includes reduced volume, intensity, or both, and therefore reduced training stress. That lighter training week allows your body time to absorb the training of the prior progressive overload weeks, resulting in a springboard effect that catapults you to a higher level of fitness after the rest week. Like I said: magic!

Training Seasons (Macrocycles)

So we have these training weeks (microcycles), which are specifically designed to effectively leverage fitness building blocks and structured to manage fatigue, combined into cycles (mesocycles) that are also specifically designed to increase fitness and manage fatigue. We then take those cycles, each having a specific purpose, and sequence them into a season of triathlon training (a.k.a. a *macrocycle*). Your training season, or macrocycle, spans your preseason preparation cycles; your in-season, race-specific fitness and skill development and peak-and-taper cycles; and potentially one or more transition cycles that bridge the training plans for multiple races.

Preseason Cycles

Preseason cycles are optional cycles that can be used before the in-season portion of your season in order to prepare for that training. Preparing for the season can take on various forms, and the specific purpose of this cycle (or cycles) will reflect your preseason preparation goal.

General Preparation Cycles

General preparation cycles (see the preseason phase-in training plan in part V) are used to gradually build toward the base fitness and workout frequency required by the first week of your in-season, or race-specific, training plan. Remembering our boiling frog, we want that first week of in-season training to feel like lukewarm water – like our current environment – so if your room temperature is currently cold, you'll want to turn the heat up a bit before you jump into your training plan. Or, to explain it without relying on an overly complicated metaphor, if the first week of your training plan includes, for example, 5 hours of weekly training, and you're currently working out 2 hours a week, you'll want to spend a few weeks gradually increasing your training from 2 to nearly 5 weekly hours in preparation for the first week of your in-season training plan.

Sport-Specific Preparation Cycles

Sport-specific preparation cycles (see the preseason level-up training plan in part V) are used to improve your fitness in a single sport prior to starting your in-season training plan. These cycles offer an excellent way to utilize any extra weeks you have between when you're ready to start training and when your training plan actually begins. A sport-specific cycle can be especially useful when you are new to one of the three sports or feel far less confident or capable in one sport than the others.

In-Season Cycles

Your in-season, or race-specific, training cycles (see the sprint-distance, Olympic-distance, and Olympic- to half-distance training plans in part V) prepare you for your triathlon. Depending on your race distance and prior training, a single round of in-season cycles (the cycles designed to prepare you for one race, or a single training plan) will include two, three, or possibly up to five 4-week fitness and skill development cycles followed by a single peak-and-taper cycle.

Fitness and Skill Development Cycles

Your fitness and skill development cycles incorporate well-constructed weeks that follow the pattern of progressive overload and supercompensation – 3 weeks of increasing training stress (volume, intensity, or both) followed by 1 week of reduced training stress. These cycles are the bread and butter of triathlon training and incorporate pretty much everything we've discussed about fitness and skill development. Each cycle will build upon the last, culminating in a fitness and skill development cycle at near-maximum training volumes.

The Peak-and-Taper Cycle

The peak-and-taper cycle, the final cycle heading into your race, includes the training week with your greatest volume and intensity of the training plan (a.k.a. your *peak training week*), followed by three taper weeks, the third of which concludes with your triathlon. The taper weeks span a phase of training specially designed to deliver you to the start line of your triathlon both fit and rested, a state we call *race-ready*. It's a delicate balance because you will technically lose a little bit of fitness as your training stress – your weekly volume and intensity – decreases over those 3 weeks. But don't panic, because that decrease in training stress also means the cumulative fatigue you've been carrying throughout the training season will finally lift. In fact, this is when you get enough recovery that the cumulative fatigue will lift completely, and that freshness will more than compensate for the relatively minor loss of fitness.

Transition Cycles

If you have more than one race planned for your triathlon season, you may use a transition cycle to bridge the training plans for those races. A transition cycle is a week (or occasionally 2 weeks) of no training, little training, or moderate training – training similar in volume and pattern (but not necessarily intensity) to a week in the middle of your prior training plan. This cycle can provide recovery after completing a particularly taxing race or fill extra weeks in between finishing one plan and starting the next. An Olympic-distance race should generally be followed by a transition week of little or moderate training, and a half-distance race should generally be followed by one transition week of no to little training and a second transition week of little to moderate training.

And that's how we do it: We take your fitness building blocks and structure them with purpose and intention across a training week, stack those training weeks to create cycles, and layer those cycles to create a season. Now, let's use the training plans of part V to plan *your* triathlon training season.

10

BUILDING YOUR TRAINING SEASON

If you are a planner – and you know who you are – then this chapter will help you feel settled and grounded, with a clear vision for how to move toward achieving your Big, Scary, Awesome Goal of completing a triathlon. If you are not a planner – and that's okay too – this chapter may feel a bit less natural, not quite in line with your usual way of moving through the world. But I encourage you to get a little out of your comfort zone and follow along.

We're going to walk step by step through the process of planning your triathlon training season using the training plans found in part V of this book. There are umpteen training season variations due to differing numbers, distances, and timing of races, so we won't be able to cover each and every permutation. But we can establish guidelines and use examples to provide a basis for you to lay out the training plans to fit the specifics of your individual triathlon training season. These guidelines will help you create the framework for your training season, schedule the training plan for your primary – or only – triathlon of the season, schedule training plans for any additional races, and tailor the plans to your athletic background and fitness level.

Create the Framework for Your Training Season

The framework for your training season defines the weeks you'll be training, the weeks (if any) you are unavailable to train, and the date or dates you will be racing. If we think of your training season as a puzzle, those parameters define the size of the puzzle and allow you to see how the puzzle pieces – the training plans – will fit.

To develop the framework for your training season, we'll identify the start of your season, the end of your season (your final race of the season), and any significant milestones that occur between those start and end dates. And because triathlon training looks at the world in terms of weeks, and specifically weeks that start on Monday, we'll outline your training season in terms of the Mondays of training weeks. With that in mind, note the Monday of your start week – the week you intend to start training – and the Monday of the week of your (last-of-the-season) triathlon. Then add the date and distance of your triathlon (or of each triathlon), noting the Mondays of the race weeks for any midseason races. Finally, note any weeks between your start week and your (last-of-the-season) triathlon where you anticipate major interruptions to training, such as a planned vacation; we'll label those *interrupted weeks*. (Single interrupted days can generally be worked around and don't need to be noted; weeks with three or more interrupted days generally count as interrupted weeks.)

Sample Season Frameworks

Scenario 1: One Triathlon and An Interrupted Week

- Week of April 15: Start week
- Week of June 24: Interrupted week (Vacation)
- Week of July 22: Sprint-distance triathlon (July 28)

Scenario 2: Two Triathlons

- Week of April 1: Start week
- Week of June 17: Sprint-distance triathlon (June 23)
- Week of September 9: Olympic-distance triathlon (September 15)

Plan for Your "A" Race

With the puzzle of your season framework defined, we now place the first puzzle piece: the training plan for your primary, or "A," race of the triathlon season. Triathletes look at their "A" race as the most important triathlon of the season, their biggest goal, the event at which they want to perform their best, or possibly all of the above. We'll define your "A" race as your only triathlon, your longest triathlon, or – if you are doing multiple events at your longest distance – the first triathlon at your longest race distance. Identify your "A" race and the corresponding race week in your season framework, and then determine the start week of your training plan by counting back 11 weeks for a sprint-distance triathlon, 15 weeks for Olympic-distance, or 23 weeks for half-distance (12/16/24 weeks if you include the race week in your count; note that the training plan for a half-distance race will consist of the first 8 weeks of the Olympic-distance training plan plus the 16 weeks of the Olympic- to half-distance training plan). Schedule your training plan to start on the determined start week and end on your "A" race week.

Best-case scenario, planning your season is that simple. But because life almost never *is* that simple, let's walk through the specific steps involved in addressing the most common complications: misaligned

Figure 10.1 Sample Single-Race Season Plans

	Sample scenario 1a: Sprint-distance training plan with an interrupted week	Sample scenario 1b: Olympic-distance training plan with a late start and an interrupted week	Sample scenario 1c: Olympic-distance training plan with an early finish and an interrupted week
April 15: Start week		Training plan: Week 2	Training plan: Week 1
April 22		Training plan: Week 3	Training plan: Week 2
April 29		Training plan: Week 4	Training plan: Week 3
May 6	Training plan: Week 1	Training plan: Week 5	Training plan: Week 4
May 13	Training plan: Week 2	Training plan: Week 6	Training plan: Week 5
May 20	Training plan: Week 3	Training plan: Week 7	Training plan: Week 6
May 27	Training plan: Week 4	Training plan: Week 8	Training plan: Week 7
June 3	Training plan: Week 5	Training plan: Week 9	Training plan: Week 8
June 10	Training plan: Week 6	Training plan: Week 10	Training plan: Week 9
June 17	Training plan: Week 7	Training plan: Week 11	Training plan: Week 10
June 24: Vacation week	Interrupted week	Interrupted week	Interrupted week
July 1	Training plan: Week 9	Training plan: Week 11	Training plan: Week 10
July 9	Training plan: Week 10	Training plan: Week 12	Training plan: Week 11
July 15	Training plan: Week 11	Training plan: Week 13	Training plan: Week 13
July 22	Training plan: Week 12 – Sprint-distance race	Training plan: Week 14	Training plan: Week 15
July 29		Training plan: Week 15	Training plan: Week 16 – Olympic-distance race
August 5		Training plan: Week 16 – Olympic-Distance Race	

start weeks and interrupted weeks. Figure 10.1 illustrates, week by week, how a training plan puzzle piece can fit into your season puzzle using example scenarios that demonstrate training plans adjusted to accommodate a late start, an early finish, and an interrupted week. The following guidelines offer a detailed explanation of how to adapt your training plan to address each of those possible hitches in your season planning.

Handling Misaligned Start Weeks

With your training plan start week determined, we need to run an important plan check: Does your training plan begin before, at, or after your training season start week? If the plan begins at or after your season start week, you're all set (Sample scenario 1a; figure 10.1). If, however, your training plan begins before your planned season start, you've got a choice to make. You can either (1) back up your season start week to align with your training plan start week or (2) modify your training plan using the following guidelines:

- If your current training volume across all three sports is similar to or exceeds the training volume in week 1 of your training plan, you can consider a late start, beginning the plan in week 2, 3, 4, or 5 (Sample scenario 1b; figure 10.1). (It is not recommended to begin a training plan after week 5; instead, consider a late start combined with an early finish.)
- If the training in week 1 of the plan exceeds your current training volume, you'll be better off implementing an early finish, beginning the training plan in week 1 (Sample scenario 1c; figure 10.1). In that case, reschedule the training plan so its start week aligns with your season start week. Work through the plan as written through 3 weeks before race week, then execute the training plan during the final 3 weeks as follows:
    - Race week is always the final week of the training plan (week 12 or 16).
    - The week before race week is always the second-to-last week in the training plan (week 11 or 15).
    - If you are doing a half-distance race, 2 weeks before race week is always week 14 of the Olympic- to half-distance training plan.
    - If you are doing a sprint-distance race and week 8 falls 2 weeks before race week, or are doing an Olympic-distance race and week 12 falls 2 weeks before race week, skip that week and complete week 9 (sprint-distance) or 13 (Olympic-distance) instead (Sample scenario 1c; figure 10.1). Otherwise, complete whichever week of the training plan falls 2 weeks before race week.
    - If your schedule doesn't allow you to complete the plan through week 11 (week 7 for a sprint-distance triathlon), consider combining a late start with an early finish to ensure sufficient fitness development for your triathlon.

Handling Interrupted Weeks

If your training plan will overlap an interrupted week, we need to account for that in your season plan:

- If the interrupted week falls on week 4, 8, 12, or the second- or third-to-last week of your training plan, you're in luck – no modifications are necessary! Those are recovery weeks or taper weeks. You can simply do whatever training you can during that week, allowing the planned week to be interrupted, and return to your training plan as scheduled the following week (Sample scenario 1a; figure 10.1).

- If the interrupted week falls on any other week in the training plan, you'll stay in touch with your fitness by doing whatever swimming, biking, and running you can during the interrupted week, and then return to your training plan the following week and repeat the training week you completed pre-interrupted week (Sample scenarios 1b and 1c; figure 10.1). You can achieve this by either backing up your training plan start week, possibly requiring a late start (Sample scenario 1b; figure 10.1), or by implementing an early finish (Sample scenario 1c; figure 10.1).

With your "A" race identified and the training plan scheduled and modified as needed to account for interrupted weeks and misaligned start weeks, you now have the most important puzzle piece of your training season set in place. If you have only one triathlon scheduled for the season, then your season plan is nearly finalized; you can jump ahead to learn about training plan levels. If you have more than one triathlon scheduled for the season, keep reading.

Plan for Multirace Seasons

Now that we have placed your first puzzle piece for your "A" race, we need to add the puzzle pieces for any additional races in your season. These additional triathlons are your "B" races; a "B" race might be used to prepare for your "A" race, might be an opportunity to improve upon your performance after your "A" race, or might be an extra race just for fun. Planning for multiple triathlons in a season can be done seamlessly using the training plans because they are specifically designed to fit together – just like puzzle pieces.

Figure 10.2 illustrates, week by week, how multiple training plans can be combined to create your multirace season plan. Three scenarios demonstrate several versions of multirace seasons that include an "A" race and a "B" race, either before or after the "A" race, and use of the training plans to support them. The following guidelines walk through the fine print of combining the training plans for a range of multirace season scenarios.

Figure 10.2 Sample Multirace Season Plans

	Sample scenario 2a: Sprint-distance + Olympic-distance races	Sample scenario 2b: Olympic-distance + half-distance races	Sample scenario 2c: Two Olympic-distance races
April 1: Start week		Olympic-distance plan: Week 1	Olympic-distance plan: Week 1
April 8		Olympic-distance plan: Week 2	Olympic-distance plan: Week 2
April 15		Olympic-distance plan: Week 3	Olympic-distance plan: Week 3
April 22		Olympic-distance plan: Week 4	Olympic-distance plan: Week 4
April 29	Sprint-distance plan: Week 1	Olympic-distance plan: Week 5	Olympic-distance plan: Week 5
May 6	Sprint-distance plan: Week 2	Olympic-Distance Plan: Week 6	Olympic-distance plan: Week 6
May 13	Sprint-distance plan: Week 3	Olympic-Distance Plan: Week 7	Olympic-distance plan: Week 7
May 20	Sprint-distance plan: Week 4	Olympic-Distance Plan: Week 8	Olympic-distance plan: Week 8
May 27	Sprint-distance plan: Week 5	Olympic-Distance Plan: Week 9	Olympic-distance plan: Week 9
June 3	Sprint-distance plan: Week 6	Olympic-Distance Plan: Week 10	Olympic-distance plan: Week 10
June 10	Sprint-distance plan: Week 7	Olympic-Distance Plan: Week 11	Olympic-distance plan: Week 11
June 17	Sprint-distance plan: Week 8 – Sprint-distance race week! ("B" race)	Olympic-distance plan: Week 12 – Olympic-distance race week! ("B" race)	Olympic-distance plan: Week 12
June 24	Olympic-distance plan: Week 5	Half-distance plan: Week 5	Olympic-distance plan: Week 13
July 1	Olympic-distance plan: Week 6	Half-distance plan: Week 6	Olympic-distance plan: Week 14
July 9	Olympic-distance plan: Week 7	Half-distance plan: Week 7	Olympic-distance plan: Week 15
July 15	Olympic-distance plan: Week 8	Half-distance plan: Week 8	Olympic-distance plan: Week 16 – Olympic-distance race week! ("A" race)

	Sample scenario 2a: Sprint-distance + Olympic-distance races	Sample scenario 2b: Olympic-distance + half-distance races	Sample scenario 2c: Two Olympic-distance races
July 22	Olympic-distance plan: Week 9	Half-distance plan: Week 9	Week off
July 29	Olympic-distance plan: Week 10	Half-distance plan: Week 10	Olympic-distance plan: Week 10
August 5	Olympic-distance plan: Week 11	Half-distance plan: Week 11	Olympic-distance plan: Week 11
August 12	Olympic-distance plan: Week 12	Half-distance plan: Week 12	Olympic-distance plan: Week 12
August 19	Olympic-distance plan: Week 13	Half-distance plan: Week 13	Olympic-distance plan: Week 13
August 26	Olympic-distance plan: Week 14	Half-distance plan: Week 14	Olympic-distance plan: Week 14
September 2	Olympic-distance plan: Week 15	Half-distance plan: Week 15	Olympic-distance plan: Week 15
September 9	Olympic-distance plan: Week 16 – Olympic-distance race week! ("A" race)	Half-distance plan: Week 16 – Half-distance race week! ("A" race")	Olympic-distance plan: Week 16 – Olympic-distance race week! ("B" race)

Planning for Races Before Your "A" Race

If you have a triathlon on your calendar before your "A" race, you'll likely need to add a training plan to your schedule to prepare you for that first "B" race. You can prepare for a sprint-distance triathlon before an Olympic-distance triathlon using the following guidelines:

- If the sprint-distance triathlon falls on week 7 or later within the Olympic-distance training plan, adding all or a portion of the sprint-distance training plan before the Olympic-distance training plan is optional.
- If the sprint-distance triathlon falls before week 7 of the Olympic-distance training plan or you'd prefer to have more weeks to prepare for the sprint-distance triathlon, schedule the first 8 weeks up to the entire sprint-distance training plan before transitioning to the Olympic-distance training plan. You can schedule the Olympic-distance training plan to begin in week 5, given that extra preparation (Sample scenario 2a; figure 10.2).

You can prepare for an Olympic-distance triathlon before a half-distance triathlon using the following guidelines (keeping in mind that the first 8 weeks of the Olympic-distance training plan are always completed before starting the Olympic- to half-distance training plan):

- If the Olympic-distance triathlon falls during week 5 or later within the Olympic- to half-distance training plan, completing more than the required first 8 weeks of the Olympic-distance training plan before beginning the Olympic- to half-distance training plan is optional.
- If the Olympic-distance triathlon falls before week 5 of the Olympic- to half-distance training plan or you'd prefer to have dedicated training to prepare for the Olympic-distance triathlon, schedule the first 12 weeks up to the entire Olympic-distance training plan before transitioning to the Olympic- to half-distance training plan. You can schedule the Olympic- to half-distance training plan to begin in week 5, given that extra preparation (Sample scenario 2b; figure 10.2).

In these scenarios, if you schedule only the first [X] weeks of the training plan for your "B" race rather than the entire "B" race training plan, your "B" race will fall on a regular training weekend during a regular training week. When that happens, you'll utilize that "B" race as the optimal race simulation training day for your "A" race, adjusting the training for the weekend when the "B" race occurs using the following guidelines:

- Best-case scenario, your "B" race falls on an actual planned race simulation weekend, and you won the jackpot. No rearranging needed! Complete the "B" race instead of the planned race simulation, switching Saturday and Sunday workouts if your "B" triathlon is on a Sunday, and continue with the training plan.
- If that's not the case, compare the total planned training time for the "B" race weekend by sport relative to your estimated "B" race swim, bike, and run splits. If the two are roughly equivalent or the triathlon provides greater volume than the training plan includes, you can do the "B" triathlon and take the rest of the weekend off. If your estimated "B" race splits are substantially lower than the planned training volume over the weekend – 500+ yards or meters shorter on the swim, 30+ minutes on the bike, or 15+ minutes on the run – then complete the balance of the planned training time on the day of the weekend that you are not racing.

Planning for Races After Your "A" Race

Adding a "B" triathlon after your season's "A" triathlon is relatively simple. Align the last week of the training plan for the "B" race with your "B" race week and schedule the weeks before the "B" race week using the "B" race training plan. Stop the plan before it overlaps your "A" race training plan; you can even incorporate a week off from training between your "A" race and starting the abbreviated plan for your "B" race (Sample scenario 2c; figure 10.2).

Handling Interrupted Weeks and Misaligned Start Weeks

In all of these scenarios, you might have a "B" race training plan that overlaps an interrupted week, or a "B" race training plan with a start week earlier than your planned season start week. Use the same guidelines we used for your "A" race to address these scheduling challenges.

Once you've completed this process for all of your planned races – you've fit all of the training plan puzzle pieces into your season plan puzzle – then your season plan is complete.

Determine Training Plan Level

Each athlete begins their triathlon training season with their individual athletic background and experience, as well as varying degrees of current fitness. And that background, experience, and fitness typically differ across swim, bike, and run. The training plans, therefore, are designed to allow you to tailor the training to your specific triathlon profile, offering three options for each swim, bike, and run workout – Level 1, Level 2, and Level 3. At the beginning of your season, you'll determine your training levels for swimming, biking, and running – they don't have to be the same for all three, and in all likelihood, they won't be. You'll stick with those training levels throughout the season, so that your first week of training meets you where you are and develops your fitness from there. And if you come back next season – which I truly hope that you do – you'll most certainly select new levels given the progression in your background and experience for each sport. Here are the guidelines for selecting training plan levels:

- Use *Level 1* for a sport if you have no prior background in that sport and are not currently training in that sport. Think of it as the "brand new and off-the-couch" training level.
- Use *Level 2* for a sport if you have a background in the sport but no current training volume *or* no background, but your current training volume is equivalent to the sport's training volume in week 1 of your (first) training plan.
- Use *Level 3* for a sport if you have a background in that sport *and* your current weekly training volume is equivalent to or greater than that sport's training volume in week 1 of your (first) training plan.

Preseason Training Options

Once you've scheduled the training plans for your triathlon or triathlons, you may find your season plan includes some empty weeks before the start week of your (first) training plan. If you have the luxury of 4 to 8 weeks available for training before your (first) training plan begins, such as in sample scenario 2a in figure 10.2, I have some suggestions for how you might use that time.

Preseason Phase-In Training

A typical sprint- or Olympic-distance triathlon training week incorporates 6 days of training – two swims, two bikes, and two runs. If you are not currently active 6 days a week, the first week of training can feel like a shock to the system. If you have 4 weeks available prior to the start of your (first) training plan, the preseason phase-in training plan in part V will gradually transition you from your current training routine – anything from 0 to 4 days a week of training – to a full triathlon training week.

Preseason Level-Up Training

If you read the description of the training plan levels and thought "humph, I would like to start at a higher level than I'm currently at," and you have 8 weeks available before starting your (first) training plan, we can do something about that. The preseason level-up training plan in part V specifically addresses sport-specific fitness, helping you "level up" before beginning your triathlon training season. You can use the preseason level-up training plan for one, two, or all three sports in Levels 1 or 2 and then start your season in Levels 2 or 3.

For example: Let's say that you did a few years of swim team as a kid but are not currently swimming; are brand new to cycling; and have been running 5K's and 10K's for years and currently run a few hours each week. Given your background and current training for each sport, you would use Level 2 for swimming, Level 1 for cycling, and Level 3 for running.

Phew! We did it. Your triathlon training season is now fully planned, incorporating the number, distance, and timing of your race or races; your calendar; and your athletic background and current fitness. Next step: Complete the training plans! Moving through those training weeks on your own can feel like a daunting, lonely adventure, so bring the next two chapters along with you for some company.

11

EXECUTING YOUR TRAINING PLAN

At this point in the program, you have learned all about swimming, biking, running, and triathlon-ing, and you are fully up to speed on how you become triathlon fit. You've constructed your triathlon training season using the training plans in part V, and it's time for you to get to work. It's also time for my role to become that of a guide; just think of me as your own personal Obi-Wan Kenobi, Gandalf, Morpheus, Mr. Miyagi, or even as Dorothy guiding the Lion, the Scarecrow, and the Tin Man on their journey of self-discovery. Because your journey from today to the start line of your triathlon will involve more than just building triathlon fitness – it will also include highs and lows, successes and struggles, and progress and setbacks.

A big part of my role as your coach is to support you along that journey by helping you recognize your successes and learn from your struggles. So this chapter contains all the conversations I typically have with my athletes, from the first day of their – and your – training plan, through the many weeks of fitness development, and up to the final weeks leading into race day. Keep me in your pocket (more metaphorically than literally) as you mark the weeks off your training plan, and keep my voice in your head as you execute your workouts. Because even if it sometimes feels like you're doing all this on your own, I see how hard you're working, and I'm here to catch you if you stumble.

Guidelines for the First Weeks of Your Training Plan

The first few weeks of your training plan lay the groundwork for everything that follows. So we'll start with two top priorities for each workout, targeting the most important aspects of a successful season: First, show up. Second, complete the distance or duration specified in the training plan. That's it – those are the two biggest contributors to a successful training season. Over the coming weeks, you'll have plenty of time to fine-tune the workout details – your effort levels, the pattern of the swim workouts, and the timing of the bike and run intervals. For now, you just want to get a rhythm going with your training. Simply showing up

Time to Talk Time Management

Even the most luxurious of weekly schedules will likely get stretched when adding in the hours for triathlon training. This is where excellent, or at least decent, time management skills come in handy.

Time management has both a strategic element and a tactical element. Strategically, time management is all about prioritization, and specifically about knowing what to prioritize on any given day and within any given week. Certain things, like family time and work deadlines, almost always require prioritization. Other things, like laundry and home-cooked meals, can sometimes be deferred or substituted if necessary. Triathlon training generally lives somewhere in the upper-middle of the priority list; it moves toward the top of the list when you are in the final, biggest training weeks of your season.

Your time management tactics provide practical ways to implement your priorities. Some athletes find that completing their training first thing each morning allows them to avoid having their plans hijacked by the unexpected. Other athletes will block out time for training on their calendar just as they would for a meeting or appointment. The most important tactic is to respect your prioritization of the training and not treat it like an optional part of your day – as soon as it's optional, it's less likely to get done.

may be half the battle, but it's the entire recipe for success when you are first getting started.

Showing up, though, requires intention. Most people don't magically have an extra hour in their day, so showing up is less about finding space for training than it is about *creating* space for training. It's about deciding that the workout will happen, then prioritizing and protecting the time you've set aside so it *does* happen. Eventually, there will come the inevitable day when there are too many other priorities and your workout time gets overwritten by the rest of your life, but by setting clear priorities and sticking to them over these first few weeks, you can make that the exception rather than the norm.

ESTABLISHING ROUTINE CUE

Objective: To develop a weekly training routine that allows you to complete your workouts alongside everything else going on in your life.

Coaching Direction: First, fit your triathlon training schedule into your life, rather than rearranging your life to fit your training schedule. Then, make it your top priority to complete each and every workout over the first several weeks of training. It will only take a few weeks for the new pattern to feel routine.

Guidelines for the Middle of Your Training Plan

After 2 or 3 weeks of training, when you've found your rhythm and training feels like a part of your routine, all the rest of the details come into play: everything from workout execution to your mindset approaching and within workouts to those days when you just can't drag yourself out the door for training. It's all part of the journey and spans all the aspects of training that I routinely discuss with my athletes. So let's have those conversations now, and give you the tools you'll need to handle whatever your journey might throw at you.

The Big-Picture Principles of Training

Our first, big-picture conversation lays out three principles for you to remember as you move through your training plan:

- *Something is always better than nothing*. There will be days when the workout details are just too much, days when your workout time gets cut short, and days when everything feels like a struggle. Show up, break a sweat, and get done what you can. Because: Something is always better than nothing.
- *We care about progress, not perfection*. Developing your sport-specific skills, dialing in your fueling plan, learning the nuances of effort levels, and managing training challenges are a constant work in progress. No one expects you to become an expert triathlete overnight. If you are making progress each week, in one or many areas, then you are doing great. Progress, not perfection.
- *Consistency is key*. Many athletes place extreme importance on the long weekend workouts and not nearly enough on their day-in, day-out training consistency. Yes, those long days serve a purpose, but the day-to-day consistency contributes at least as much, if not more, toward building fitness. Additionally, excellent workout consistency builds fitness that can withstand the occasional lapse in consistency. So, as I said, consistency is key.

Your Workout Execution

Our next conversation focuses on workout execution. Effective workout execution serves two key purposes: It ensures fitness development and supports skill development. We covered fitness development in chapter 8, discussing how training zones allow us to accurately target specific energy systems and achieve our desired fitness adaptations. Proper workout execution ensures you're actually training in the right zones for each workout and therefore developing the fitness we want for race day. Developing the discipline to stick with those intended zones within a workout is a skill, honed in workout execution and then leveraged on race day.

The Fundamentals

The basis of all workout execution is accurately following the workout directions: the distances or durations and training zone targets for each workout segment. Let's talk about those training zone targets first. Over time, you want to develop an excellent sense of how each training zone *feels* so that you are always training or racing in your intended zone. Table 8.1 provided the first clues for the feel – or rate of perceived exertion (RPE) – of each zone. Chapter 8 added further sport-specific color to those descriptions, and you will continue to fine-tune your RPE for each sport and zone in practice. Even if you are using heart rate, pace, or power to define your training zones, your RPE provides the first indication of your effort level and training zone – the data should confirm it more than dictate it. Additionally, remember to only use heart rate-, pace-, or power-based training zones if they have been determined recently (in the past several months) using a lab- or field-based threshold test; zones determined through software, apps, and calculators without an accompanying threshold test are less reliable.

When it comes to following the distances or durations of intervals and the overall workout outlined in a workout description, though, technology can be very helpful. Many multisport watches and indoor bike training apps let you program your intervals as a workout and will alert you to the start of each interval (or the end of each interval, depending on how you look at it). Multisport watches also great for counting laps in the pool. If you don't want to or just aren't good at dealing with tech, any watch can be used to track time, and any watch with a GPS function can track distance (outdoors); if you go this route, aim to adhere to the spirit of the workout and don't stress about a few minutes here or there.

The Art of Warming Up

With the fundamentals in place, it's time to talk specifics. Let's start with the warm-up. All workouts are designed to begin with a zone 1 warm-up, but in my experience, virtually no athlete instinctively starts their workouts with one. So here's my case for why you should really, truly, start your workout in zone 1 even though it often feels excruciatingly easy and slow: Our bodies are like a 1970s-era car engine. Back in the day, specifically a cold, winter day, you couldn't simply pull out of the driveway and head out into the world because the engines would get very cranky if you ran them cold. Instead, you would first need to let the car idle in the driveway for 5 or 10 minutes to warm up the engine. And if you really wanted to make sure that engine was warm before heading out, you'd pump the gas a few times before shifting into drive.

This is exactly how we need to treat our bodies, just like those old car engines. We need to spend 5, 10, 15, or even 20 minutes moving at idling-equivalent effort levels – in Zone 1 – to let our cardiorespiratory system and muscles warm up before shifting into zone 2. And if we want to shift into, say, zone 4, our bodies will respond best if we rev the engine with some high-intensity priming efforts before starting those longer, harder effort intervals. The benefit of a proper warm-up is that it allows your cardiorespiratory system and aerobic energy production time to acclimate to the workload, helping your heart rate to stay aligned with your pace and power rather than decoupling. Leaving the lingo aside, this means your pace or power will feel easy at the beginning, and then only as hard as it's supposed to feel in the later minutes or miles. Without that proper warm-up, your pace or power will feel disproportionately challenging in the final minutes or miles, which is as disheartening as it is uncomfortable.

WARMING UP THE ENGINE CUE

Objective: To execute a proper warm-up.

Coaching Direction: With great focus and discipline, keep your effort level extremely low – properly in zone 1 – for the duration of the warm-up, just barely breaking a sweat by the end of the warm-up. Swimming will feel lazy, biking will feel like you're hardly pressing on the pedals, and running will feel like you're barely even moving, which is how you'll know you're doing it correctly.

Proper Workout Pacing

After your warm-up, you will feel primed and ready to tackle the workout ahead. It's all too easy, at this point, to start off strong – maybe too strong – and then find yourself fading in those later minutes or miles. That's why it's important to remember that the exact same pace or power will feel easy at the beginning of a workout, appropriate in the middle, and a bit more challenging at the end. Proper workout pacing, then, involves holding back a bit in the beginning, settling into the pace in the middle, and keeping a bit in reserve for the final push to the finish.

In training, you'll develop the discipline to keep your effort level easy during the first minutes and miles and moderate in the middle, when you still feel fresh and before the fatigue makes its appearance. On race day, this translates to the discipline to keep your effort level easy during the first minutes of the swim and miles on the bike and run, when

You Will Race the Way You Train

This chapter focuses on developing the skills and mindset that you will bring to your training, day in and day out. All the skills, the guidance on how to approach your workouts, and the direction on how to mentally move through your workouts will raise the overall quality of your training, increase your fitness development, and help you feel like you are succeeding as you progress through your training plan. But even beyond that, by incorporating all the skills, guidance, and direction in this chapter into your training, you will create habits within your workouts that directly translate to your execution on race day.

My daughter's third-grade lacrosse coach would tell her team that they would "play the way they practice," a quote widely attributed to Hall of Fame forward and three-time NBA champion Larry Bird. In other words, if the girls focused and gave their best effort at practices, those habits would transfer directly to game day. And if they were distracted and lackluster at practices, those habits would *also* carry over to game day. In triathlon, we say that you will race the way you train. As in, the habits that you cultivate within your workouts – whether they are constructive habits or self-defeating ones – will carry over to race day. So even the simplest, shortest, and easiest workouts are an opportunity to hone your execution skills and mindset, laying the foundation for a successful triathlon.

you feel fresh and excited to start swimming, biking, or running. That discipline pays off in the final minutes and miles, allowing you to work hard to run fast rather than just to keep running.

SAVE THE BEST FOR LAST CUE

Objective: Moderate your effort level at the beginning and middle of each workout so that you can finish feeling strong.

Coaching Direction: Use the following workout-specific guidelines when completing each workout:

- *Endurance (steady-state) bike and run workouts*: Approach each workout knowing that your final 10 minutes must be your strongest. Stay within zone 2 or at your endurance effort level for the majority of the workout, but aim to just slightly increase your pace, power, or effort level as you finish the workout, or hold your pace, power, or effort level but *feel* strong.
- *Interval bike and run workouts and all swims*: Even though you have consistent targets for all the intervals, aim to come in slightly below (slower than) the target for the first one or two intervals, on target

for the middle intervals, and slightly above (faster than) the target for the final one or two intervals. You should always complete an interval set feeling like you could complete one more interval.

- *Runs off-the-bike*: Complete each run off-the-bike knowing that the second half of the run must be faster than your first. The difference only needs to be a few seconds per mile (or kilometer), but it must be faster.

TRAIN YOUR RACE SKILLS CUE

Objective: Develop habits in training that will translate to success on race day.

Coaching Direction: As you approach and perform each workout, remember that you will race the way you train. Given that, consider your execution, your mindset, and your response to challenges. Do you approach and complete your workouts in the manner that you want to approach and complete your triathlon? If not, now is the time to make changes.

Your Training Mindset

We always have conversations about your training mindset because what goes on in between your ears greatly affects how you perform during workouts. It influences whether you get off the couch (or desk chair or out of bed) to do your workouts, your attitude during the workouts, and how you respond when the workout doesn't go as planned. So let's talk through some of the most common internal dialogues for athletes, anticipating what those voices in your head might say and lining up responses that'll keep you on track.

Pre-Workout Dialogues

The most common pre-workout whisper (sometimes even a scream) from your internal voice is something along the lines of "do we have to?" or "but I don't want to." You're not going to convince that internal voice, whoever they are, of the merits of doing your training. But here are some strategies that can help you get your workout done anyway:

- Know that getting out the door – overcoming the inertia of your current state – is often the hardest part of doing the workout. Instead of thinking about the workout, just focus on lacing up your shoes, pumping up your bike tires, or grabbing your swimsuit.
- Tell yourself you only have to do the first 5 to 10 minutes of the workout, and if you still don't want to, then you can stop. When

swimming, biking, or running for [X] meters or minutes feels overwhelming, this strategy shrinks the task to something more manageable – and usually once you get started, completing the workout doesn't feel as daunting.

- Think ahead 12 to 24 hours and consider how you'll feel if you *don't* do the workout. The visceral sense of that crummy feeling can be a great motivator.
- If all else fails – or as a backdrop from the very beginning – dissuade yourself of the idea that your training is optional. That concept renders the original musings of "do we have to?" or "but I don't want to" moot.

MOTIVATION CUE

Objective: Effectively combat lack of motivation.

Coaching Direction: First, recognize that the occasional lack of motivation across the weeks and months of a training season is *normal.* Don't beat yourself up, question your commitment, or get down about it. Recognize it for what it is, and use one of the tools provided – or whatever gets you out the door – to counteract the inertia and get the training done.

Early-Minute or -Mile Dialogues

Often, the whining voice in your head during the early minutes and miles of a workout comes from a place of fatigue. And that's understandable – there will be days when you *do* start your workout tired from yesterday's workout, or maybe from the whole week of workouts. Starting a workout fatigued isn't in and of itself problematic, so here are some ways to get through those initial minutes and miles:

- Always start your workout with an open mind. Just because you feel fatigued doesn't mean your body won't respond when asked.
- For runs specifically, remember that triathlon is running on tired legs. Learning to run on tired legs – learning that you *can* run on tired legs – will help you tremendously on race day.
- Don't judge the workout based on the warm-up. The warm-up – which extends through the prep set – serves to work through any lingering fatigue, and often you'll feel better after the warm-up (or prep set) than when you started.
- Ultimately, though, the most important workout is always tomorrow's. If you are so fatigued going into today's workout that completing it will jeopardize tomorrow's, better to abort the workout and focus on recovery.

Mid- and Late-Workout Dialogues

Sometimes workouts start perfectly fine and then take a turn toward the middle or later minutes or miles. In fact, it's nearly impossible to make it through an entire triathlon training season *without* having a workout that gets really, really hard. I never root for an athlete to have a particularly challenging workout, but I always value what an athlete can learn from the experience. Race day will undoubtedly, inevitably involve some minutes or miles that are anywhere from generally uncomfortable to downright miserable. And the only way to truly prepare for them, to practice in advance how you'll handle that challenge, is to face a similar challenge in training. So when you do have that rough workout, remember the opportunity it presents and use it intentionally to prepare for the potential rough patches in your triathlon. The following guidelines provide tactics and strategies to help you face that challenge head-on.

Tactical Strategies for Managing Rough Patches You'll first approach the rough patch from a problem-solving perspective. Ask yourself why your workout has gone sideways: Is it fatigue, is it fueling or dehydration, are you bored, or is it just hard? Many of these challenges can be addressed from a tactical perspective. Start by adjusting your effort level: If your workout incorporates efforts in zone 3 or above, skip those and stick to an endurance effort level (zone 2). If it's an endurance workout, drop your effort level to easy (zone 1). Alternatively (and counterintuitively), endurance efforts sometimes feel easier after a brief (1-3 minute) increase in effort to zone 3. If none of that works, allow yourself a break of just a minute or two to reset – pause, catch your breath, right your mind, and start again.

Along with adjusting your effort level, sugar can do wonders for both your body and your mindset. Grab whatever you've brought with you or stop at home, your car, or a convenience store – you can even stray from your standard workout fueling if you spot a more enticing option (candy can be a great pick-me-up!). You may find yourself drawn to a salty snack more than sugar – respect those cravings; they are telling you what your body needs. When in doubt, guzzling a bottle of a sports drink can provide the full spectrum of pick-me-ups: fluids, salt, *and* sugar. Finally, don't underestimate the power of caffeine – a cola or energy drink has the power to salvage a workout even when it feels like all hope is lost.

Mental Strategies for Handling Rough Patches If the rough patch stubbornly persists even with solid problem solving, then you'll need to break out your mental skills toolbox – your strategies for taming your inner dialogue. Start by listening carefully to your inner voice to assess and adjust its messaging, if needed. Does your voice speak in the first person (I) or in the second person (you)? First-person messaging tends to be more positive than second-person, but it depends on exactly what your voice is saying. If your inner voice tends toward negative thoughts ("you can't do this"), try to reframe anything it says as a positive ("I *am* doing this").

Sometimes, though, it's more helpful to get out of your own head. Distraction can be a surprisingly effective mental tool, moving your thoughts away from your discomfort onto something more productive. You can exchange your negative thoughts for just about anything, but common strategies include focusing on your form or your breathing; counting your footsteps, pedal strokes, swim strokes, trees, or the cones bordering the course; singing a song; thinking of friends and loved ones; or imagining yourself in a different location altogether. Physical distraction can also be effective – tapping your forefinger and thumb, for example, provides a new physical sensation to focus on.

You can also trick your brain into triggering a spike of dopamine – a neurotransmitter (or chemical messenger) that is released when you experience something rewarding, like reaching a goal. When dopamine is released, it provides a rush of satisfaction or even a brief sense of euphoria, which can help to combat that rough patch. And the thing is, your brain releases dopamine whether you reach a real goal (like the end of an interval or the finish line) or a completely made-up one (like reaching the next aid station, mile marker, street light, or tree). You can force regular dopamine spikes by segmenting the remaining distance – breaking it down into manageable chunks, each one providing a milestone that you will reach far quicker than the finish. Each time you achieve the completely fictional but real-to-your-brain goal of reaching the next milestone, the resulting dopamine spike will boost your motivation, increase your focus, and reduce your perceived effort, helping you reach the milestone after that and ultimately the finish line.

YOUR MENTAL SKILLS TOOLBOX CUE

Objective: To intentionally stock your mental skills toolbox.

Coaching Direction: As you complete your training, pay attention to the mental strategies you naturally use and gravitate toward during your workouts. Mentally catalog them, so you have an inventory of tools you can turn to when you hit a low point during a workout or race. Additionally, consider what you can add to your toolbox, and intentionally practice those strategies in training.

Getting Comfortable With Being Uncomfortable While all of these tactical and mental strategies provide excellent resources for managing the discomfort of training and racing, they won't allow you to completely avoid the discomfort of hard training sessions or the final miles of your triathlon. Acclimating to that sensation – getting comfortable with being uncomfortable – helps you understand how uncomfortable you can be

The Two-Thirds Rule

A fascinating and consistent phenomenon occurs right around two-thirds of the way through nearly any arduous task, whether that task spans an hour, a day, a month, or even longer. That phenomenon is a predictable slump – fatigue, lack of motivation, and an I-don't-know-if-I-can-do-this mental low – that occurs when you've been working on the task for long enough that you are *tired*, but the task's endpoint is not yet in sight. As in: right around two-thirds of the way to the finish.

In triathlon, the two-thirds rule comes into play in several contexts. You may find yourself at a low point two-thirds of the way through any workout or set of intervals. You will often find that you hit a low two-thirds of the way through the bike leg, run leg, or both, during your triathlon. And it's incredibly common to bottom out two-thirds of the way through your triathlon training season or race-specific training plan.

When you find yourself at that low point, it's helpful to pick your head up and realize where you are: at or around that two-thirds mark, and therefore exactly on schedule with your fatigue, lack of motivation, and I-don't-know-if-I-can-do-this inner dialogue. Once you understand where you are, all you have to do is hold on long enough to get *past* that two-thirds point. Because once you're 70 percent or maybe three-quarters of the way through the task, the endpoint finally comes into view. And when you can see the end and know you can make it there, the fatigue will lift, the motivation will return, and adrenaline and excitement will carry you to the finish.

and for how long. And that understanding helps you dig deep during workouts and on race day, ensuring that you don't leave anything on the table in those final intervals or miles of your triathlon. So yes, use those tactical and mental strategies to help you manage the discomfort, but don't shy away from it altogether. Getting outside your comfort zone is where the magic happens.

Guidelines for the Peak Weeks of Your Training Plan

The peak weeks of your training plan – the final fitness and development cycle and the first week of the peak-and-taper cycle – often feel like the most intense and focused weeks emotionally as much as they present the biggest training challenge of your season physically. Between managing those emotions, checking the final boxes in preparation for your triathlon, and appreciating all that you've accomplished, there are quite a few conversations to have over these several weeks.

Gaining Perspective on Your Peak Training Weeks

By the time you arrive at your peak training weeks, your consistency throughout your training season and across your training plan has inevitably led to increased fitness. And, understandably, you'll look to your workout performance during peak training weeks for evidence of your fitness – and your ability to thrive on race day. But the work you've done to develop that fitness, those weeks upon weeks of training, has also created fatigue – fatigue that you will inevitably carry into those biggest training weeks and seemingly critical training days.

When you have both fitness and fatigue, sometimes your workouts reflect your fitness – but other times they reflect your fatigue. That fatigue can lead to one of those rough workouts that we discussed previously, rattling your confidence exactly when you're hoping to build it. This is the time to trust your training, trust me as your coach, and believe that your fitness is there, even if you can't see it. As a friend and fellow coach always says, "There is fitness behind your fatigue." And on race day when the fatigue has lifted, you will see that fitness shine through.

Adding Race Specificity to Your Peak Training Weeks

Given the proximity of your peak training weeks to race day, we use this window to incorporate race specificity into your training. By race specificity, I mean tailoring your training sessions to simulate race conditions as closely as possible in order to maximize your preparedness for race day. We incorporate race specificity into your training in three different ways: race-specific training environments, race-specific gear, and race-specific workouts.

Race-Specific Training Environments

Race-specific training environments sounds like a fancy, technical term but really just means that we want to have your training – or at least several workouts – simulate the race-day environment as closely as possible. So if your triathlon includes an open-water swim, you'll want to swap out a scheduled pool swim for an open-water swim once, if not several times, during peak training weeks. Similarly, you'll want to complete a few of your long bikes and runs on terrain that mimics your triathlon bike and run courses in terms of riding or running surface, especially if you've completed a substantial portion of your training indoors. (If you reach the end of your peak training weeks and want additional opportunities to train in race-specific environments, you can incorporate them into your taper weeks, too.)

You can get even more race-specific by considering the details of your triathlon's venue and course. A swim in a closed body of water like a lake or reservoir differs from a swim in a river, bay, or the ocean, and a flat or technical (lots of turns or U-turns) bike or run course differs considerably from a hilly or straight one. You may not be able to find a perfect simulation of your triathlon's venue and course nearby – and no one expects you to drive for hours to find it – but try to get as close as possible given the training environments available to you.

Race-Specific Gear

In triathlon, we have a saying: "Nothing new on race day." In other words, don't use anything on race day – any piece of clothing or equipment or any fueling, hydration, or electrolyte product – that you have not used at least once in training (and ideally more than once). So use your peak training weeks to test out every single piece of clothing, each piece of gear, every fueling product, every hydration product, and every electrolyte product that you plan to use or even *might* use on race day. You can wear your wetsuit in the pool for your warm-up or to your open-water swim, wear your race-day outfit for a long bike and run off-the-bike, use your bike and helmet and sunglasses for a ride, wear your run shoes and race belt on a run, and fuel your longest workouts just like you will on race day. Because: nothing new on race day.

Race-Specific Workouts

In triathlon training, you mostly complete standalone swim, bike, and run workouts – single sport workouts each completed separately from the workouts for the other two triathlon sports. While we do include several runs off-the-bike in training, we rarely schedule a day when you swim then bike then run all in a row, like on race day. And it doesn't get more race-specific than completing a swim-bike-run workout. A swim-bike-run workout (a.k.a. a *race simulation day*) offers an opportunity to practice and experience swimming then biking then running, so you have a better sense of what to expect during your triathlon. Additionally, a race simulation day of approximately two-thirds your planned race distance provides confirmation of your triathlon fitness and serves as an excellent boost of confidence as you approach your triathlon.

Crossing the Training Finish Line

When all the peak training weeks are behind you – the biggest training weeks, the long workouts in race-specific training environments using race-specific gear, and especially the final race simulation day – you have reached the training finish line. While your ultimate finish line is still a few weeks away, reaching the training finish line is an accomplishment worth acknowledging and celebrating. You've put in weeks and months of hard work and sacrifice, managing fatigue and juggling schedules along the way, and arriving at this finish line is arguably more arduous than getting to the finish line on race day. So when you get here – and you will get here, no matter how distant it feels when you read this – I want you to take a moment to recognize and be proud of how far you've come.

Guidelines for Your Taper Weeks

The taper weeks serve up a distinct phase in your training season. On one hand, you survived your peak training weeks (yay!), and now you get to rest and recover in preparation for your triathlon. On the other hand, you don't feel rested, your knee feels a bit odd, the weather forecast keeps changing, and there's not enough training left on the calendar to distract you from the fact that *very shortly you are going to do a triathlon*. Which is why our conversations during the taper phase often shift from focusing on the training to focusing on your emotions. *Breathe*. This is all perfectly normal, and you will be okay.

The Mechanics of Taper

The first 10 days of taper might be my least favorite 10 days of the entire triathlon training season. I wake up the first morning of the taper phase so excited because I've crossed my training finish line, and then look at the calendar to discover that rather than lots of rest, I still have quite a bit of training planned. After seasons of this, I finally started referring to the first 10 days of taper as *fake taper* so I would get less cranky about them.

A typical taper phase – and the taper phase in each of the training plans in this book (barring an early finish) – spans 3 weeks: race week, the week before race week, and the week before that (20 days not including race day, assuming your triathlon is on a Sunday). The goal of these 3 weeks is to deliver you rested and ready to unleash all of your fitness on your triathlon course. This requires two things: first, you need to be rested, and second, you need to still be fit. Taper accomplishes that by spending the first 10 days holding onto your hard-earned fitness, maintaining near-peak training volume and intensity. Then it transitions to reduced volume and intensity for the second 10 days of taper, a duration long enough to provide the necessary rest and recovery but short enough that your fitness remains strong come race day. Done properly, taper will achieve the perfect balance of recovery and fitness – not 5 days before your triathlon or 3 days after, but exactly on the day of your event.

The Emotions of Taper

Taper encompasses *all* the emotions, so prepare yourself for a bit of a rollercoaster over these 3 weeks. You may find yourself alternatingly excited, nervous, confident, insecure, calm, and freaking out. You may become obsessed with the weather forecast, go to extreme lengths to avoid exposure to any possible cold or illness, and consider wrapping yourself in bubble wrap to prevent injury. You may be extra impatient or short with coworkers, friends, and family (I try to apologize in advance for that). All of this simply means that you have put a lot of work toward your Big, Scary, Awesome Goal and you care about the outcome. So, while you want to try to let go of things out of your control and be mindful of any snippiness, your rollercoaster of emotions is totally normal.

The Physical Manifestations of Taper

Along with all sorts of emotions, the taper phase also brings along a range of physical experiences. Do you remember back when you were in high school or college (or maybe you have kids who are now in high school or college), and right after exams you (or they) would get sick? Same phenomenon. When your body is under stress – stress from lots of hours of triathlon training or stress from studying for exams, for example – it somehow knows that it has to hold it together, that you cannot afford to break down while you're already under all that stress. Once the stress is lifted – you finish your peak training weeks or exams – your body feels like it finally has the opportunity to fall apart. And so it does.

During a triathlon taper, that falling apart can take on lots of different forms. Almost universally, athletes tend to feel fatigued and run-down during the first week or two of taper, possibly more fatigued and run-down than they've felt throughout their entire triathlon season or training plan. Athletes also often catch a cold or other minor illness, develop a small niggle (minor discomfort in a muscle or joint that causes concern about a possible injury), or feel like a prior injury could be resurfacing. The fatigue, cold or illness, niggle, or other concern always (or at least with only the rare exception) clears up before race day, but that doesn't mean it won't contribute to your already volatile emotional state during your taper weeks.

A Final Word on Taper

One final, important word about taper: Respect it. The reduction in training volume combined with the *oh-my-goodness-it's-almost-race-day* focus on your triathlon can transform the calmest, most rational athlete into a frenetic *tapering* athlete with nowhere to deposit all that energy. And sometimes people decide to put that extra energy into a little extra training – a few more yards or meters in the pool or a few extra miles on the bike or run. But here's the thing: The hay is in the barn. The impact of that bonus or panic training won't be realized in time for your triathlon, and by doing that extra work you are deferring your rest and recovery. So don't extend those workouts or add in a hike or decide to reorganize your garage or expend that energy in any way, shape, or form. As hard as it is, hold onto it and save it all up for race day.

NAVIGATING YOUR TAPER WEEKS CUE

Objective: Successfully manage the highs and lows of your taper weeks.

Coaching Direction: As you enter your taper weeks, keep in mind everything we discussed surrounding these unique 3 weeks of training. Remember that you will likely feel worse before you feel better. Try to keep perspective on your wide range of emotions. And be sure to save all your extra energy for your triathlon, rather than directing it toward other activities or additional training. The hay is in the barn – trust the fitness you've built.

All these conversations and all this information will help you navigate your triathlon season or training plan with wisdom, grace, and grit. You understand your priorities, know how to navigate the details and the ups and downs, will celebrate your milestones, and manage the challenges. And if life throws a monkey wrench into your training plan, the next set of conversations will help you handle those disruptions and get back on track with your training.

12

ADAPTING YOUR TRAINING PLAN

There are many great quotes about how things don't always go according to plan, but Mike Tyson, one of the greatest heavyweight boxers of all time, might have said it best: "Everyone has a plan until they get punched in the face." And while I'm not anticipating that you'll get punched in the face while training for your triathlon – that would be highly unusual – it's entirely likely that at some point during your carefully crafted training season, life will throw something your way that disrupts your training plan.

Even the best-planned triathlon season, an impeccable training routine, and a perfectly honed mindset do not make your training plan immune to disruptions. Illness, injury, and aspects of your life beyond your control can wreak havoc on your carefully constructed season. Overall consistency outside of these interruptions will allow your fitness to weather the storm, and the conversations and guidelines in this chapter will help you adapt your training plan and navigate the details of whatever life throws your way.

How to Handle a Disruption Due to Illness

An illness can often – but doesn't always – disrupt your training. The nature of the illness and the details of how your body reacts to it dictate both the extent of the disruption and the road back to your training routine. Generally speaking, if your energy level remains normal, you don't have a fever and aren't vomiting, and your symptoms are isolated to your throat and head, you can train as planned. (Yay!) If you do have a fever, vomiting, or chest congestion, though, you'll need to ignore your training calendar until you are symptom-free for 24 hours and focus on rest and recovery instead. Those are the simple, black-and-white guidelines.

When you don't have a fever, vomiting, or chest congestion but your energy level has dropped, you'll need to use some judgment to determine how to proceed. If you feel crummy but not truly awful (very nebulous terms, as we're living in a decidedly gray area here), you can start your planned workout and see how it goes. Generally speaking, you'll want to lower your effort level for workouts done while nursing a cold, so ignore any planned intensity (intervals or segments in zone 3 or higher) and stick with an easy to endurance effort level (zones 1 and 2). If you do, however, feel truly awful – or if all training feels hard – then you are actually sick, and we're back to the rest and recovery plan.

Whether you were I-have-a-note-from-my-doctor sick or just run down from a cold, your return to training should follow a gradual trajectory. Start with an endurance-effort bike or swim to confirm that your body is back to normal. If that goes well, then you're cleared to return to normal activity. If your energy levels are still lagging, though, stick to endurance-effort training until you feel like yourself again.

How to Manage a Disruption Due to Injury

Here's the typical injury lifecycle for an athlete (yes, you are an athlete): a slight injury-related discomfort comes on during training, you ignore it until it can't be ignored, and then you take a few days off from training. But you grow impatient, assume the injury has resolved, and start training again, just to realize the discomfort is still there and maybe worse. At this point, you finally acquiesce and take enough time off from training to let the injury actually heal.

While this may be the lifecycle for a typical athlete, you will be a *wise* athlete. You will first be wise by knowing how to recognize an injury that requires rest. If you are swimming, biking, or running and you notice any point-specific discomfort in your muscles or joints, pay close attention. If the discomfort level does not increase during the workout and is mild enough that it does not affect your swim stroke, bike position, bike pedaling motion, run stride, or facial expression, then you are not (yet) injured. You will still benefit from paying some extra attention to the area of discomfort – stretching, foam rolling, or bodywork can all provide relief – but you can typically safely continue training.

If, on the other hand, the discomfort gets steadily worse or alters your swim, bike, or run form or facial expression (as in a wince or grimace), then the discomfort is actually pain, and you are officially injured. Unlike with illness, though, an injury does not require a complete halt of all training. You do need to skip workouts for the affected sport while the injured body part heals, but you can usually substitute those workouts and continue to train the other two sports while recovering. Cycling, time on the elliptical or similar piece of gym equipment, and pool running are all great substitutes for running. The rowing machine provides an excellent full-body, cardiovascular workout if your swimming or cycling is affected. Don't, though, substitute runs for bike or swim workouts, because a sudden increase in run volume could lead to a second injury – and runs aren't great substitutes for those sports anyway. And since rest is not always sufficient to address an injury, consider seeing a sport-focused physical therapist who can both speed up your healing process and reduce the likelihood of reinjury.

In addition to giving yourself rest when needed, you will also be a wise athlete by practicing patience. Once you feel that you've rested the injury sufficiently and are ready to return to training, you will remember the typical injury lifecycle and wait at least 1 – if not 2 or 3 – days beyond that. And then, when you do actually return to training, you'll start with an easy- to endurance-effort workout at one-half to two-thirds the planned volume, to test out the body and ensure that you are pain-free before returning to the full volume and intensity prescribed in the training plan. By substituting workouts, seeing a physical therapist, and returning to training only after it has truly healed, you will have minimized the duration of the interruption due to injury and maintained your fitness while managing it.

How to Deal With Life Disruptions

Life – work or family or the weather or something else – will inevitably show up and make a mess of your training routine at some point (or many points) within your training season. So, let's talk through guidelines that will help you understand when and how to rearrange, substitute, or – if all else fails – skip a workout as you balance your triathlon training with everything else in your life.

When and How to Rearrange Your Workouts

If the life disruption limits your time available for training over 1 or 2 days, then rearranging workouts can allow you to salvage most, if not all, of the planned training for the week. You can move workouts from one day to another, shifting them either earlier or later as your schedule allows. Use the following guidelines when considering how to rearrange your weekly training calendar to manage a disruption:

- You can swap a training day with an "off" or rest day, or – if you have two workouts scheduled on one day – complete one workout and move the other to your normal rest day.
- You can do two workouts in a single day, with the following exceptions:
    - Don't do two workouts of the same sport in a single day.
    - Don't do your longest bike and your longest run on the same day.
    - Ideally, avoid doing interval-based bike and run workouts on the same day.
- Avoid doing swim, bike, and run workouts all in one day (other than race simulation days). Two sport sessions plus a strength workout

can be completed in one day only if your regular schedule includes training days with two cardio-based (swim, bike, or run) workouts.

- If possible, avoid doing workouts for the same sport on back-to-back days. (This is most important for running and least important for cycling.)
- You can rearrange workouts *within* a week, but you cannot move the workouts from one week to the next.

When and How to Substitute Your Workouts

If the life disruption takes you away from home or otherwise limits your access to your normal training environments, then substituting workouts – or even just workout equipment – can allow you to stay in touch with your fitness until you're back to your standard routine. Start by figuring out what resources you *do* have at your disposal, then use the following guidelines to determine how to substitute your workouts:

- A gym or recreation center offering day passes can provide indoor training options when traveling or when outdoor training isn't possible due to weather.
- Hotel gyms often include exercise machines such as treadmills, ellipticals, or exercise or spin bikes as well as strength training equipment. The quality of these facilities can sometimes be surprisingly good, and calling ahead allows you to pack accordingly for the options available.
- As with injuries, time on a spin bike, elliptical machine, or similar piece of equipment can be substituted for run workouts if a treadmill or outdoor run isn't available, and time on a rowing machine can replace a swim or bike workout if you can't find a pool or an exercise bike.

As you assess your options, remember that something is always better than nothing, and do the best you can with what you have to work with. Also, keep in mind that you can rearrange workouts to take advantage of easier substitutions.

When to Skip a Workout

Sometimes you just can't rearrange and substitute your way through a training week, and one or more workouts will have to fall off the calendar. Use the following guidelines to help determine what to keep and what can go:

- Prioritize your long weekend training days first.
- Prioritize your weakest sport – the lowest level in your training plan – second.

When to Reign in Your Emotions and When to Feel Them All

You fell ill or found yourself injured or had a work, family, or life crisis crop up and pull you away from training for several days. And now you're panicked – your emotions are spiraling, and you're convinced that you've lost grasp of the Big, Scary, Awesome Goal you've been working so hard to achieve. *Breathe. You will be okay.* Your response is completely understandable, but also inaccurate. Remind yourself that your excellent training consistency has provided you with a buffer against exactly this type of disruption, and that fitness development requires progress, not perfection. Pick yourself up, dust yourself off, *breathe,* and get back to work.

Unless, of course, you can't get back to making progress because your illness, injury, or other disruption was so significant that it derailed your training season altogether. This does happen sometimes; I am truly sorry. And while nonathletes may not understand what you are feeling, I do. You are experiencing a loss – the disappointment of plans being taken away from you, the frustration of working so hard toward a goal that won't come to fruition, and the void from the absence of the training that had taken up so much of your time. Know that it's natural to feel *all* of these things, to grieve the loss of your triathlon and your season. Allow yourself to process these emotions over whatever time you need – and then pick yourself up, dust yourself off, and get to work preparing for your next triathlon season.

- Prioritize your high-quality (interval) training days third.
- Balance skipped workouts across sports, rather than skipping one sport altogether in favor of the other two.

And, I've said it before, but it bears repeating (for a third time): Something is always better than nothing, so shortening a workout is preferable to skipping it altogether.

With this final set of conversations behind us, you really, truly have everything you need to manage your training season. Now go forth and train. Follow your plan. Be consistent. Be intentional. Ride the highs and weather the lows. Hold firm when required, but adapt when necessary. Remember that showing up is at least half the battle, and marvel at your progress across weeks and months. Then, when you're ready, we can talk about race week.

PART IV

PREPARING, COMPETING, AND COMPLETING

> Showing up at the start line of a triathlon makes you a badass. Crossing the finish line makes you a triathlete.
>
> Coach Alison

Oh. My. Goodness. Race week is finally here! You've done all the things – worked on your swim, bike, and run technique; faithfully executed your training plan; developed your execution, mental, and race skills; and learned to fuel effectively while doing all of those things. Now it's time to put everything together, all in one day. The culmination of all your hard work can bring out all the emotions – excitement, nervousness, and sometimes a bit of what-the-heck-was-I-thinking. The best way to manage all of those emotions is with preparation, so these final chapters will help you understand and anticipate everything that you'll do over race week and on race day itself.

We'll start by discussing why and how to write a race plan, and then we'll spend time filling in all the details you need so that you *can* write your race plan. We'll cover your pre-race schedule, logistics, tasks, packing, and fueling. And we'll walk through race day in excruciating detail, so that you can visualize the day even before you step into it. Finally, we'll talk about what you might feel and think about and do *after* your race – but save that chapter until you're actually on the other side of the finish line. Let's tackle this Big, Scary, Awesome Goal before we look beyond it.

13

PRE-RACE: PLANNING AND PREPARATION

Well – gulp – it's really happening. Your triathlon has been in the future for weeks and months, but now it sits squarely in the present. The date looms large in the weekly view of your calendar, with very little standing between this moment and race morning. The next few days will likely be full of nervous energy – energy you will feel mentally as much as physically. And since you don't want to channel that energy into extra training or other physical activity, the most productive outlet for your nervous energy lies in race preparation.

Race preparation generally involves a series of tasks, some done at home and some at the race venue or associated location, along with the mental preparation of deciding how you want to approach and execute your triathlon. A race plan – more appropriately called a *race week plan* – captures all of these tasks and thoughts and lays out a blueprint for everything that will happen before (part one of the plan) and during (part two of the plan) your triathlon. Much like scheduling your training season, writing your race week plan may feel natural – even comforting – to some, and possibly more like a chore to others. Either way, I require all my athletes (yes, including you) to write a race week plan. Need some extra incentive to complete this exercise? Your race week plan tames pre-race nerves by removing the uncertainty that drives them, and it's easy to get on board with just about anything that tames pre-race nerves.

Writing Part One of Your Race Week Plan

Writing part one of your race week plan – outlining all of your pre-race tasks – forces you to think through logistics, gear, and timing, helping you picture how the weekend will unfold and reducing the likelihood of any "uh-oh" moments. It front-loads all the decisions about what you're going to eat and when you're going to leave the house and what you should pack, so that not only do you know ahead of time what decisions you'll need to make, you've also already made them. Then, having made those decisions and thought through logistics, gear, and timing in advance, you'll have a better sense of what to expect in the days and hours leading up to your triathlon. Plus, once you've written part one of your race week plan, you can turn off your brain and simply follow the instructions you've written for yourself.

A thorough part one will cover everything you need to do or think about from several days before the triathlon, all the way through the moment you cross the start line. The plan will include a detailed itinerary, covering everything from when to pick up your athlete packet to when to leave your house or hotel on race morning to when you'll queue up for the swim start, along with all the tasks you'll complete over those days and hours. If this is your first triathlon, you might feel like you don't have all the information you need to write this (clearly very helpful) portion of the race week plan. That's completely understandable, but not a problem. We'll spend the rest of this chapter painting the picture of the days and hours leading up to your triathlon, so you can use this information as the backbone for part one of your race week plan.

WRITE YOUR RACE WEEK PLAN CUE

Objective: Write a thorough and detailed race week plan.

Coaching Direction: Use the content in chapters 13 and 14, along with the sample plan provided across the two chapters, to write your race week plan. Make sure it includes the timeline and tasks for the days leading into race day as well as race morning; your effort-level targets for swim, bike, and run; your race-day fueling plan; details on the race course; and any cues to help you focus on your execution and goals.

Preparing for Your Triathlon: Race Week

Getting ready for race day begins a week or so before your triathlon, when you first start to draft your race week plan. But most of the pre-race preparation itself takes place in the few days leading up to the triathlon.

Travel

If you are traveling for your race, you'll want to think through the timing and details of your travel logistics as well as transportation, lodging, and meals at your destination. If you are driving, use the drive time to the race venue and your desired arrival time to determine your departure time. If you are flying or taking the train or a bus, note its departure time and plan your departure from home accordingly. Think through food for the day you are in transit, so your meal quality and timing aren't negatively affected by travel. You'll also want to gather all the details for your stay at the race venue, including your rental car, hotel or rental home, and especially details about the nearest grocery store and restaurants, so you know how you'll handle your pre-race meals and race-morning breakfast.

Tasks

Prepping for a race that covers three sports, including the gear-intensive sport of cycling, requires quite a few tasks. They all serve a purpose, so let's walk through each of them.

Read the Athlete Guide

Every race director will publish an athlete guide, usually at least a week in advance of race day. The athlete guide will typically include information such as the athlete check-in times and locations; when transition opens and closes on race morning; the start time and format; and the swim, bike, and run course details. You know, all of the important stuff. Whether this is your first time doing a triathlon – or this triathlon – or your fifteenth, *read the athlete guide*, preferably a week or more before race day. If you've done this event before, you'll be reassured that nothing has changed, and if the event is new to you, then you'll learn everything you need to know about the logistics and details for this particular event. Keep in mind that race directors are typically unforgiving if you miss something because you didn't take the time to read the athlete guide.

Setting Your Support Crew Up for Success

As you think through your schedule and tasks for race weekend and start to anticipate how race day might unfold, you can also think through how your support crew – your friends, family, or other individuals who will accompany you over race weekend – can support you. Because while they are eager and well-meaning, unless they are a triathlete, they likely won't have a clue about what the weekend or race day will involve. And unless they know you exceptionally well, their best intentions may not align with what you need.

The best way to set your support crew up for success is to explain what support looks like to you. So, as you run through your tasks and schedule, note where you'd value their help and in what form – whether it's carrying gear, parking the car, pumping your tires, or picking up dinner. And as you think through race day, share information about spectator-friendly points on the course, along with the words you would find most encouraging – and even what you'd prefer *not* to hear. Make sure to share the athlete guide, because it often provides helpful information about road closures and spectator access to the race venue. Sharing your race plan and your ideas on where and how their support will be most meaningful will give your support crew the tools they need to succeed – and will help you feel supported rather than distracted by their presence.

Athlete Check-In

Athlete check-in (also called packet pick-up) is when you receive the packet containing the athlete-identifying items required on race day: typically a swim cap, stickers for your bike frame and helmet, a race bib, and a timing chip. Your athlete packet also usually includes race swag, such as a T-shirt (we love race swag!). Most triathlons offer athlete check-in the day before the race, and sometimes multiple options over multiple days beforehand. Some triathlons also offer athlete check-in on race morning, while others explicitly do not. Be sure to *read the athlete guide* to confirm the athlete check-in times and locations for your event. Virtually all triathlons will require that you show identification to verify that you are picking up your own packet and may also require proof of your annual membership or a one-day membership (typically purchased at the time of registration) with the event's national governing body for triathlon.

Athlete Briefing

If your race director offers an athlete briefing, whether this is your first time doing a triathlon – or this triathlon – or your 15th, *attend the briefing*. These sessions often cover much of the information in the athlete guide but typically provide additional information on the specifics of the race course. Those details, along with other helpful hints and tidbits, can improve your understanding of what to expect on race day, how to handle race-day logistics, and how to approach the course.

Bike Drop-Off

Most sprint- and Olympic-distance triathlons, as well as locally-produced half-distance triathlons, will have you bring your bike into transition on race morning. Races organized by large-scale race production companies, however, may require that you drop off your bike in transition the day before the race. Be sure to *read the athlete guide* to learn whether you need to drop off your bike before race day and, if so, during what time window.

Gear Prep

Triathlon involves a lot of gear, and prepping it for race day is a crucial component of race preparation. Use the following list to confirm that your gear is ready for your event, ideally a week before your triathlon, so you have time to address any issues that come up during your gear check:

- Tri kit (or whatever you're wearing for race day) fits and isn't overly worn.
- Wetsuit (if you're using one) fits and is free from tears. If you haven't worn your wetsuit in over 6 months, soak it for 15 minutes to loosen the neoprene.

- Goggles are leak-free and reasonably fog-resistant. (A drop of baby shampoo, smeared into each lens and then rinsed out, helps immensely in combating fog.)
- Bike is clean and in good working order, including the drivetrain, shifting, brakes, and tires. You can pump your tires to your desired air pressure the day before the race. If your bike has electronic shifting or a power meter, charge them to full the night before the race.
- Bike helmet is free of cracks and buckles securely.
- Run shoes aren't overly worn and have sufficient tread.
- Watch (if you use one) is functioning properly – and you know how to use the multisport mode, if available. Charge it to full the night before the race.
- Fueling, hydration, and electrolyte product supplies are sufficient for race-day needs.

Race-Day Packing

The afternoon before your race – or in advance of traveling – you'll want to lay out and pack all of your race-day gear. You want to avoid at all costs the possibility of showing up race morning without a key piece of equipment, so make a list and check it twice. (Fun fact: My showing-up-for-an-exam-without-having-studied dreams morphed into showing-up-for-a-triathlon-without-my-bike dreams once I entered the sport.) You can think through your packing list by imagining your race day from start to finish: pre-race attire, fueling, and hydration; transition gear; swim attire and gear; bike attire, gear, fueling, and hydration; run attire, gear, fueling, and hydration; and post-race attire, fueling, and hydration.

Race-Day Packing List

This list encompasses just about everything a triathlete might need for their event. You may not – and likely will not – need to bring everything on the list, but in some instances, you may need an item not included on it. Use the list as a starting point, edit it, and make it yours.

Personal Items

- ☐ ID
- ☐ Phone
- ☐ Credit card, cash, or both
- ☐ Keys
- ☐ Registration confirmation
- ☐ Directions to venue
- ☐ Athlete guide
- ☐ Race plan
- ☐ National governing body membership card

(continued)

Race-Day Packing List *(continued)*

Pre-Race

Many of these items will be worn race morning

- ☐ Triathlon kit, triathlon bottoms, or swimsuit
- ☐ Casual shoes
- ☐ Sweatpants or shorts
- ☐ Sweatshirt or other top
- ☐ Timing chip
- ☐ Multisport watch
- ☐ Hair ties
- ☐ Sunscreen
- ☐ Pre-race hydration
- ☐ Headphones

Transition

- ☐ Transition or duffel bag
- ☐ Towel or transition mat
- ☐ Small towel for face
- ☐ Water bottle (or from pre-race)

Swim

- ☐ Race-issued swim cap
- ☐ Second swim cap (for cold water)
- ☐ Goggles
- ☐ Wetsuit
- ☐ Body glide
- ☐ Pre-swim fueling
- ☐ Throwaway socks to wear to the swim start

Bike

- ☐ Bike with race number stickers
- ☐ Helmet with race number sticker
- ☐ Sunglasses
- ☐ Bike shoes
- ☐ Bike socks
- ☐ Bike gloves
- ☐ Bike jersey (if changing)
- ☐ Bike shorts (if wore swimsuit for swim)
- ☐ Chamois cream
- ☐ Bike computer
- ☐ Flat kit
- ☐ Bike hydration and fueling

Run

- ☐ Run shoes
- ☐ Run socks
- ☐ Hat or visor
- ☐ Run top (if changing)
- ☐ Run shorts (if wore swimsuit for swim)
- ☐ Race bib
- ☐ Race belt or other bib fastener
- ☐ Run fueling
- ☐ Run hydration (if needed in addition to aid stations)

Post-Race

- ☐ Post-race fueling
- ☐ T-shirt or post-race outfit

Meals

Chapter 7 discussed pre-race fueling and hydrating in detail, so this is your reminder to revisit that chapter and translate your pre-race fueling plan to part one of your race week plan. Remember that your pre-race fueling is as much about what to eat as it is what *not* to eat, especially for those with a more sensitive stomach. And be sure to hydrate, hydrate, hydrate, increasing electrolytes along with fluids.

Sleep

Sleeping the night before your triathlon can be anywhere from mildly challenging to extremely difficult. Thankfully, the night *before* the night before your triathlon is actually the more important night of sleep. So, start by setting yourself up for a solid 8 hours – or whatever a good night of sleep looks like for you – 2 nights before your triathlon. Then, the night before, don't let worrying about not sleeping compound your pre-race anxiety. You'll get as much sleep as you get, and you will be fine. Do try to get to bed early and ensure a calm environment that supports good sleep habits. And as you're in bed waiting to fall asleep – the night before the race and the whole week leading into it – use the time to visualize your race day, from the time you arrive at the race venue through the moment you cross your finish line.

A Few Words On Pre-Race Nerves

Everyone gets nervous before a race – and that's okay. Those nerves show that the race means something to you. But that doesn't mean the nervous feelings are enjoyable, particularly when they manifest as a pesky voice that amplifies several – often unwarranted and irrational – concerns. Your instinct may be to engage with this pesky voice in an attempt to silence it, but that strategy is unlikely to succeed. It turns out this voice acts much like a toddler: It throws tantrums that are wholly disproportionate to the situation, and it cannot be reasoned with.

The best course of action when your toddler throws a tantrum is typically just to let it happen. (Because if you try to reason with an irrational toddler, you get nowhere.) So when you hear the toddler whining in the background, go ahead and give it the floor to spell out all of its concerns and misgivings. And then just listen as the toddler expresses its largely unwarranted and irrational concerns, on repeat. After a few minutes, you'll realize the toddler actually doesn't have anything terribly meaningful to say, and the toddler will get tired and quiet down. At that point – because you trust your training and preparation for your Big, Scary, Awesome Goal – you can tell the toddler, "Thanks, but I've got this," and move on with your day.

VISUALIZATION CUE

Objective: Use visualization to prepare for race day.

Coaching Direction: Close your eyes and picture your race day, from the time you arrive at the venue through the moment you cross the finish line, incorporating all the race-morning preparation and race execution notes from chapters 13 and 14 and parts one and two of your race week plan:

- Visualize arriving at the race venue, setting up your transition area, and walking to the swim start.
- Visualize the swim start, the first 200 adrenaline-fueled yards or meters, settling into your planned effort level, sighting to find the buoys, executing buoy turns, reaching the swim finish, standing up, and exiting the water.
- Visualize the swim-to-bike transition: taking off your cap and goggles, finding your transition spot, taking off your wetsuit, putting on your bike gear, grabbing your bike, and walking or jogging to the bike start.
- Visualize the bike start, riding with confidence, fueling along the way, and ultimately returning to transition.
- Visualize the bike-to-run transition: walking or jogging through transition to your spot; reracking your bike; trading your bike gear for your run gear; and walking, jogging, or running toward the run start.
- Visualize the run start, running with discipline, fueling along the way, and ultimately the finish line.

MANAGING PRE-RACE NERVES CUE

Objective: To work with, instead of against, your pre-race nervous energy.

Coaching Direction: Be cognizant of your pre-race inner dialogue, observing it and recognizing it for what it is rather than being drawn into unhelpful internal conversations. Acknowledge your fears and give space to your feelings rather than shying away from them, while simultaneously sitting in the confidence you have earned through your hard work and dedication to your training.

For as much fuss as I've made about everything involved in pre-race preparation, the day before your triathlon will actually be very quiet. You'll pick up your athlete packet, maybe drop off your bike, and prep and pack your gear. That's it. The remainder of the day, you'll stay off your feet, out of the sun, and sip your electrolyte drink. You can also use this time to review everything race-day specific in your race week plan, since you won't be bringing it along with you on race morning.

Incorporating Race Week Preparation Into Part One of Your Race Week Plan

You'll want to capture all of the race week preparation details we discussed – the travel logistics, wide range of tasks, and notes about fueling and hydrating – within part one of your race week plan. And you'll want to do this with a high level of detail and precision, as the more you put into part one, the less you'll need to think when it's time to kick off the race week activities.

Given the amount of information and level of detail we're planning to include in part one, starting with a template or sample plan can be really helpful. Good thing we can reference part one of our friend Alex's Race Week Plan for their first Olympic-distance triathlon as an example.

Preparing for Your Triathlon: Race Morning

Given your excellent organization and preparation over the days leading up to race day, your race-morning preparation will be limited to only those things that you could not have done in the days prior. You'll wake up, eat breakfast, tie up any loose ends, and leave for the race venue. Once at the race venue, you'll tackle those final tasks specific to the race site and get ready to start the event. (Get ready to start your triathlon! You're going to do a triathlon!)

Alison Freeman

Alex's Race Week Plan

Part One: Race Week Preparation

Travel: Leave house Saturday at 11 a.m., 2-hour drive time, arrive at hotel by 2 p.m., including a stop for lunch at my favorite sandwich shop

Athlete Check-In: 1 to 5 p.m. at race venue - leave hotel at 3 p.m., packet pick-up by 3:30 p.m.

Athlete Briefing: 4 p.m. first-timer briefing at race venue

Bike Drop-Off: n/a - bring bike on race morning

Gear Prep: Charge watch, bike computer, pump tires to 95 psi, lube chain

Race-Day Packing

Wear: Tri kit, sweatpants, hoodie, flip flops, watch, timing chip

Pre-Race: Bottle of water with 5 X 300-mg electrolyte tablets and 1 gel

Transition: Towel for transition area, small towel for face, sunscreen, body glide

Swim: Wetsuit, goggles, race swim cap

Bike: Bike, shoes, sunglasses, helmet, gloves or socks?, chamois cream, bike computer, 1 bottle with carbs + electrolytes, 1 bottle with electrolytes, 1 package of chews, flat kit

Run: Shoes, socks, race belt with run bib, visor, 2 gels, bag with 10 salt tablets

Post-Race: Recovery shake mix, t-shirt

Pre-Race Fueling

- Saturday breakfast at home: pancakes with syrup
- Lunch on the road: sandwich on sourdough bread, no tomato or lettuce, bag of chips
- Pre-race dinner: microwavable rice, precooked chicken, dark chocolate bites for dessert
- NOTE: before or after packet pick-up, go to grocery store (5-minute drive from hotel) to get food for Saturday dinner and Sunday breakfast

Pre-Race Hydration

- Saturday morning: 1 additional bike bottle of water with 300-mg electrolyte tablet
- Saturday afternoon: 1 bike bottle of water with 5 X 300-mg electrolyte tablets

Sleep: In bed by 8:30 p.m., read for 30 minutes, eyes shut by 9 p.m.

Race-Morning Timeline

Work backward from the official race start time to calculate when to depart for the race venue, and then backward from that to determine your wake-up time. Set your departure time so that you arrive at the race venue 90 minutes before the race start, or even earlier if you need to complete athlete check-in that morning. Add in time for breakfast and a few minutes for final prep and packing to determine your wake-up time, ensuring that you'll eat breakfast 2 to 3 hours before your anticipated race start time.

Breakfast

Plan for a race-day breakfast following the guidelines provided in chapter 7. Given the "nothing new on race day" maxim, stick with breakfast foods that you've consumed in the past, and ideally those you have consumed before big training days or on your race simulation days.

Final Prep and Packing

The final race preparation tasks before departing for the event typically include pumping up your tires, if you didn't do so the day before, and mixing your fueling bottles. Keeping your pre-departure task list short reduces stress and doesn't force you to set your wake-up alarm any earlier than absolutely necessary. Limiting your race-morning packing helps avoid forgotten items, and putting your keys or phone with the small pile of items you do need to grab that morning serves as a great reminder to actually bring them when you depart for the race. (Yes, forgetting your race fueling or timing chip does happen.)

Transition Area Setup

Once you arrive at the race site, your first task is to find or select your transition spot and set up your transition area. Some races will assign your exact transition spot by race number, others will assign ranges of race numbers to each bike rack and allow you to pick a spot anywhere on the rack, and others will allow athletes to select any transition spot on a first-come, first-served basis. (Given the choice, I look for a spot close to the bike exit and entrance, so that I spend less time running in my bike shoes. I also prefer a spot at the end of a bike rack, because the space between or at the end of racks provides extra room for my gear.) Once you've got your transition spot, you'll rack your bike: If the transition is set up with A-frame bike racks, hang your bike on the rack using the nose of the saddle. If the transition is set up with standard bike racks, place your rear tire in the bike rack. In both cases, your front tire will be facing you. Bikes are typically racked in alternating directions, so that the bikes racked on either side of yours will face the opposite transition aisle.

You'll organize your gear in a small area to the right of your front tire. (To the right of the tire as you're looking at it, not on the tire's right side. When in doubt, mimic the setup of the bikes surrounding yours.) And by small, I mean *small* – you'll have an area approximately 18 inches wide and 36 inches deep (45 × 90 cm) in which to lay out all of your bike and run gear. I recommend bringing a brightly colored bath or beach towel to use as your "transition mat" – it will both define your transition space and differentiate it from those around you. Place your bike gear on the front half of the towel, neatly organized and ready for use: bike shoes open, helmet upside down and unclipped, and sunglasses unfolded. (Your bike computer, fueling, etc., can be placed directly on your bike, with the bike computer turned on and paired to all accessories.) Place your run gear on the back half of the towel in a similar fashion: run shoes unlaced and open, one sock in each shoe, and additional items, including your race belt or race bib, run hat or visor, and race fueling, neatly piled together. Your transition bag, bucket, or container can be placed directly behind your transition mat.

Alison Freeman

Flow of Transition

Once you have set up your transition spot, your next task is to understand the flow of the transition area (figure 13.1). The transition area has two entry points and two exit points:

- Swim In, where you enter transition after completing the swim.
- Bike Out, where you exit transition to begin the bike.
- Bike In, where you enter transition after completing the bike.
- Run Out, where you exit transition to begin the run.

The entrances and exits will be clearly marked, usually with large inflatable arches. Bike Out and Bike In typically pass under an arch on one side of transition, while Swim In and Run Out usually pass under an arch on a different side of transition.

Once you have identified Swim In, Bike Out, Bike In, and Run Out, you want to determine the position of your transition spot relative to those locations, so that you can avoid an I-can't-remember-where-I-parked-my-car type of situation. First, walk from Swim In to your transition spot, noting the location of your bike rack and your bike's position on the rack relative to Swim In. Then walk from your transition spot to Bike Out and from Bike In back to your transition spot, again noting the location of your bike rack and your bike's position on the rack relative to Bike In. Finally, note Run Out's location relative to your transition spot, so that you don't sprint off in the wrong direction after putting on your run shoes.

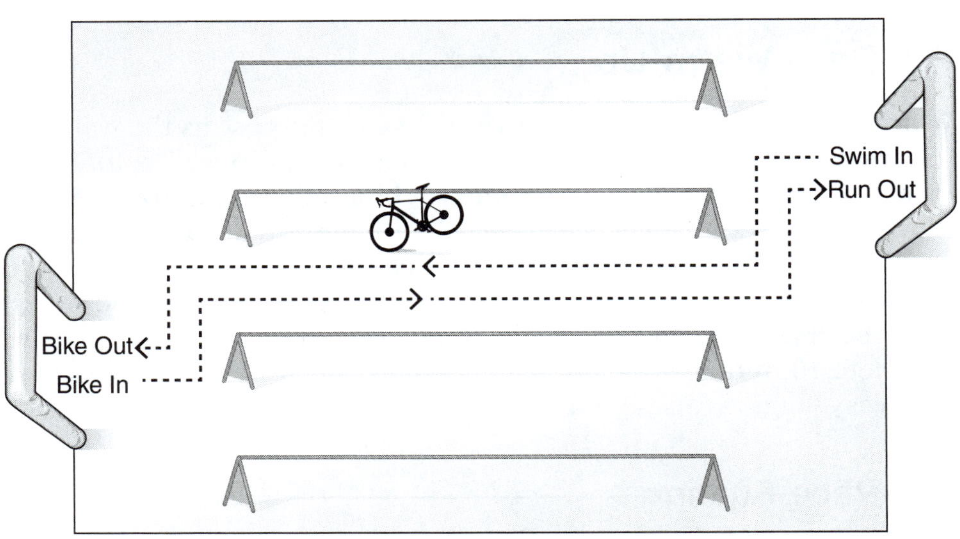

FIGURE 13.1 The flow of the transition area.

Final Prep at Race Site

After completing your transition walk-through, you now have time to apply sunscreen and wrap up any loose ends in your transition area preparation. Then you'll head to body marking, where volunteers write your race number on your arms with a permanent marker. Body marking can also include writing your age on your calf, which increases athletes' awareness of their fellow competitors within their age group. Many, but not all, triathlons use body marking to help identify athletes. Occasionally, body marking is done with temporary tattoos instead of a permanent marker. (In all cases, body marking can be worn as a badge of honor for several days if you don't put a lot of effort into scrubbing it off post-race.) If your timing chip wasn't provided during athlete check-in, you can usually get it at the same time and near the body marking area.

Next, you'll get in line for the all-important port-o-potty visit; be prepared for long lines, as this ritual unites all triathletes. After your trip to the port-o-potty, you are ready to put on your wetsuit. If you're able to do a swim warm-up (see Pre-Race Warm-Up), you'll want to put on your wetsuit at least 40 minutes before the race start – that allows 10 minutes to put on your wetsuit (yes, 10 whole minutes) and 30 minutes to walk over to the swim area, warm up, and be out of the water well in advance of the start. If you'll be doing a dry-land warm-up (see Pre-Race Warm-Up), complete it after your port-o-potty trip, and put on your wetsuit 30 minutes before the race start. In all scenarios, you want to be at the swim start 10 to 15 minutes before the event begins, so you can calm your nerves and settle yourself before the race starts. (Before your triathlon starts! You're going to do a triathlon!)

Pre-Race Warm-Up

Warming up before your race serves the same purpose as the warm-up for any workout, even if you complete that warm-up well before your race start. Best-case scenario, your triathlon allows you to get in the water pre-race, and you'll warm up with 10 minutes of easy swimming, including a few 30-second efforts at race pace in the final few minutes. If your triathlon doesn't allow for a swim warm-up, then a dry-land warm-up is your backup plan. Start with your favorite mobility exercises, then complete 10 minutes of easy jogging – no race efforts needed because even easy jogging raises your heart rate sufficiently for a warm-up.

Pre-Race Fueling

Your final pre-race task is to fuel your swim. As we discussed in chapter 7, you'll want to consume 25 to 30 grams of carbs 15 to 30 minutes before

Alex's Race Week Plan

Part One: Race Morning Preparation

Alarm Set For: 4:30 a.m.

Breakfast: At 4:45 a.m.: bagel with peanut butter and honey and black coffee (review race-day details from race week plan while eating)

Final Prep and Packing: Mix fueling and electrolyte bottles for bike, electrolyte bottle for pre-race – and add to gear bag

Leave / Arrive: Leave by 5:15 a.m., arrive by 5:35 a.m., allow 10 minutes to park, at transition by 5:45 a.m.

Set Up Transition: Transition set up by 6:00 a.m. – put fueling bottles on bike, turn on bike computer, pre-open package of chews, put gels in race belt loops and bag with salt tablets in race belt pocket

Transition Walk-Through: At 6:00 a.m., walk through transition: Swim In to transition spot, spot to Bike Out, Bike In to spot, spot to Run Out – sip bottle with electrolytes; put on sunscreen when finished

Body Marking: At 6:10 a.m.

Use Port-o-Potty: Between 6:10 a.m. and 6:20 a.m.

Put On Wetsuit: At 6:20 a.m.

Pre-Race Warm-Up: Swim warm-up open from 6:30-7:00 a.m. – walk over at 6:30 a.m., swim warm-up from 6:40-6:50 a.m.

Walk to Swim Start: transition closes at 7:00 a.m., race briefing at 7:10 a.m. – I will be at swim start at 7:00 a.m.

Pre-Race Fueling: 1 gel at 7:10 a.m.

Race Starts: First swim wave is at 7:15 a.m. – I am in wave 4

your start time. Gels, chews, and other sport-specific fueling products are often packaged in 25-gram servings, making them an easy option for pre-race fueling. As always, stick with products that you've used previously in training so you know they work for you without causing gastrointestinal distress.

Incorporating Race Morning Preparation Into Part One of Your Race Week Plan

All the details of the race-morning timeline and tasks were captured to round out part one of Alex's Race Week Plan. Having a concrete list of things to remember race morning helped Alex sleep better than expected the night before the race.

That was quite a big conversation about all the pre-race tasks that take place over the days and hours leading up to your triathlon. All those details painted a picture of what to expect and what to do as you prepare for race day and the event itself; you can now visualize moving through those days and hours and anticipate what it will feel like to inhabit that space. You also now have the information you need to write part one of your race week plan. With that all squared away, it's time to have a similar conversation about the triathlon itself, so that – like the pre-race activities in part one – you know what to anticipate and how to think through your event ahead of time, and can use that information to develop part two of your race week plan.

14

RACE DAY: STRATEGY AND EXECUTION

Once you're standing at the swim start, your preparation is complete. You've done all the training, practiced all the skills, and have checked every race-specific box available. You've prepped your gear, fueled your engine, and set up transition. Now it's time to let your body do what you've trained it to do over weeks and months of training – swim, then bike, then run. Now, *now*, it's time to do a triathlon.

Knowledge of what lies ahead and how to move through the miles of swim-bike-run on race day comes with experience – which, if this is your first triathlon, you don't yet have. So let's talk through your upcoming race in incredible, excruciating detail. We'll cover the swim start, the final miles of the run, and everything in between. By the time we're done, you'll feel like you actually *have* experienced a triathlon. You'll be able to show up race morning with an excellent understanding of what to expect and how to execute each leg of your triathlon, and you'll be ready to complete part two of your race week plan.

Writing Part Two of Your Race Week Plan

When you show up at the start line of your triathlon (you're going to do a triathlon!), your dedicated training season will have built all the fitness you need to get to the finish line. Your job at this point is to keep your engine fueled, maintain an effort level appropriate for your fitness and the race distance, and get out of your own way so your body can do what you've trained it to do.

Getting out of your own way, however, is harder than it sounds. The excitement and adrenaline on race morning lead most athletes to start their race as if they were shot out of a cannon. Plus, thanks to a great couple of taper weeks, you're rested and race-ready, and the speeds and paces all feel almost effortless at the beginning. So, if you decide during the race how fast you can go and how hard you can push, the excitement and adrenaline will almost always lead you astray, and you can find yourself running out of energy and fitness far before the finish line.

That's where part two of your race week plan comes into play. By thinking through how you want to approach your race ahead of time, when you are rational and unbiased rather than swept up in the moment, you can ground your execution in the reality of the fitness you've developed in training. Writing part two gives you the opportunity to define your race-day effort levels and to outline everything else you want to think through in advance of the triathlon: your race goals (yes! finally!), your race-day fueling and hydration plan, any course-specific notes, and your intended mindset for each leg of the race. Writing part two creates the blueprint for a smart, disciplined race, one that keeps your engine fueled, your mind focused, and your effort level appropriate for your fitness and your race distance. And much like with part one, writing part two puts all the thinking and decision making behind you, so that once you cross the start line, all you need to do is follow your plan to the finish.

Determining Race-Day Effort Levels

Your race-day effort levels represent a key component of part two of your race week plan. So, let's talk about how to define yours based on your race distance and your training plan level for each triathlon sport. Ultimately, you want to target effort levels for swim and bike that will allow you to feel strong on the run, and a run effort level that you can sustain even after swimming and biking. Those swim, bike, and run effort levels need to be both appropriate for your race distance and aligned with the sport-specific effort levels you developed in training. With that in mind, table 14.1 provides guidelines for race-day effort levels for each training plan level and race distance.

Defining Race Goals

We have deferred setting race goals until this moment – until your training is behind you and you have a good understanding of both the race distance and the fitness that you have built to cover it. But now I will remove the handcuffs and finally let you think about your goals for your triathlon. However, I do want you to think about your goals in terms of process goals (how you want to execute your race) rather than outcome goals (your sport splits, overall finish time, or finishing position). Process goals represent all the things you can control – your effort, your execution, and your attitude – whereas outcome goals are often influenced by factors outside of your control, such as the weather.

TABLE 14.1 Target Effort Levels by Training Plan Level and Race Distance

	Sprint-distance	Olympic-distance	Half-distance
Level 1	Moderate (zone 2)	Moderate (zone 2)	Moderate (zone 2)
Level 2	Strong (zone 3)	Moderate (zone 2)	Moderate (zone 2)
Level 3	Hard (zone 4)	Strong (zone 3)	Moderate (zone 2)

If this is your first triathlon (or even if it's your 15th), an appropriate and worthy top goal is to have fun and finish with your head held high and a smile on your face. Another excellent race goal, regardless of your level of experience, is to execute part two of your race-day plan just as you wrote it. For any additional goals, instead of focusing on speed or pace, think about how you want to feel during each leg of the race, because a race where you have fun, execute well, and finish strong is always one you will be proud of.

Capturing the Final Details

Having determined your race-day effort levels and defined your race goals, there are just a few remaining items left to round out part two of your race week plan. First, you want to translate the fueling and hydration plan that you've tested and solidified through training into your race week plan. Next, jot down any course-specific notes, such as the start format for the swim or specific features (like hills or aid station locations) of the bike and run courses. Finally, include any cues or reminders for yourself (like "stay present" or "don't forget to use all your gears") that you want to keep top of mind during each leg of the race. We can look at part two of Alex's Race Week Plan for their first triathlon as an example.

Part two of your race week plan details how you want to execute your triathlon, but it won't paint the full picture of the triathlon experience, help with visualization, and ease your nerves by taking away some of the uncertainty. So let's wade into that promised excruciating level of detail and cover everything you want to know – and everything you never knew you needed to know – about race day.

The Swim

Despite your consistent training and strong swim fitness, you may still be most nervous about the swim leg of your triathlon. If so, you are in good company. By my estimate, around 75 percent of all triathletes – regardless of fitness, swim pace, or experience level – have some degree of anxiety about an open-water swim. The following discussion may help alleviate some of those nerves, and the tools provided will help you manage them when they do bubble up.

The Start Format

Your triathlon will, in all likelihood, use one of three standard swim start formats. Each has its pros and cons, but all of them lead to you swimming along the designated swim course, surrounded by your fellow triathletes.

Alex's Race Week Plan

Part Two: The Triathlon

Goals

#1 – Have fun and finish strong.

#2 – Follow the effort levels and fueling notes in the plan, especially on the run.

#3 – Feel calm and steady in the swim, comfortable on the bike, and in control early in the run, so I can run hard for the final third!!

The Swim

Start Format/Time: Wave start – my wave is wave 4, at about 7:30 a.m.

Effort Level: Moderate, just like the endurance swims

Course Notes: Buoys every 200 yards, two right turns at red buoys

Think About: Settle into moderate effort before first buoy, remember to sight every 6 to 8 strokes, if I feel anxious, list snack foods or desserts or candy

T1: Swim-to-Bike Transition

Notes: Remember to start taking off wetsuit while jogging to transition spot, don't dawdle!, take stuff off, put stuff on, and go

The Bike

Effort Level: Moderate – remember that you still have to run!

Fueling: 1 bottle with 60 g carbs + 500 mg sodium (drink 1/3 bottle every 30 min), 1 bottle with 900 mg sodium (drink 1/3 bottle every 30 min), 1 package of 6 chews (eat 1 chew every 20 min)

Course Notes: Most of the hills are in the first half of the course

Think About: Remember to use all my gears on the hills – not too hard going up, not too easy going down; outside foot down then inside hand heavy around the corners

T2: Bike-to-Run Transition

Notes: Remember that bike goes back rear wheel first, don't dawdle!, take stuff off, put stuff on, and go – put on visor and race belt while heading to Run Out

The Run

Effort Level: Overall – strong; first 2 miles run with grandma + stare at my watch, then strong (but not too strong) to the 4-mile mark, then GO FOR IT

Fueling: One gel coming out of T2, one at the halfway point, 1 cup of water from each aid station, 1 salt tablet with each cup of water

Course Notes: Long hill in the middle, not much shade, aid stations every mile

Think About: Final mile has to be my fastest! think about three gears: one for the first 2 miles, another for the middle, and a final gear to finish

Wave Starts

Wave starts are used in many local and short-course triathlons. This start format places participants into starting groups based on factors such as age, gender, and race category (if multiple distances or formats are offered for the same race). The athletes in each group, or wave, start together, with several minutes between each wave start. The waves may use a beach start, where athletes wait on the beach for the starting horn and then run into the water to begin the swim, or an in-water start, where athletes wait at a designated spot in the water until the starting horn sounds.

When participating in a wave start for your triathlon, think carefully about where you position yourself within the group. If you are a strong and confident swimmer, go ahead and take a place at the front. If you feel anxious about the swim, and especially about swimming while surrounded by other athletes, positioning yourself in either back corner gives you the best opportunity for more space while swimming. And there's no rule that says you have to start swimming when the horn blows, so feel free to let your fellow triathletes get moving, count to 3, and then start your swim with clean water and a bit less chaos.

Rolling Self-Seeded Starts

Rolling self-seeded starts are similar to the start format for many running races. Athletes line up according to their anticipated swim time, with the fastest swimmers at the front of the queue. When the starting horn sounds, the first batch of athletes – typically three to six people – enters the water and their "race clock" starts. After a few seconds, the next batch of athletes enters the water, and so on until everyone has started their race. (Coach tip: Seed yourself as accurately as possible, because surrounding yourself with athletes at similar paces provides a relatively calm swim experience.)

Mass Starts

Think of the mass start like a wave start, except there's only one wave. Mass starts were very common in the early years of triathlon, but are less so now. If your triathlon includes a mass start, think very carefully about where to position yourself within the group. Your front-to-back position will be similar to that for a self-seeded rolling start: toward the front for faster swimmers and toward the back for slower swimmers. If you are less keen about swimming surrounded by other athletes, position yourself on an outer edge rather than in the middle of the pack.

Estimating Your Swim Time

Not sure how to estimate your anticipated swim time? Use the following process to arrive at a good ballpark estimate:

1. Take the distance of your triathlon swim in meters and divide that by 100 to determine the number of hundreds in your swim distance (e.g., 1500 divided by 100 is 15 100s).
2. Note your average swim pace in the pool at your intended race effort level in seconds per 100 meters, adding 10 seconds to a seconds-per-100-yards pace to get a rough metric conversion (e.g., 1:40 pace per 100 yards is 100 seconds per 100 yards; 100 seconds + 10 seconds = 110 seconds, so roughly 110 seconds per 100 meters).
3. Add 10 seconds per 100 meters to your average per 100 meters pace in the pool to account for the difference between your pool swim pace and your likely open-water swim pace (e.g., 110 seconds + 10 seconds = 120 seconds, so 120 seconds per 100 meters).
4. Multiply the number of hundreds in your swim distance by your open-water swim pace per 100 meters to find your anticipated time in seconds (e.g. 15 100s × 120 seconds per 100 = 1,800 seconds).
5. Divide by 60 to convert your anticipated time from seconds to minutes (e.g., 1,800/60 = 30 minutes).

Water Safety

Water safety is top-of-mind for every triathlon race director, so a good number of volunteers will be in the water to support you during your swim. You will typically see volunteers in kayaks, on stand-up paddleboards, and on jet skis scattered throughout the swim course. These volunteers function as lifeguards and their vessels as floating rest areas, and there's no need to be shy about asking for support. At every single triathlon, you will find athletes – regardless of fitness, swim pace, or experience level – taking a break and hanging onto a kayak or stand-up paddleboard.

Swim Execution

Swimming in a straight line in a pool requires little execution instruction. Swimming a course requiring turns in an open body of water where you often can't see the bottom, and which won't have painted lines to follow even if you could see them, will benefit from some additional guidelines.

The First 200 Yards or Meters

Before we worry about swimming in a straight line and following the swim buoys, let's talk about your swim start effort level. The start of your triathlon (you're going to do a triathlon!) is filled with adrenaline – lots and lots of adrenaline, stemming from days and weeks and months of anticipation of this exact moment. That adrenaline typically makes it next to impossible to begin your swim at anything resembling your planned race effort. So your goal in those first 200 yards or meters is to, as quickly as possible, recognize that you are far exceeding your planned effort level, *breathe*, and drop down to a comfortable, sustainable pace.

Sighting

We discussed sighting – what it is and how to do it – in chapter 4. So this is your reminder to actually incorporate sighting into your triathlon swim. Pick your head up and "sight" the next buoy every 6 to 8 swim strokes. Yes, that often. And be sure you actually see the buoy when you lift your head; don't just go through the motions.

Buoy Turns

Turns on the swim course will be marked with buoys, typically ones that differ in color from the this-is-the-swim-course buoys, and can be very dense and congested points on the swim course. For some reason, athletes who were previously spread out comfortably in the water condense into a narrow stream, practically swimming on top of each other. You, however, will be a smart triathlete and execute your turn wide of the buoy – wide enough that you stay away from the melee right alongside it. You may find it easiest to swim Tarzan-style or switch to breaststroke as you execute your turn so that you can always see where you're going. This will also help with the most important part of your buoy turn: sighting the next buoy along the course.

The Swim Exit

As long as the swim may feel in the moment, eventually you will arrive at the swim course finish. Remember to increase your kick rate in the final 50 to 100 yards or meters to avoid feeling lightheaded when you transition to standing. You'll make that transition to standing once your fingers touch the bottom, because at that point you can stand up and have the water at or beneath your knees, making it easier to walk or run out of the water and to the transition area.

Open-Water Swim Anxiety

As I mentioned earlier, around 75 percent of all triathletes feel some degree of anxiety about an open-water swim. When swimming, this anxiety often manifests as the feeling that you cannot catch your breath, and – if you're wearing a wetsuit – that your wetsuit specifically is constricting your breathing. In reality, the wetsuit is seldom the culprit. These sensations generally stem from two triggers: cold water temperatures and your nervous system's fight-or-flight response.

Our Mammalian Dive Reflex

The mammalian dive reflex occurs in mammals – and therefore us humans – when submerged in water, especially when your face comes into contact with cold water. The reflex elicits several physiological responses designed to keep you alive underwater, which is generally a good thing. One of the physiological responses, though, causes you to hold your breath, even if you are trying to breathe. This mammalian dive reflex is why you feel like you can't catch your breath when you put your face in cold water and try to start swimming.

The sensation that you can't breathe when you're in a large body of water where you can't touch the bottom is a profoundly disturbing feeling, and one you want to avoid if at all possible. Two things can help avert this: First, if possible, splash water on your face before starting the swim, giving your face time to acclimate to the water temperature and limiting the future dive reflex response. Second, to combat the reflex, *exhale*, focusing on long, slow exhales to the count of 3 or 4, like you're blowing bubbles. The diving reflex will naturally cause you to hold your breath – holding onto the oxygen at first, and then the carbon dioxide produced as your

T1: The Swim-to-Bike Transition

After completing the swim (yay! phew!), you will walk, jog, or run to your transition spot. During that time, unzip your wetsuit and pull it down to your waist. Then take off your cap and goggles. (You can, of course, lift your goggles to your forehead before removing the top half of your wetsuit, but taking off your cap and goggles first means you're holding them while trying to remove your wetsuit. We don't need to make that any harder than it already is.) Once you arrive at your transition spot, drop your cap and goggles behind your gear, remove your wetsuit, and place it with them.

body uses that oxygen – so exhaling the carbon dioxide both opposes the reflex and rids your body of the carbon dioxide, making room for a full, deep intake of oxygen on your next breath.

Grounding Techniques

When feelings of anxiety swell – from feeling like you can't breathe or general open-water anxiety – your nervous system moves into a fight-or-flight state. That can create a surge of adrenaline, amplify the sensation of shortness of breath, and lead you down a spiral that you can't reason your way out of. Grounding techniques help bring your nervous system out of the fight-or-flight state, returning it to a state of calm.

Grounding techniques can be sensory, physical, or mental. Beyond long, deep breaths – inhaling for a count of 2 and exhaling for a count of 4 – sensory and physical techniques present some challenges while swimming, so plan to have a few mental grounding techniques in your back pocket if you're concerned about open-water anxiety (or even if you're not):

- Pick a category, like cars or flowers or vegetables, and name as many items as you can from that category.
- Recite the steps for a routine task or activity, like making a sandwich or prepping your bike for a long ride.
- Count your swim strokes, or recite multiplication tables.

These techniques may seem odd, but seeing as no one recites multiplication tables as they're fleeing a burning building, they tell your nervous system that you are safe and there's no need to panic.

Put on your bike shoes, sunglasses, helmet, any other attire needed for your bike, and race belt if your race bib is required on the bike leg. (If you want, you can towel off your face, but don't worry about drying off completely; you'll dry off while cycling.) Once your helmet chinstrap is fastened, you may take your bike and walk, jog, or run with it to Bike Out. After crossing under the Bike Out arch, you will see the mount line, the location of which is generally made abundantly clear by loud volunteers stationed to ensure you follow the mount line rule. Cross the mount line with your bike and move to one side so that you don't impede the progress of another athlete. Mount your bike, look over your shoulder to confirm that there's no one barreling toward you, and begin your bike leg.

Triathlon Rules

The rules for a triathlon will be dictated by the national governing body that sanctions the event and by the race production organization. While they may differ slightly from race to race and from country to country, the rules generally include the following:

Overall Rules

- You must complete the course in its entirety and as designed. (Duh!)
- No nudity, indecent exposure, public urination, or littering is permitted. (Fun fact: Urinating in your wetsuit, in transition, while riding your bike, and while running is generally considered to be acceptable behavior in triathlon and within the rules as long as you do it without disrobing.)
- No headphones are allowed (I know, I know, but really no headphones).
- No one may receive outside assistance. Outside assistance does not include aid from volunteers, but it does include receiving support such as fueling, fluids, or pacing on the course from your friends and family. Outside assistance specifically prohibits any assistance with forward progress from volunteers, other participants, or anyone else.
- Typically, you may carry a phone with you, but you are prohibited from using it.
- You may not impede the progress of another athlete.
- You must treat race officials, volunteers, other athletes, and spectators with respect and courtesy.

Swim Rules

- Triathlon-certifying organizations have very specific rules regarding the use of wetsuits, which have common themes but do vary slightly by organization.
    - Generally speaking, wetsuits are permitted if the water temperature is below a stated number, usually between 76 °F and 78 °F (24.5 °C and 25.5 °C) (specific to the tenth of a degree). If the water temperature falls between that cutoff and a second temperature, typically around 84 °F (28.9 °C), wetsuits are optional, meaning you can wear one but won't be eligible for awards or championship qualification. Wetsuits are typically prohibited if the water temperature exceeds the second temperature cutoff.
    - Triathlon wetsuits typically must be no more than 5 millimeters thick.
- Neoprene caps are permitted, but neoprene booties are only allowed if the water temperature is "wetsuit legal" or below a specific cutoff (generally 65 °F [18.3 °C]), depending on the certifying organization.
- Swim gloves, snorkels, and fins are prohibited.

Bike Rules

- Your race number must be visible at all times. In some regions, the provided bike sticker satisfies this rule, but in other regions race bibs are required during the bike leg.
- You must put on your bike helmet and fasten the chinstrap before you first touch your bike in T1 and keep it fastened – and therefore on – until you've reracked it in T2.
- You must ride on the right and pass on the left; riding on the left constitutes a blocking violation and can be subject to a time penalty. (Unless your triathlon takes place in a left-hand traffic country, in which case the rules are opposite.)
- Most triathlons are non-drafting triathlons and have clearly defined rules surrounding drafting and passing. Similar to wetsuit rules, they are very specific but vary slightly by certifying organization. Violation of any of these rules is subject to a time penalty. (Drafting and passing rules – specifically draft zone distances and passing time constraints – are periodically updated; be sure to check the current rules before your triathlon.)
    - To keep from drafting, you must ride at least 12 meters (39.3 ft), or six bike lengths, behind the bicycle in front of you.
    - Once you enter the draft zone of the bike in front of you, you must execute a pass, and that pass must be completed within 25 seconds.
    - A completed pass is defined by your front wheel overtaking the leading edge of the front wheel of the bicycle you passed.
    - If another athlete passes you, you must immediately drop back out of that athlete's draft zone. You cannot pass that athlete without first dropping out of their draft zone.
- You cannot make forward progress without your bike.

Run Rules

- Your race bib must be visible at all times.
- You may run or walk. Some certifying organizations allow you to crawl, others do not. Either way, let's hope it doesn't come to that.

Transition Rules

- Spectators are not allowed in transition.
- Glass containers are not allowed in transition.
- Your gear must be contained within your transition spot.
- You may not mess with another athlete's bike or gear.
- You may not ride your bike in transition. Your bike must be mounted after the mount line and dismounted before the dismount line.
- You must return your bike to its original location and position after finishing the bike leg.

The Bike

For many triathletes, the fun begins on the bike: You've made it through the swim, the pre-race nerves and open-water swim anxiety are behind you, and now it's time to *go*. But the perfect triathlon bike leg strikes the ideal balance between riding well enough to demonstrate your bike fitness and holding back enough to still showcase your run fitness once you're done cycling. So your entire bike leg can be guided by a simple question: "Is what I am doing right now setting myself up to run well later?"

Bike Aid Stations

Depending on the length of the bike course – typically for long-course races, occasionally for Olympic-distance races, and rarely for sprint-distance races – your triathlon may offer aid stations along the course. Aid stations are always stocked with water and may also offer sport-specific fueling and hydration products. You can "roll through" the aid station on your bike by slowing down, making eye contact with a volunteer, hand-signaling or verbally communicating with them, and grabbing the outstretched bottle as you pass. If you prefer to stop, be sure to pull to the side of the course so that you don't impede another athlete's progress. And if you find yourself in need of a port-o-potty, most aid stations will offer one along with a friendly volunteer to hold your bike – and maybe even fill your water bottle – while you take care of business.

Thomas Frey/picture alliance via Getty Images

Bike Execution

Remember back when I mentioned that triathlon success is built off of bike fitness? This is where that bike fitness pays off: not by using up all your fitness on the bike course, but by leaving some in the tank so it can be repurposed for the run.

The First Miles

The initial few miles of the bike are often a bit congested, as the clumps of athletes who came out of the water together work to settle into their bike pace and their single-file order along the bike course. You may often find yourself in a competitor's draft zone during this window, and race officials usually extend a bit of grace during these first miles, but you will work to find your position in line while still staying within your planned bike effort level. Note that the operative phrase here is "while still staying within your planned bike effort level" – you want to avoid burning through a big chunk of your hard-earned bike fitness passing people during these early miles!

The Remaining Miles

Once the field has spread out and you've settled into your place in the single-file line of cyclists, your job is simply to execute the bike leg at your planned effort level. Sometimes athletes look to "bank" time during the bike leg by riding above their planned effort level, believing this will improve their overall time. But here's the thing about triathlon math: For every minute you save on the bike, you will lose 2, 3, or 5 minutes on the run. And virtually no triathlete gets to the halfway point of their run and wishes they'd biked harder. Stick to your planned effort level, ask yourself that key bike execution question regularly, and set yourself up for success on the run – and at the finish line.

Executing Passes

You may end up exceeding that planned effort level, though, if you find yourself needing to overtake a fellow competitor. And I do mean need – if your planned effort level brought you to the back of another cyclist's draft zone, you need to pass them; if you saw them ahead and a fire got lit inside you, then you *want* to pass them and will likely burn through a chunk of fitness if you try to make that happen. Plus you will potentially have to slow down after executing the pass, given that extra effort, and all you will have accomplished is initiating a game of leapfrog.

To execute a pass without expending more energy than necessary, only increase your effort level as much as is required to complete the pass within the required timeframe – 25 seconds (or however long your triathlon's certifying organization allows) is a surprisingly long time.

A well-executed pass does not demand a recovery after the effort; you want to simply slide back into the same bike effort level you were originally using.

Fueling and Hydrating

Along with adhering to your planned effort level, staying on top of your fueling and hydration plays a critical role in setting yourself up to run well off the bike. You practiced and fine-tuned your bike fueling and hydration plan in training, but it still requires diligence to ensure you execute your plan on race day. Pay careful attention to your watch or bike computer to stay on pace with your fueling and hydration so that you arrive at T2 with a body that's ready to run.

Flat Tires and Mechanical Issues

Flat tires and mechanical issues are a risk any time you ride your bike, including on race day. Your pre-race gear check can minimize the risk, but cannot eliminate it entirely. Most triathlons will have one or several roaming bike techs on the course. However, most triathlons have hundreds, if not thousands, of athletes and miles and miles of road, so the likelihood of a bike tech being available and at your side the moment you have a flat tire or mechanical issue is slim, to say the least. Always carry a flat kit and multitool, and make sure you know how to fix a flat tire; a pre-race tune can also limit the likelihood of a mechanical issue. Athletes are permitted to assist other athletes, and a bike tech may appear in a few minutes, but self-sufficiency provides the quickest return to riding.

T2: The Bike-to-Run Transition

Upon finishing the bike leg (yay!), you'll stop and dismount your bike just before the dismount line, which is generally the mount line approached from the opposite direction, and also made abundantly clear by loud volunteers there to ensure that you follow the dismount line rule. You'll walk, jog, or run with your bike to your transition spot and rerack it just as it started. Only then will you unclip your chinstrap, remove your helmet, and take off any other bike attire that won't be coming along with you for the run.

Then you'll quickly pull on your run shoes (assuming you're switching shoes) and take care of any other major clothing changes that can't be done while moving. You'll grab whatever else you need for your run, including your race belt with the attached run bib number (if you don't already have it on from the bike leg), and head toward the run course. You can clip your race belt, don your hat or visor, stuff gels in your pockets,

Understanding Course Cutoffs

Course cutoffs are the unfortunate reality at all triathlons (and all endurance events). Race directors can only procure permits, keep roads safe, and ask volunteers to staff aid stations for so long. The race director will typically communicate all cutoffs in the athlete guide (yet another great reason to *read the athlete guide*). Cutoffs can be defined by an athlete's elapsed time on the course, the time of day, or a combination of these two factors. If an athlete does not finish a specific discipline or reach an intermediate point on the course by the cutoff, they are generally not allowed to complete the event. You can estimate your swim, bike, and run splits using your average swim, bike, and run paces to gauge whether you might be affected by course cutoff times.

and take care of any other necessary run prep as you walk, jog, or run toward Run Out and even during your first steps on the run course.

The Run

No matter how you're feeling and how your race has gone up until this point, the way you'll ultimately feel about your triathlon largely rests on how you perform during the run. Fueling, hydrating, and sticking to your planned run paces and effort levels remain crucial through the majority of the run course, so that you can run strong over the final miles and cross the finish line standing tall, with your arms raised in victory.

Run Aid Stations

Most triathlons position aid stations approximately every mile (every 1.5-2 km) along the run course. These aid stations always offer water, typically portioned into roughly half-full 8-ounce (240 mL) cups. They may also provide a second beverage option with electrolytes and possibly carbohydrates, as well as fueling products like gels or bars, fruit such as oranges or bananas, and snacks like pretzels or potato chips. Most run aid stations additionally have enthusiastic, helpful volunteers, a first aid kit, and a port-o-potty.

Run Execution

Your run execution can be divided into three phases: the first 1 mile (1.5 km) for sprint-distance races or 2 miles (3 km) for all other distances, the middle miles, and the final push to the finish – 1 mile (1.5 km) for a sprint-distance triathlon, 2 miles (3 km) for an Olympic-distance event, or 3 miles (5 km) for a long-course event.

Phase I

During the first phase of the run, you exist within the T2 reality distortion field discussed in chapter 7. Because you cannot trust your body's feedback or your rate of perceived exertion, you will set a "not to exceed" pace target approximately 30 seconds per mile (20 seconds/km) slower than your expected race pace. You will rely on factual information – the pace shown on your watch – for accurate feedback, and you will stare at your watch, adhere to your pace target, and use the Running with Grandma cue until you escape the reality distortion field. Not sure about your expected race pace? It will typically range from your run pace in training at your planned effort level to 30 seconds per mile (20 seconds/km) slower than that pace. The higher your planned effort level and the longer the triathlon, the more likely your race pace will differ from your training pace.

Phase II

Once you've left the reality distortion field and can return to trusting your rate of perceived exertion, you will stop looking at your watch and run entirely by feel. Even with perfect training and race preparation, accurately predicting your race-day pace is difficult at best, so defining a pre-set pace target for this phase of your race can either push you too hard or hold you back. And seeing your pace in real time can mess with your head, either because you believe you're running too fast or too slow. So stop looking at the data and trust yourself to find the correct effort level for you, on this day and in this moment – with one important caveat.

Because here's the thing: Your effort level during this phase of the run *cannot* be your maximum effort level. Remember all the work you did learning how to Save the Best for Last? *This* is why you practiced that skill: So you can run consistently in this middle phase while still having more for the finish. You will find the correct effort level for you, on this day and in this moment, that allows you to run well in this phase *and* still increase your effort and pace in the final phase of your run.

Phase III

You've been disciplined all day – staying comfortable in the swim, demonstrating control on the bike, and holding back in the early miles of the run – to set yourself up for this moment. Once you reach the final phase of your run, you can finally let go of the reins and pour the remaining depth of your energy onto the run course. You'll let the adrenaline carry you through to the finish line, where you will finally celebrate your victory over the Big, Scary, Awesome Goal that you worked so hard to achieve.

Completing your first triathlon, your first triathlon at a new distance, or really any triathlon, requires a leap of faith. While you likely trained up to or beyond the distance for each individual discipline during your season and executed one or several race simulation days, putting all three sports together at their full distances in a single day often represents new territory. You may not be able to see how all your hard work comes together to provide the fitness necessary to comfortably cover your race distance at a speed appropriate for that distance, but I do.

So when you toe the line on race morning, trust your training. Trust that you've done the work and that you have the fitness you need to get the job done. Control what you can – your effort, your execution, and your attitude – and let go of the rest. And remember, just by showing up, you are braver than most.

15

POST-RACE: WHAT TO EXPECT AND WHAT COMES NEXT

YOU DID IT! You completed your triathlon! You set a Big, Scary, Awesome Goal for yourself, worked hard toward that goal, and your focus and dedication carried you across the finish line. With the completion of your goal – and, if this was your first triathlon, your newfound title of triathlete – often comes a wide range of thoughts and emotions. So, let's have one final conversation to talk through what you might be thinking and feeling post-race – from reflecting on your triathlon to the very common post-race letdown to thoughts on your next Big, Scary, Awesome Goal.

Your Post-Race Reflection

At some point after you cross the finish line – maybe minutes after, maybe days after – you will inevitably look back and evaluate your day and your performance. Before we dive into a structure that guides productive takeaways from your experience, I want to emphasize two important points to keep in mind as you reflect on your triathlon: First and foremost, whether your day went perfectly or was a far cry from what you expected, *you completed a triathlon*. You set a goal, and you accomplished it. All the rest of the details are secondary to this Big, Scary, Awesome achievement.

Second, nearly everyone looks back and wonders if they could've pushed just a bit harder on the run. I have learned from hundreds of my athletes' races and dozens of my own that this question only pops up once you are sitting comfortably post-race, hours or days later, and the tangible discomfort of those run miles has faded from your memory. Because those miles *were* uncomfortable. And 99 percent of the time, if you could've pushed just a bit harder on the run, you would have. So trust that you did the best you could with what you had to give in the moment, and leave it at that.

The rest of your "I wonder" questions, though, are part of the fabulous puzzle that is racing triathlon. Just about every triathlete looks back at their triathlon and wonders whether doing this a little differently in

Justin Tafoya/Getty Images for IRONMAN

training or that a little differently on race day could have shaved a few extra minutes off their finish time. And at every race, you learn something – about pacing, about fueling, about gear, or maybe about all of those things. The things we learn and the questions we ask keep us coming back, race after race and season after season, in search of the perfect race. So, to aid you on that journey, let's walk through a post-race reflection exercise.

Your post-race reflection will serve as an addendum to your race week plan, capturing where you stuck to the plan and where you went off-script, what worked well, and what you would like to do differently next time. Recording this now, while the experience and your thoughts on it are fresh in your mind, helps you fine-tune your race week plan for your next triathlon, incorporating everything you did well and adjusting for those things you'd like to approach differently. Because while many moments from your race will stay fresh in your memories for months or even years, your recollection of many details will fade over time, and you want to ensure you can take what you learned from this experience and apply it to your next.

Much like with the race week plan, a template or sample reflection can provide guidance when writing your post-race reflection. So, let's take a look at Alex's Post-Race Reflection from their first triathlon. Alex already captured the details of their pre-race preparation and race execution in their race week plan, so they used a similar overall structure to note what worked, what didn't, and what they'll change next time. For the race itself, Alex recorded their results and added specific notes on how they felt about their effort level, fitness, and fueling plan, since those are areas that often evolve from race to race. Beyond documenting everything they learned during the race, writing the post-race reflection was an excellent way for Alex to process the experience (since nontriathlete friends have limited interest in hearing about every detail of the race). Once they were done, Alex filed the reflection away with the race week plan, so both will be available when it comes time to prep for their next triathlon.

Alex's Post-Race Reflection

Race Week Preparation

Travel: The afternoon felt rushed, next time plan to arrive earlier

Race Week Preparation and Tasks: Overall good, glad I went to the athlete briefing

Pre-Race Fueling and Hydration: Plan worked great – but going to the grocery store on Saturday took more time than anticipated, maybe go to the grocery store at home next time and bring food in a cooler to take a task off the list

Sleep: Might get into bed a little earlier next time, so I have more time to wind down

Race Morning Preparation

Timing: Left earlier than planned, but timing was good, I was happy not to be rushed, LONG line at the port-o-potty – need to allow more time for that

Breakfast: Might try oatmeal with maple syrup next time, bagel and peanut butter felt a bit heavy

The Triathlon

Results: 3:08:09 total time – swim 29:32, T1 4:07, bike 1:34:16, T2 2:51, run 57:23; 12th in my age group

The Swim

Effort and Execution: Started fast, and I felt a little panicky, need to work on this – eventually found my moderate effort level

Fitness: Was happy I did those swims that seemed unnecessarily long in training, didn't feel tired at all coming out of the water

Notes: Tinted goggles would've been nice, the sun was really bright; swam breaststroke a few times to find the buoys, so should probably keep practicing sighting

T1: The Swim-to-Bike Transition

Notes: Walk-through was helpful, took more time than needed to dry off

(continued)

Alex's Post-Race Reflection *(continued)*

The Bike

Effort and Execution: Faded the second half

Fitness: Missed a few long rides, wondering if that's part of why I faded

Fueling: Only drank about half of each bottle

Notes: Could do better here – fitness, sticking to fueling plan

T2: The Bike-to-Run Transition

Notes: Almost forgot to take my helmet off! oops – loved the no-tie laces

The Run

Effort and Execution: Tougher than expected (maybe because I didn't drink all my bottles on the bike?), happy that I didn't walk other than aid stations and still finished strong

Fitness: Legs had plenty of endurance, would like to find some more speed though

Fueling: Stayed on plan, seemed to work well

Notes: Not sure if I need to work on my run speed or if I need to do better on the bike, so I am not so tired on the run – or maybe both?

Overall Thoughts

I think my race day performance pretty accurately reflected my training and fitness, and I'm really happy with how the day went – but I also think there are lots of areas where I can do better

Next season, I want to really work on bike fitness and get better at fueling

I want to work on my run speed over the off-season

I need to get better about hydrating after workouts and especially after race day – I forgot about that post-race hydration bottle and I felt it the next day

The Post-Race Letdown

Once the glow of the finish line has dimmed, you've told the story of your day to everyone who's willing to listen, and life has returned to normal, many athletes find themselves in a bit of a post-race letdown. If this sounds like you, know that a letdown, even a bit of depression, is very common and completely normal after your triathlon season concludes. Because over the weeks and months of your training season, you devoted a lot of time toward preparing for your triathlon – toward training and showering and doing laundry and eating all the things. And you spent a lot of time thinking about your triathlon – about your training and your gear and your fueling and all the other triathlon things. So now that you've completed your triathlon season, there's not really anything triathlon-related to do or think about, and that feels . . . odd, almost like a void.

For some, regaining the mental space and time on your calendar will be a relief, allowing room for hobbies and obligations that you placed on the back burner during your triathlon training. For others, this void feels downright uncomfortable – like you're wandering aimlessly, lacking purpose and direction. Often that feeling passes with time . . . but instead of waiting for that to happen, sometimes athletes look to fill the void with a new Big, Scary, Awesome Goal. And hey, I *want* you to do another triathlon, but let's be sure not to jump into your next challenge too quickly. Force yourself to take at least a week, if not two or more, to celebrate your accomplishment and enjoy the extra time in your schedule before we talk about what's next. You want to ensure that you dive into your next big thing because of that thing itself, not just because you're looking to fill the void.

So, What Now?

Once you've given yourself a moment just to be, without agenda or direction, you are in a space to start thinking about what's next. What's next could be absolutely anything, but I'm hoping it's another triathlon. Because I'm hoping that you *loved* doing your triathlon. That you loved the puzzle of training three sports simultaneously, maybe adding a sport or two to your repertoire, and growing as an athlete and a person. That the routine and structure of your training weeks became a part of you, and that continuing to swim, bike, and run feels as natural and obvious as continuing to breathe. That you found your people in training and on race day, swimming and biking and running, in transition and out on the course, and celebrating after the finish line. That you now feel like you are not only a triathlete but also a part of the triathlon community.

But also know that it's okay if you didn't. You are a triathlete, and you will be a triathlete for life, even if you never cross another triathlon finish line. That badge and your accomplishment don't fade with time. Maybe you have a different Big, Scary, Awesome Goal in mind, or maybe you're done with Big, Scary, Awesome Goals for a while – or forever. That's okay. There's no rule that says you have to follow one Big, Scary, Awesome Goal with another, or that your next goal has to look anything like your last one.

If you *did* fall in love with triathlon (yay!), you may already be thinking about your next race. Know that there is no rule that says your next triathlon has to be a longer distance, or a faster finish, or different in any way from your last. You can come back next year and follow the exact same training plan and do the exact same race with the exact same gear, and that will be wonderful. If you are, though, looking to progress your journey in the sport, here are a few principles to keep in mind:

- Master one race distance before progressing to the next – and don't skip over any of them.
- Challenge yourself to develop your endurance or your speed, but not both at the same time.
- Progress is rarely made across all three sports simultaneously; prioritize your weakest sport first.
- Incredible gains can be made in the off-season; use that time wisely, and you'll be amazed at where you can be when you *start* your next season, let alone finish it.

Keeping all of this in mind, you can return and use the training plans in this book again next season. Plus, if you used Level 1 for one or more sports this season, you'll begin next season at Level 2 or 3 across all sports – the "brand new" designation will no longer apply to you.

As you toss around ideas for your next Big, Scary, Awesome Goal – be it a triathlon or something completely different – keep in mind the one rule I *do* have for my athletes' goals and races: they must always excite you. You want your next goal or race to draw you toward it, just as the last one did. You want to understand your "why" for this next goal or race just as clearly as you understood your "why" for the last one – whether they're the same or completely different. And if part of what excites you about your goal or race also scares you, don't turn away from it. That's how you know it's a worthy goal.

No Matter What Comes Next, You Are Now – and Forever – a Triathlete

We've talked a lot about you conquering your Big, Scary, Awesome Goal and completing a triathlon, but we haven't yet talked about what it means to be a triathlete. You are part of a pretty exclusive club – only about one-tenth of 1 percent of the world's population has completed a triathlon (about 5-10 times fewer than those who have finished a marathon). This club, this community, is filled with people who *get it*. Who get what it's like to have a calendar filled with workouts, who think it's completely normal to do a workout after having done a workout, and who also look at an opportunity and say, "That sounds crazy. Where do I sign up?"

We are the people who want to hear *every detail* about your last race. We want to hear about the fueling products you recently tried and your bike ride in gusty winds and the really tough workout you did last Wednesday. We are here for all of your stories and excited to share all of ours. We can't wait to nudge you along the path toward your next Big, Scary, Awesome Goal, whatever that means for you. But mostly, we're glad to have you here with us. We hope you stick around for a while.

PART V

PLANNING AND PROGRAMMING

A goal without a plan is just a wish.

Antoine de Saint-Exupéry

This is it: The training plans are how we put words into action, where all the conversations about swim form, bike cornering, and run posture translate to you actually doing the swimming, biking, and running – to you training for and completing a triathlon. I know you're excited to get moving, both literally and figuratively, but let's walk through the "fine print" of the training plans before you do.

How the Training Plans Are Structured

All training plans are based on a 4-week training cycle, typically incorporating 3 weeks that build training volume, intensity, or both, and one recovery week. The final training cycle in each triathlon plan – the peak-and-taper cycle – includes a peak week (your biggest volume training week), two taper weeks, and race week. With the exception of the preseason training plans, all weeks have six scheduled training days, with Monday as your "off" day. If you prefer Friday as your "off" day, you can shift the Tuesday through Friday workouts back one day to rearrange your weekly workout pattern. (If you are doing the Olympic- to half-distance training plan, you can execute the Sunday swim session on Sunday or your scheduled "off" day.)

All triathlon plans include two race simulation days, where you will swim, then bike, then run, simulating the workout order, the physical demands, and the quick transitions of race day. Additionally, triathlon plans include options for open-water swim practice sessions in the final weeks leading up to the triathlon. All plans include optional strength and mobility sessions. If you are injury-prone or over 40 years old, please read "optional" as "recommended" and maybe even interpret that as "mandatory."

The triathlon plans assume a Sunday race day. You can modify the plan for a Saturday race day with some minor adjustments: For sprint- and Olympic-distance races, replace the Friday workout (if you have one) with the Saturday pre-race workout, opening up Saturday for race day. For half-distance races, you can do one or both of the Friday and Saturday pre-race workouts on Friday, and then race on Saturday. In either case, be sure to rest and enjoy your achievement on Sunday!

How to Follow the Training Plans

Each week in every plan begins with your Coach Cues for the week. The Coach Cues draw from the sport-specific, execution, and race-specific cues included throughout the book. Think of these as the big-picture concepts and details of technique that we'd be talking through if I were working with you one-on-one to prepare for your event. They are your weekly areas of focus – the aspects of execution and racing and the sport-specific skills that should be top of your mind as you move through your week and complete your workouts.

Each day in every plan lists the workout or workouts scheduled for that training day. Actually, each day in every plan typically lists multiple options for each workout scheduled for that training day: a Level 1 option, a Level 2 option, and a Level 3 option. We'll talk through using levels to tailor the training plans later, but for now, just know that as you look at each day, you'll complete *one* option for each workout listed.

Because listing all the workout options for every day is already a lot of information, the training plans use abbreviated workout titles to succinctly deliver the workout programming for each day. All workouts use the same naming convention: descriptor + sport + distance (swim and race simulation workouts) or descriptor + sport + duration (bike, run, and run off-the-bike workouts). For example, EndB60 is an endurance bike with a duration of 60 minutes. Some workout titles may include additional information, such as a workout progression number or distance target. For example, ThR45.2 is the second in a series of threshold-effort runs, with a duration of 45 minutes; EndR35(3) is a 35-minute endurance run with a minimum distance of 3 miles (4.8 km). Detailed instructions for each workout can be found in appendix A.

How to Tailor the Training Plans

All the training plans are specially designed for athletes with varying degrees of swim, bike, and run experience and fitness. To tailor each plan to match your individual athletic profile, you'll select Level 1 (L1), Level 2 (L2), or Level 3 (L3) for each of the three triathlon sports based on the following guidelines. Once you select a level for each sport, stick with that level for the entire training plan – or plans, if you are using several in combination; it is not necessary to use the same level for all three sports – in fact, most athletes won't.

- **Use Level 1** for a sport if you have no prior background in that sport and are not currently training in that sport. Think of it as the "brand new and off-the-couch" training level.
- **Use Level 2** for a sport if you have a background in the sport but no current training volume *or* no background but current training volume equivalent to the sport's training volume in week 1 of your (first) training plan.
- **Use Level 3** for a sport if you have a background in that sport *and* your current weekly training volume is equivalent to or greater than that sport's training volume in week 1 of your (first) training plan.

For example: Let's say that you did a few years of swim team as a kid but are not currently swimming; are brand new to cycling; and have been running 5K's and 10K's for years and currently run a few hours each week. Given your background and current training for each sport, you would use Level 2 for swimming, Level 1 for cycling, and Level 3 for running. Note that for those athletes at Level 3 for a sport, the plan's single-sport volume in week 1 may be less than your current training volume for that sport. Remember that you are adding training volume for new sports, and give yourself a week or two at the plan's training volumes before extending the workouts to match your current training volume.

16

PRESEASON TRAINING PLANS

The training plans in chapters 17 to 19 provide specific preparation for your triathlon. But sometimes you want to improve your overall or sport-specific fitness before beginning a focused triathlon plan. That's where the preseason training plans come into play. The preseason phase-in training plans help you gradually adjust to the weekly training routine and training volume in your triathlon plan. The preseason level-up training plan can give your current fitness a boost in one, two, or all three sports so you can begin your triathlon plan at a higher "level." Want to take advantage of both options? Complete the phase-in plan first, the level-up plan second, and then begin your triathlon plan.

Please be sure to read the part V introduction for information on how to follow the plans and how to use the three provided training levels (L1, L2, and L3) to tailor the plans to your individual sport-specific experience and current fitness. Appendix A will help decipher the plans by providing direction on finding the Coach Cues in earlier chapters, translating workout abbreviations into workout titles, and outlining the specific details for each workout.

Preseason Phase-In Training Plans

The 4-week preseason phase-in training plans are designed to gradually transition you from your current training routine to a full week of sprint- or Olympic-distance triathlon training. If you currently exercise 0 to 2 days per week, opt for the preseason phase-in training plan: option A to prepare for 6 days per week of training. If you currently exercise 3 to 4 days per week, choose the preseason phase-in training plan: option B.

Preseason Phase-In Training Plan

TRAINING CYCLE: OPTION A

	Week 1	Week 2	Week 3	Week 4
Coach cues	E: Establishing routine S: Breathing B: Pedaling R: Hip position	E: Establishing routine S: Body position B: Pedaling R: Hip position	E: Establishing routine S: Engage your core B: Cadence R: Leg stiffness	E: Establishing routine S: Breathing B: Cadence R: Leg stiffness
Monday	OFF	OFF	OFF	OFF
Tuesday	L1: IntroS500 L2: IntroS1000	L1: IntroS500 L2: IntroS1000	L1: IntroS600 L2: IntroS1000	L1: IntroS600 L2: IntroS1000
Wednesday	OFF	OFF	L1: SklB30 L2: SklB40	L1: SklB30 L2: SklB30
Thursday	L1: SklR15 L2: SklR20	L1: SklR15 L2: SklR20	L1: SklR15 L2: SklR20	OFF
	Optional: BwSt.1 or St.1	Optional: BwSt.2 or St.2	Optional: BwSt.1 or St.3	Optional: BwSt.2 or St.4
Friday	OFF	OFF	OFF	OFF
Saturday	L1: EndB30 L2: EndB30	L1: EndB30 L2: EndB40	L1: EndB30 L2: EndB45	L1: EndB30 L2: EndB40
Sunday	OFF	L1: EndR15 L2: EndR20	L1: EndR20 L2: EndR30	L1: EndR15 L2: EndR20

Preseason Phase-In Training Plan

TRAINING CYCLE: OPTION B

	Week 1	Week 2	Week 3	Week 4
Coach cues	E: Establishing routine S: Breathing B: Pedaling R: Hip position	E: Establishing routine S: Body position B: Pedaling R: Hip position	E: Establishing routine S: Engage you core B: Cadence R: Leg stiffness	E: Establishing routine S: Breathing B: Cadence R: Leg stiffness
Monday	OFF	OFF	OFF	OFF
Tuesday	L1: IntroS500 L2: IntroS1000 L3: EndSkS1600	L1: IntroS500 L2: IntroS1000 L3: EndSkS1600	L1: IntroS600 L2: IntroS1000 L3: EndS1600	L1: IntroS600 L2: IntroS1000 L3: EndS1600
Wednesday	OFF	L1: SkIB30 L2: SkIB30 L3: SkIB45	L1: SkIB30 L2: SkIB40 L3: ThB50.2	L1: SkIB30 L2: SkIB30 L3: SkIB45
Thursday	L1: SkIR15 L2: SkIR20 L3: SkIR30	L1: SkIR15 L2: SkIR20 L3: HillR30.1	L1: SkIR20 L2: SkIR30 L3: SkIR30	OFF
	Optional: BwSt.1 or St.1	Optional: BwSt.2 or St.2	Optional: BwSt.1 or St.3	Optional: BwSt.2 or St.4
Friday	OFF	OFF	L1: IntroS500 L2: IntroS1000 L3: EndSkS1600	L1: IntroS600 L2: IntroS1000 L3: EndSkS1600
Saturday	L1: EndB30 L2: EndB30 L3: EndB45	L1: EndB30 L2: EndB40 L3: EndB60	L1: EndB30 L2: EndB45 L3: EndB60	L1: EndB30 L2: EndB40 L3: EndB45
Sunday	L1: EndR15 L2: EndR20 L3: EndR30	L1: EndR20 L2: EndR30 L3: EndR40	L1: EndR20 L2: EndR30 L3: EndR40	L1: EndR15 L2: EndR20 L3: EndR35

Preseason Level-Up Training Plan

The 8-week preseason level-up training plan allows you to build your sport-specific training volume and fitness before beginning a sprint- or Olympic-distance training plan. By completing the level-up plan for one, two, or all three sports, you can "level up" from Level 1 (no experience, no current training volume) to Level 2 (no experience but with current training volume) or from Level 2 (experience but no current training volume) to Level 3 (experience and current training volume) before beginning your triathlon plan.

Select Level 1 or Level 2 for each sport you are targeting through the plan; you can – and often will – use a different level for each sport. (For sports not being targeted through the plan, you may substitute a workout similar to your recent training in that sport.) Upon completing this plan and moving on to your triathlon training plan, you may advance one level for each sport targeted using this plan. The preseason level-up plan provides the only avenue to advance a level within the training season.

Preseason Level-Up Training Plan

TRAINING CYCLE 1

	Week 1	Week 2	Week 3	Week 4
Coach cues	E: Warming up the engine S: Breathing B: Pedaling R: Hip position	E: Warming up the engine S: Body position B: Pedaling R: Hip position	E: Save the best for last S: Engage your core B: Cadence R: Leg stiffness	E: Train your race skills S: Breathing B: Cadence R: Leg stiffness
Monday	OFF	OFF	OFF	OFF
Tuesday	L1: IntroS500 L2: IntroS1000	L1: IntroS600 L2: IntroS1100	L1: IntroS700 L2: IntroS1200	L1: IntroS500 L2: IntroS1000
	Optional: BwSt.1 or St.1	Optional: BwSt.1 or St.3	Optional: BwSt.1 or St.1	Optional: BwSt.1 or St.3
Wednesday	L1: SklB30 L2: SklB45	L1: SklB30 L2: SklB50	L1: SklB30 L2: ThB50.2	L1: SklB30 L2: SklB45
Thursday	L1: SklR15 L2: SklR30	L1: SklR15 L2: SklR30	L1: SklR20 L2: SklR30	L1: SklR15 L2: SklR30
	Optional: BwSt.2 or St.2	Optional: BwSt.2 or St.4	Optional: BwSt.2 or St.2	Optional: BwSt.2 or St.4
Friday	L1: IntroS500 L2: IntroS1000	L1: IntroS600 L2: IntroS1200	L1: IntroS700 L2: IntroS1300	L1: IntroS600 L2: IntroS1100
Saturday	L1: EndB30 L2: EndB45	L1: EndB40 L2: EndB50	L1: EndB45 L2: EndB60	L1: EndB30 L2: EndB50
Sunday	L1: EndR15 L2: EndR30	L1: EndR20 L2: EndR35	L1: EndR25 L2: EndR40	L1: EndR15 L2: EndR30

Preseason Level-Up Training Plan

TRAINING CYCLE 2

	Week 5	Week 6	Week 7	Week 8
Coach cues	E: Train your race skills S: The entry B: Gearing R: Foot strike position	E: Train your race skills S: The catch B: Gearing R: Cadence	E: Save the best for last S: The pull B: Steering and cornering R: Cadence	E: Train your race skills S: The complete pull B: Steering and cornering R: Cadence
Monday	OFF	OFF	OFF	OFF
Tuesday	L1: IntroS800 L2: IntroS1300	L1: IntroS900 L2: EndS1400	L1: IntroS1000 L2: EndS1600	L1: IntroS800 L2: EndS1400
	Optional: BwSt.1 or St.1	Optional: BwSt.1 or St.3	Optional: BwSt.1 or St.1	Optional: BwSt.1 or St.3
Wednesday	L1: SklB35 L2: SklB60	L1: SklB40 L2: ThB60.3	L1: SklB45 L2: SklB60	L1: SklB40 L2: SklB50
Thursday	L1: SklR25 L2: HillR30.1	L1: SklR25 L2: SklR35	L1: SklR30 L2: HillR40.2	L1: SklR20 L2: SklR30
	Optional: BwSt.2 or St.2	Optional: BwSt.2 or St.4	Optional: BwSt.2 or St.2	Optional: BwSt.2 or St.4
Friday	L1: IntroS800 L2: EndSkS1400	L1: IntroS900 L2: TpSkS1400	L1: IntroS1000 L2: TpSkS1600	L1: IntroS800 L2: EndSkS1400
Saturday	L1: EndB45 L2: EndB60	L1: EndB45 L2: EndB60	L1: EndB45 L2: EndB60	L1: EndB40 L2: EndB50
Sunday	L1: EndR25 L2: EndR40	L1: EndR30 L2: EndR40	L1: EndR30 L2: EndR40	L1: EndR20 L2: EndR30

17

SPRINT-DISTANCE TRAINING PLAN

This 12-week sprint-distance training plan will guide you from your first day of training through your start – and finish – line. A typical week includes two swims, two bikes, two runs, and optional strength and mobility sessions. Beginning in week 2, there is also a run after the long weekend bike (a.k.a. a *brick workout*). Weekly training volumes begin at 2.5 to 4.5 hours of training in week 1 and increase to 4 to 6 hours in weeks 7 and 9, depending on your levels for each sport.

Please be sure to read the part V introduction for information on how the plan is structured, how to follow the plan, and how to use the three provided training levels (L1, L2, and L3) to tailor the plan to your individual sport-specific experience and current fitness. Appendix A will help decipher the plan by providing direction on finding the Coach Cues in earlier chapters, translating workout abbreviations into workout titles, and outlining the specific details for each workout.

If you would like to gradually phase into the 6-day-a-week workout pattern in the plan, you can precede this plan with a 4-week preseason phase-in training plan (chapter 16). If you want to "level up" one or more sports before beginning this plan, first complete the 8-week preseason level-up training plan (chapter 16).

Sprint-Distance Training Plan

TRAINING CYCLE 1

	Week 1	Week 2	Week 3	Week 4
Coach cues	E: Establishing routine S: Breathing B: Pedaling R: Hip position	E: Establishing routine S: Body position B: Pedaling R: Hip position T: Reality distortion field	E: Warming up the engine S: Engage your core B: Gearing R: Leg stiffness T: Reality distortion field	E: Warming up the engine S: Breathing B: Steering and cornering R: Leg stiffness T: Transitions
Monday	OFF	OFF	OFF	OFF
Tuesday	L1: IntroS700 L2: IntroS1000 L3: EndS1600	L1: IntroS800 L2: IntroS1200 L3: EndS1800	L1: IntroS900 L2: IntroS1400 L3: EndS2000.1	L1: IntroS800 L2: IntroS1000 L3: EndS1600
	Optional: BwSt.1 or St.1	Optional: BwSt.1 or St.3	Optional: BwSt.1 or St.1	Optional: BwSt.1 or St.3
Wednesday	L1: SklB30 L2: SklB45 L3: ThB60.4	L1: SklB35 L2: SklB45 L3: ThB60.5	L1: SklB40 L2: SklB45 L3: ThB60.6	L1: SklB30 L2: SklB45 L3: ThB60.4
Thursday	L1: SklR20 L2: SklR30 L3: HillR45.3	L1: SklR20 L2: SklR30 L3: HillR45.4	L1: SklR20 L2: SklR30 L3: ThR45.4	L1: SklR20 L2: SklR25 L3: ThR45.2
	Optional: BwSt.2 or St.2	Optional: BwSt.2 or St.4	Optional: BwSt.2 or St.2	Optional: BwSt.2 or St.4
Friday	L1: IntroS700 L2: IntroS1000 L3: TpSkS1600	L1: IntroS800 L2: IntroS1200 L3: TpSkS1800.1	L1: IntroS900 L2: IntroS1400 L3: TpSkS2000.2	L1: OFF L2: OFF L3: IntroS1000
Saturday	L1: EndB40 L2: EndB45 L3: EndB60	L1: EndB45 L2: EndB50 L3: RcEffB60.1	L1: EndB50 L2: EndB60 L3: EndB75	ALL LEVELS: RcSimS400 + RcSimB(8) + RcSimR(1.5)
		ALL LEVELS: EndRotb10	ALL LEVELS: EndRotb10	
Sunday	L1: EndR20 L2: EndR30 L3: EndR40	L1: EndR20 L2: EndR30 L3: EndR40	L1: EndR25 L2: EndR35 L3: EndR45	L1: OFF L2: EndB30 L3: EndB45
	Optional: Mob.1	Optional: Mob.2	Optional: Mob.1	Optional: Mob.2

Sprint-Distance Training Plan

TRAINING CYCLE 2

	Week 5	Week 6	Week 7	Week 8
Coach cues	E: Save the best for last S: The entry B: Cadence R: Foot strike position T: Reality distortion field	E: Train your race skills S: The catch B: Cadence R: Cadence T: Reality distortion field	E: Your mental skills toolbox S: The pull B: Eating and drinking R: Cadence T: Fueling and hydrating	E: Train your race skills S: The complete pull B: Gearing R: Cadence T: Transitions
Monday	OFF	OFF	OFF	OFF
Tuesday	L1: IntroS1000 L2: EndS1400 L3: TpS2000.1	L1: IntroS1100 L2: EndS1600 L3: TpS2000.2	L1: IntroS1200 L2: EndS1800 L3: TpS2200.3	L1: IntroS1000 L2: EndS1400 L3: TpS2000.1
	Optional: BwSt.1 or St.1	Optional: BwSt.1 or St.3	Optional: BwSt.1 or St.1	Optional: BwSt.1 or St.3
Wednesday	L1: SklB40 L2: ThB45.1 L3: ThB60.7	L1: SklB45 L2: ThB50.2 L3: AnB60.1	L1: SklB45 L2: ThB50.3 L3: AnB60.2	L1: SklB40 L2: SklB50 L3: ThB60.4
Thursday	L1: SklR25 L2: HillR30.1 L3: HillR50.5	L1: SklR25 L2: HillR40.3 L3: ThR50.5	L1: SklR25 L2: ThR40.3 L3: ThR50.6	L1: SklR20 L2: SklR40 L3: HillR45.1
	Optional: BwSt.2 or St.2	Optional: BwSt.2 or St.4	Optional: BwSt.2 or St.2	Optional: BwSt.2 or St.4
Friday	L1: IntroS1000 L2: TpSkS1400 L3: ThSkS2000.3	L1: IntroS1100 L2: TpSkS1600 L3: ThSkS2000.4	L1: IntroS1200* L2: TpSkS1800.1* L3: ThSkS2000.5*	L1: OFF or OWSEnd800 L2: IntroS1000* L3: IntroS1200*
Saturday	L1: EndB50(14) L2: RcEffB60.1 L3: RcEffB75.2	L1: EndB55(15) L2: EndB70 L3: EndB90	L1: EndB60(16) L2: EndB75 L3: RcEffB90.3	ALL LEVELS: RcEffSimS600 + RcEffSimB(10) + RcEffSimR(2)
	L1: EndRotb10 L2: EndRotb15 L3: EndRotb15	L1: EndRotb10 L2: EndRotb15 L3: EndRotb15	L1: EndRotb15 L2: EndRotb20 L3: RcEffRotb20	
Sunday	L1: EndR25 L2: EndR40 L3: EndR45	L1: EndR30(2.5) L2: RcEffR40.1 L3: RcEffR45.2	L1: EndR35(3) L2: EndR45 L3: EndR50	L1: OFF L2: EndB30 L3: EndB45
	Optional: Mob.1	Optional: Mob.2	Optional: Mob.1	Optional: Mob.2

*Option to substitute the pool swim with an open-water swim (OWS) of equivalent distance as follows: substitute an IntroS with an OWSEnd; a TpSkS with an OWSTp; or a ThSkS with an OWSTh. You may move the OWS session to the weekend if that makes it easier to access an OWS venue.

Sprint-Distance Training Plan

TRAINING CYCLE 3

	Week 9	Week 10	Week 11	Week 12
Coach cues	E: Save the best for last S: Open-water swimming B: Eating and drinking R: Hip position T: Fueling and hydrating	E: Navigating your taper weeks S: Open-water swimming B: Steering and cornering R: Leg stiffness	S: Open-water swimming B: Gearing R: Cadence C: Write your race week plan	C: Visualization and pre-race nerves
Monday	OFF	OFF	OFF	OFF
Tuesday	L1: IntroS1300 L2: EndS2000.1 L3: TpS2200.4	L1: IntroS1400 L2: EndS1800 L3: TpS2000.3	L1: IntroS1000 L2: EndS1600 L3: TpS1800	L1: RcWkS900 L2: RcWkS1200 L3: RcWkS1500
	Optional: BwSt.1 or St.1	Optional: BwSt.1 or St.3	Optional: BwSt.1 or St.1	Optional: Mob.1
Wednesday	L1: SklB45 L2: ThB60.4 L3: AnB60.3	L1: SklB40 L2: ThB50.3 L3: ThB60.6	L1: SklB30 L2: ThB45.1 L3: ThB60.4	L1: EndB30 L2: RcWkB45 L3: RcWkB45
Thursday	L1: SklR25 L2: ThR45.4 L3: ThR50.7	L1: SklR20 L2: ThR40.2 L3: ThR45.5	L1: SklR20 L2: ThR30.1 L3: ThR45.3	L1: EndR20 L2: RcWkR30 L3: RcWkR40
	Optional: BwSt.2 or St.2	Optional: BwSt.2 or St.4	Optional: Mob.1	Optional: Mob.2
Friday	L1: IntroS1300* L2: TpSkS2000.2* L3: ThSkS2000.6*	L1: IntroS1200* L2: TpSkS1800.2* L3: ThSkS2000.4*	L1: IntroS800* L2: TpSkS1600* L3: ThSkS1800*	L1: OFF or PreRcOWS15 L2: OFF or PreRcOWS15 L3: IntroS1000 or PreRcOWS20
Saturday	L1: EndB60(16) L2: RcEffB75.2 L3: RcEffB90.3	L1: EndB45 L2: RcEffB60.1 L3: RcEffB75.1	L1: EndB40 L2: EndB45 L3: EndB60	ALL LEVELS: PreRcBrk15
	L1: EndRotb15 L2: RcEffRotb20 L3: RcEffRotb20	L1: EndRotb10 L2: RcEffRotb10 L3: RcEffRotb10		
Sunday	L1: EndR40(3.5) L2: RcEffR45.2 L3: RcEffR50.3	L1: EndR30 L2: EndR40 L3: EndR45	L1: EndR20 L2: EndR35 L3: EndR40	RACE DAY
	Optional: Mob.1	Optional: Mob.2	Optional: Mob.2	

*Option to substitute the pool swim with an open-water swim (OWS) of equivalent distance as follows: substitute an IntroS with an OWSEnd; a TpSkS with an OWSTp; or a ThSkS with an OWSTh. You may move the OWS session to the weekend if that makes it easier to access an OWS venue.

18

OLYMPIC-DISTANCE TRAINING PLAN

This 16-week Olympic-distance training plan will prepare you for your Olympic-distance triathlon. A typical week includes two swims, two bikes, two runs, and optional strength and mobility sessions. Beginning in week 5, there is also a run after the long weekend bike (a.k.a. a *brick workout*). Weekly training volumes begin at 2.5 to 4.5 hours of training in week 1 and increase to 7 to 7.5 hours in week 13, depending on your levels for each sport.

Please be sure to read the part V introduction for information on how the plan is structured, how to follow the plan, and how to use the three provided training levels (L1, L2, and L3) to tailor the plan to your individual sport-specific experience and current fitness. Appendix A will help decipher the plan by providing direction on finding the Coach Cues in earlier chapters, translating workout abbreviations into workout titles, and outlining the specific details for each workout.

If you would like to gradually phase into the 6-day-a-week workout pattern in the plan, you can precede this plan with a 4-week preseason phase-in training plan (chapter 16). If you want to "level up" one or more sports before beginning this plan, first complete the 8-week preseason level-up training plan (chapter 16). And if you just completed the sprint-distance plan, you can begin this plan in week 5, using the same levels as you did for the sprint-distance plan.

Olympic-Distance Training Plan

TRAINING CYCLE 1

	Week 1	Week 2	Week 3	Week 4
Coach cues	E: Establishing routine S: Breathing B: Pedaling R: Hip position	E: Establishing routine S: Body position B: Pedaling R: Hip position	E: Establishing routine S: Engage your core B: Gearing R: Leg stiffness	E: Warming up the engine S: Breathing B: Steering and cornering R: Leg stiffness
Monday	OFF	OFF	OFF	OFF
Tuesday	L1: IntroS700 L2: IntroS1000 L3: EndS1600	L1: IntroS800 L2: IntroS1200 L3: EndS1800	L1: IntroS1000 L2: IntroS1400 L3: EndS2000.1	L1: IntroS800 L2: IntroS1200 L3: EndS1600
	Optional: BwSt.1 or St.1	Optional: BwSt.1 or St.3	Optional: BwSt.1 or St.1	Optional: BwSt.1 or St.3
Wednesday	L1: SklB30 L2: SklB45 L3: ThB60.4	L1: SklB40 L2: SklB45 L3: ThB60.5	L1: SklB45 L2: SklB50 L3: ThB60.6	L1: SklB40 L2: SklB45 L3: ThB60.4
Thursday	L1: SklR20 L2: SklR30 L3: HillR45.3	L1: SklR25 L2: SklR30 L3: HillR45.4	L1: SklR30 L2: SklR40 L3: ThR50.3	L1: SklR20 L2: SklR30 L3: HillR40.1
	Optional: BwSt.2 or St.2	Optional: BwSt.2 or St.4	Optional: BwSt.2 or St.2	Optional: BwSt.2 or St.4
Friday	L1: IntroS700 L2: IntroS1000 L3: TpSkS1600	L1: IntroS800 L2: IntroS1200 L3: TpSkS1800.1	L1: IntroS1000 L2: IntroS1400 L3: TpSkS2000.2	L1: IntroS800 L2: IntroS1200 L3: TpSkS1600
Saturday	L1: EndB45 L2: EndB45 L3: EndB60	L1: EndB50 L2: EndB50 L3: EndB75	L1: EndB60 L2: EndB60 L3: RcEffB75.1	L1: EndB50 L2: EndB50 L3: EndB60
Sunday	L1: EndR20 L2: EndR30 L3: EndR45	L1: EndR30 L2: EndR40 L3: EndR45	L1: EndR35 L2: EndR40 L3: EndR50	L1: EndR30 L2: EndR30 L3: EndR40
	Optional: Mob.1	Optional: Mob.2	Optional: Mob.1	Optional: Mob.2

Olympic-Distance Training Plan

TRAINING CYCLE 2

	Week 5	Week 6	Week 7	Week 8
Coach cues	E: Warming up the engine S: The entry B: Cadence R: Foot strike position T: Reality distortion field	E: Train your race skills S: The catch B: Cadence R: Cadence T: Reality distortion field	E: Your mental skills toolbox S: The pull B: Eating and drinking R: Cadence T: Fueling and hydrating	E: Save the best for last S: The complete pull B: Gearing R: Cadence T: Transitions
Monday	OFF	OFF	OFF	OFF
Tuesday	L1: IntroS1200 L2: EndS1600 L3: TpS2000.1	L1: IntroS1400 L2: EndS1800 L3: TpS2000.2	L1: IntroS1600 L2: EndS2000.1 L3: TpS2200.3	L1: IntroS1400 L2: EndS1600 L3: TpS2000.1
	Optional: BwSt.1 or St.1	Optional: BwSt.1 or St.3	Optional: BwSt.1 or St.1	Optional: BwSt.1 or St.3
Wednesday	L1: ThB45.1 L2: ThB50.2 L3: ThB60.7	L1: SklB50 L2: ThB50.3 L3: ThB60.8	L1: ThB50.2 L2: ThB60.4 L3: ThB60.9	L1: SklB45 L2: SklB50 L3: EndB60
Thursday	L1: SklR35 L2: HillR40.1 L3: HillR50.5	L1: ThR40.2 L2: HillR40.3 L3: ThR50.4	L1: SklR40 L2: ThR45.3 L3: ThR55.5	L1: SklR35 L2: SklR40 L3: EndR50
	Optional: BwSt.2 or St.2	Optional: BwSt.2 or St.4	Optional: BwSt.2 or St.2	Optional: BwSt.2 or St.4
Friday	L1: IntroS1200 L2: TpSkS1600 L3: ThSkS2000.3	L1: IntroS1400 L2: TpSkS1800.1 L3: ThSkS2000.4	L1: IntroS1600 L2: TpSkS1800.2 L3: ThSkS2000.5	L1: OFF L2: IntroS1000 L3: IntroS1000
Saturday	L1: EndB70 L2: EndB75 L3: EndB90(22)	L1: EndB75 L2: RcEffB75.1 L3: RcEffB90.2	L1: EndB80 L2: EndB90(22) L3: EndB105(26)	ALL LEVELS: RcSimS1000 + RcSimB(15) + RcSimR(3)
	ALL LEVELS: EndRotb10	L1: EndRotb15 L2: RcEffRotb10 L3: RcEffRotb10	ALL LEVELS: EndRotb20	
Sunday	L1: EndR40 L2: EndR40 L3: RcEffR50.1	L1: EndR45 L2: EndR50 L3: EndR60(5.5)	L1: EndR50 L2: RcEffR50.1 L3: RcEffR60.2	L1: OFF L2: OFF L3: EndB30
	Optional: Mob.1	Optional: Mob.2	Optional: Mob.1	Optional: Mob.2

Olympic-Distance Training Plan

TRAINING CYCLE 3

	Week 9	Week 10	Week 11	Week 12
Coach cues	E: Train your race skills S: Reducing drag B: Hills and descending R: Hip position T: Fueling and hydrating	E: Motivation S: The complete pull B: Eating and drinking R: Hip position T: Reality distortion field	E: Your mental skills toolbox S: Breathing B: Gearing R: Leg stiffness T: Fueling and hydrating	E: Train your race skills S: Body awareness B: Cadence R: Leg stiffness T: Transitions
Monday	OFF	OFF	OFF	OFF
Tuesday	L1: EndSkS1600 L2: EndS2000.2 L3: ThS2000.1	L1: EndSkS1800 L2: EndS2000.3 L3: ThS2200.2	L1: EndSkS2000.1 L2: EndS2200.4 L3: ThS2400.3	L1: EndSkS1600 L2: EndS1800 L3: ThS2000.1
	Optional: BwSt.1 or St.1	Optional: BwSt.1 or St.3	Optional: BwSt.1 or St.1	Optional: BwSt.1 or St.3
Wednesday	L1: ThB50.3 L2: ThB60.5 L3: AnB60.1	L1: SklB60 L2: ThB60.6 L3: AnB60.2	L1: ThB60.4 L2: ThB60.7 L3: AnB60.3	L1: SklB60 L2: SklB60 L3: EndB60
Thursday	L1: SklR45 L2: HillR50.5 L3: HillR55.6	L1: ThR45.3 L2: ThR50.4 L3: ThR55.6	L1: SklR50 L2: ThR50.5 L3: ThR60.7	L1: SklR45 L2: SklR50 L3: EndR50
	Optional: BwSt.2 or St.2	Optional: BwSt.2 or St.4	Optional: BwSt.2 or St.2	Optional: BwSt.2 or St.4
Friday	L1: TpSkS1600 L2: TpSkS2000.3 L3: AnSkS2000.1	L1: TpSkS1800.1 L2: TpSkS2000.4 L3: AnSkS2000.2	L1: TpSkS1800.2* L2: TpSkS2000.5* L3: AnSkS2000.3*	L1: OFF or OWSEnd800 L2: IntroS1000* L3: IntroS1200*
Saturday	L1: EndB90(22) L2: RcEffB90.2 L3: RcEffB105.3	L1: EndB105(26) L2: EndB105(26) L3: EndB120(30)	L1: EndB120(30) L2: EndB120(30) L3: RcEffB120.4	ALL LEVELS: RcEffSimS1200 + RcEffSimB(18) + RcEffSimR(4)
	L1: EndRotb20 L2: RcEffRotb20 L3: RcEffRotb20	L1: EndRotb25 L2: EndRotb30 L3: EndRotb30	L1: EndRotb30 L2: EndRotb30 L3: RcEffRotb30	
Sunday	L1: EndR55(5) L2: EndR60(5.5) L3: EndR70(6.5)	L1: EndR60(5.5) L2: RcEffR60.2 L3: RcEffR70.3	L1: EndR65(6) L2: EndR70(6.5) L3: EndR75(7)	L1: OFF L2: EndB30 L3: EndB30
	Optional: Mob.1	Optional: Mob.2	Optional: Mob.1	Optional: Mob.2

*Option to substitute the pool swim with an open-water swim (OWS) of equivalent distance as follows: substitute an IntroS with an OWSEnd; a TpSkS with an OWSTp; or a ThSkS with an OWSTh. You may move the OWS session to the weekend if that makes it easier to access an OWS venue.

Olympic-Distance Training Plan

TRAINING CYCLE 4

	Week 13	Week 14	Week 15	Week 16
Coach cues	E: Save the best for last S: Open-water swimming B: Steering and cornering R: Foot strike position T: Fueling and hydrating	E: Navigating your taper weeks S: Open-water swimming B: Cadence R: Cadence	S: Open-water swimming B: Gearing R: Cadence C: Write your race week plan	C: Visualization and pre-race nerves
Monday	OFF	OFF	OFF	OFF
Tuesday	L1: EndSkS2000.2 L2: EndS2200.5 L3: ThS2400.4	L1: EndSkS1800 L2: EndS2000.3 L3: ThS2200.2	L1: EndSkS1600 L2: EndS1600 L3: ThS2000.1	L1: RcWkS1200 L2: RcWkS1200 L3: RcWkS1500
	Optional: BwSt.1 or St.1	Optional: BwSt.1 or St.3	Optional: BwSt.1 or St.1	Optional: Mob.1
Wednesday	L1: ThB60.5 L2: ThB60.8 L3: AnB60.4	L1: ThB60.3 L2: ThB60.5 L3: ThB60.6	L1: SklB50 L2: ThB50.3 L3: ThB60.4	ALL LEVELS: RcWkB45
Thursday	L1: ThR50.4 L2: ThR50.6 L3: ThR60.8	L1: SklR45 L2: ThR45.5 L3: ThR50.6	L1: SklR40 L2: ThR40.3 L3: ThR45.4	L1: RcWkR30 L2: RcWkR30 L3: RcWkR40
	Optional: BwSt.2 or St.2	Optional: BwSt.2 or St.4	Optional: Mob.1	Optional: Mob.2
Friday	L1: TpSkS2000.3* L2: TpSkS2000.6* L3: AnSkS2000.4*	L1: TpSkS1800.2* L2: TpSkS1800.2* L3: AnSkS2000.2*	L1: TpSkS1600* L2: TpSkS1600* L3: ThSkS1800*	L1: OFF or PreRcOWS15 L2: OFF or PreRcOWS15 L3: IntroS1000 or PreRcOWS20
Saturday	L1: EndB120(30) L2: RcEffB120.3 L3: RcEffB120.5	L1: EndB90 L2: RcEffB90.1 L3: RcEffB90.3	ALL LEVELS: EndB60	ALL LEVELS: PreRcBrk15
	L1: EndRotb30 L2: RcEffRotb30 L3: RcEffRotb40	L1: EndRotb15 L2: RcEffRotb15 L3: RcEffRotb15		
Sunday	L1: EndR70(6.5) L2: RcEffR70.3 L3: RcEffR75.4	ALL LEVELS: EndR60	ALL LEVELS: EndR45	RACE DAY
	Optional: Mob.1	Optional: Mob.2	Optional: Mob.2	

*Option to substitute the pool swim with an open-water swim (OWS) of equivalent distance as follows: substitute a TpSkS with an OWSTp; or an AnSkS or ThSkS with an OWSTh. You may move the OWS session to the weekend if that makes it easier to access an OWS venue.

19

OLYMPIC- TO HALF-DISTANCE TRAINING PLAN

This 16-week Olympic- to half-distance training plan will ensure you develop the fitness necessary to carry you through the many race-day hours of a half-distance triathlon. A typical week includes two or three swims, three bikes, three runs, and optional strength and mobility sessions. Beginning in week 5, there is also a run after the long weekend bike (a.k.a. a *brick workout*). Weekly training volumes begin at 6 to 7 hours of training in week 1 and increase to 12 to 13 hours in week 13, depending on your levels for each sport.

Please be sure to read the part V introduction for information on how the plan is structured, how to follow the plan, and how to use the three provided training levels (L1, L2, and L3) to tailor the plan to your individual sport-specific experience and current fitness. Appendix A will help decipher the plan by providing direction on finding the Coach Cues in earlier chapters, translating workout abbreviations into workout titles, and outlining the specific details for each workout.

This plan builds upon the fitness developed within the Olympic-distance training plan. If you have not recently completed the Olympic-distance training plan, complete the first 8 weeks of the Olympic-distance plan before beginning this one. If you just completed 12 or more weeks of the Olympic-distance plan, start this plan in week 5, using the same levels as you did for the Olympic-distance plan.

Weekly Workout Pattern and Order of Workouts

The plan reflects the recommended pattern for distributing the training across your week. Ideally, you will complete the workouts on the days they are scheduled, but for any number of reasons that schedule may not work for you. Table 19.1 provides alternative workout patterns to help you find your optimal weekly workout pattern.

TABLE 19.1 Alternative Weekly Workout Patterns

	As planned	Alternate #1	Alternate #2	Alternate #3
Monday	OFF	OFF	S: Intro	B: End/Skills BwSt/St
Tuesday	S: Longest B: Intervals/End	B: Intervals/End BwSt/St	B: Intervals/End R: End/Skills	R: End/Skills S: Longest
Wednesday	R: Intervals/End BwSt/St	R: Intervals/End S: Longest	S: Longest BwSt/St	B: Intervals/End BwSt/St
Thursday	S: Skill Focus B: End/Skill	B: End/Skill R: End/Skill	B: End/Skills R: Intervals/End	R: Intervals/End S: Skill Focus
Friday	R: End/Skill BwSt/St	S: With Skills BwSt/St	S: Skill Focus BwSt/St	OFF
Saturday	B: Longest R: Off the bike	B: Longest R: Off the bike	B: Longest R: Off the bike	B: Longest R: Off the bike
Sunday	R: Longest S: Intro	R: Longest S: Intro	R: Longest	R: Longest S: Intro

The plan also lists the daily workouts in the recommended order of completion. Similar to the training pattern, ideally, you will complete each day's workouts in the order they appear in the plan, but completing the workouts is more important than completing them in order, so don't sacrifice actually getting the training done to the concept of perfection. For those days that include two workouts, you can complete them back-to-back, do one in the morning and one in the evening, or just complete them whenever works best for your schedule.

Olympic- to Half-Distance Training Plan

TRAINING CYCLE 1

	Week 1	Week 2	Week 3	Week 4
Coach cues	E: Establishing routine S: Reducing drag B: Pedaling R: Hip position	E: Establishing routine S: Body awareness B: Cadence R: Leg stiffness	E: Warming up the engine S: Breathing B: Eating and drinking R: Foot strike position	E: Warming up the engine S: The entry B: Gearing R: Cadence
Monday	OFF	OFF	OFF	OFF
Tuesday	L1: EndSkS1600 L2: EndS2000.1 L3: ThS2000.1	L1: EndSkS1800 L2: EndS2000.2 L3: ThS2200.2	L1: EndS1800 L2: EndS2200.3 L3: ThS2400.3	L1: EndSkS1600 L2: EndS2000.1 L3: ThS2000.1
	L1: ThB50.3 L2: AnB50.1 L3: AnB60.2	L1: EndB60 L2: AnB60.2 L3: AnB60.3	L1: ThB60.4 L2: AnB60.3 L3: AnB60.4	L1: EndB45 L2: EndB60 L3: AnB60.1
Wednesday	L1: EndR40 L2: HillR40.1 L3: HillR40.3	L1: ThR40.3 L2: HillR40.2 L3: HillR50.4	L1: EndR45 L2: HillR50.3 L3: HillR50.5	L1: EndR40 L2: HillR40.1 L3: HillR40.2
	Optional: BwSt.1 or St.1	Optional: BwSt.1 or St.3	Optional: BwSt.1 or St.1	Optional: BwSt.1 or St.3
Thursday	L1: TpSkS1600 L2: TpSkS2000.3 L3: AnSkS2000.2	L1: TpSkS1800.1 L2: TpSkS2000.4 L3: AnSkS2000.3	L1: TpSkS1800.2 L2: TpSkS2000.5 L3: AnSkS2000.4	L1: TpSkS1600 L2: TpSk2000.3 L3: AnSkS2000.1
	L1: SklB45 L2: SklB45 L3: EndB45	L1: SklB50 L2: SklB50 L3: EndB50	L1: SklB50 L2: SklB60 L3: EndB60	L1: SklB45 L2: SklB50 L3: EndB50
Friday	L1: SklR30 L2: SklR30 L3: EndR40	L1: SklR30 L2: SklR40 L3: EndR40	L1: SklR40 L2: SklR45 L3: EndR50	L1: SklR30 L2: SklR40 L3: EndR40
	Optional: BwSt.2 or St.2	Optional: BwSt.2 or St.4	Optional: BwSt.2 or St.2	Optional: BwSt.2 or St.4
Saturday	L1: EndB60 L2: EndB60 L3: EndB75	L1: EndB75 L2: EndB75 L3: EndB90	L1: EndB90 L2: EndB90 L3: EndB105	L1: EndB75 L2: EndB75 L3: EndB90
Sunday	L1: EndR50 L2: EndR60 L3: EndR60	ALL LEVELS: EndR60	ALL LEVELS: EndR60	ALL LEVELS: EndR50
			L1: IntroS1000 L2: IntroS1000 L3: IntroS1000 (optional)	L1: IntroS1000 L2: IntroS1000 L3: IntroS1000 (optional)
	Optional: Mob.1	Optional: Mob.2	Optional: Mob.1	Optional: Mob.2

Olympic- to Half-Distance Training Plan

TRAINING CYCLE 2

	Week 5	Week 6	Week 7	Week 8
Coach cues	E: Establishing routine S: The catch B: Pedaling R: Cadence T: Reality distortion field	E: Establishing routine S: The pull B: Cadence R: Cadence T: Reality distortion field	E: Train your race skills S: The finish B: Steering and cornering R: Hip position T: Fueling and hydrating	E: Save the best for last S: The complete pull B: Eating and drinking R: Hip position T: Transitions
Monday	OFF	OFF	OFF	OFF
Tuesday	L1: EndSkS2000.1 L2: TpS2200.1 L3: TpS2400.4	L1: EndS2000.1 L2: TpS2200.2 L3: TpS2400.5	L1: EndS2200.2 L2: TpS2400.3 L3: TpS2600.6	L1: EndSkS2000.1 L2: TpS2200.1 L3: TpS2200.3
	L1: EndB60 L2: ThB60.4 L3: ThB60.6	L1: ThB60.5 L2: ThB60.5 L3: ThB60.7	L1: ThB60.6 L2: ThB60.6 L3: ThB60.8	ALL LEVELS: EndB60
Wednesday	L1: ThR40.4 L2: ThR45.3 L3: ThR50.5	L1: EndR45 L2: ThR45.4 L3: ThR50.7	L1: ThR45.5 L2: ThR50.5 L3: ThR55.8	ALL LEVELS: EndR45
	Optional: BwSt.1 or St.1	Optional: BwSt.1 or St.3	Optional: BwSt.1 or St.1	Optional: BwSt.1 or St.3
Thursday	L1: ThSkS1800 L2: ThSkS2000.1 L3: ThSkS2200.5	L1: TpSkS2000.3 L2: ThSkS2200.2 L3: ThSkS2200.6	L1: ThSkS2000.1 L2: ThSkS2200.3 L3: ThSkS2400.7	L1: IntroS1000 L2: IntroS1000 L3: EndSkS1400
	L1: SklB60 L2: SklB60 L3: EndB60	L1: SklB60 L2: SklB60 L3: EndB60	L1: SklB60 L2: SklB60 L3: EndB60	L1: SklB50 L2: SklB50 L3: EndB60
Friday	L1: SklR40 L2: SklR45 L3: EndR45	L1: SklR45 L2: SklR45 L3: EndR50	L1: SklR45 L2: SklR50 L3: EndR50	L1: SklR40 L2: SklR45 L3: EndR45
	Optional: BwSt.2 or St.2	Optional: BwSt.2 or St.4	Optional: BwSt.2 or St.2	Optional: Mob.2
Saturday	L1: EndB110 L2: EndB110 L3: EndB120	L1: EndB130 L2: EndB130 L3: EndB135	ALL LEVELS: EndB150(40)	ALL LEVELS: RcSimS1200 + RcSimB(30) + RcSimR(6)
	ALL LEVELS: EndRotb15	ALL LEVELS: EndRotb15	ALL LEVELS: EndRotb20	
Sunday	ALL LEVELS: EndR70	ALL LEVELS: EndR80	ALL LEVELS: EndR90	L1: EndB30 L2: EndB45 L3: EndB60
	L1: IntroS1200 L2: IntroS1200 L3: IntroS1200 (optional)	L1: IntroS1200 L2: IntroS1200 L3: IntroS1200 (optional)	L1: IntroS1400 L2: IntroS1400 L3: IntroS1400 (optional)	
	Optional: Mob.1	Optional: Mob.2	Optional: Mob.1	Optional: Mob.1

Olympic- to Half-Distance Training Plan

TRAINING CYCLE 3

	Week 9	Week 10	Week 11	Week 12
Coach cues	E: Motivation S: Breathing B: Gearing R: Foot strike position T: Fueling and hydrating	E: Your mental skills toolbox S: Body awareness B: Hills and descending R: Leg stiffness T: Reality distortion field	E: Train your race skills S: Reducing drag B: Steering and cornering R: Cadence T: Fueling and hydrating	E: Your mental skills toolbox S: The complete pull B: Eating and drinking R: Cadence T: Transitions
Monday	OFF	OFF	OFF	OFF
Tuesday	L1: EndS2200.3 L2: TpS2400.4 L3: TpS2600.7	L1: EndS2400.4 L2: TpS2600.5 L3: TpS2800.8	L1: EndS2600.5 L2: TpS2800.6 L3: TpS3000.9	L1: EndS2400.2 L2: TpS2400.3 L3: TpS2600.6
	L1: ThB60.7 L2: TpB60.1 L3: TpB60.2	L1: EndB60 L2: TpB60.2 L3: TpB60.3	L1: ThB60.8 L2: TpB60.3 L3: TpB60.4	ALL LEVELS: EndB60
Wednesday	L1: EndR50 L2: ThR50.6 L3: HillThR50	L1: ThR50.6 L2: ThR55.7 L3: ThR60.9	L1: EndR60 L2: ThR60.8 L3: HillThR60	ALL LEVELS: EndR50
	Optional: BwSt.2 or St.4	Optional: BwSt.2 or St.2	Optional: BwSt.2 or St.4	Optional: BwSt.2 or St.2
Thursday	L1: TpSkS2200.4 L2: ThSkS2200.4 L3: ThSkS2400.8	L1: ThSkS2200.2 L2: ThSkS2200.5 L3: ThSkS2400.9	L1: TpSkS2400.5 L2: ThSkS2400.6 L3: ThSkSk2400.10	L1: IntroS1000 L2: IntroS1000 L3: EndSkS1400
	L1: SklB60 L2: SklB60 L3: EndB60	L1: SklB60 L2: SklB60 L3: EndB60	L1: SklB60 L2: SklB60 L3: EndB60	L1: SklB50 L2: SklB50 L3: EndB60
Friday	L1: SklR50 L2: SklR50 L3: EndR50	L1: SklR50 L2: SklR50 L3: EndR50	L1: SklR50 L2: SklR50 L3: EndR60	L1: SklR45 L2: SklR45 L3: EndR50
	Optional: BwSt.1 or St.1	Optional: BwSt.1 or St.3	Optional: BwSt.1 or St.1	Optional: Mob.1
Saturday	ALL LEVELS: EndB170(45)	ALL LEVELS: EndB190(50)	ALL LEVELS: EndB210(56)	ALL LEVELS: RcSimS1500 + RcSimB(40) + RcSimR(8)
	ALL LEVELS: EndRotb20	ALL LEVELS: EndRotb30	ALL LEVELS: EndRotb30	
Sunday	ALL LEVELS: EndR100	ALL LEVELS: EndR110	ALL LEVELS: EndR120	L1: EndB30 L2: EndB45 L3: EndB60
	L1: IntroS1400* L2: IntroS1400* L3: IntroS1400 (optional)*	L1: IntroS1600* L2: IntroS1600* L3: IntroS1600 (optional)*	L1: IntroS1600* L2: IntroS1600* L3: IntroS1600 (optional)*	
	Optional: Mob.2	Optional: Mob.1	Optional: Mob.2	Optional: Mob.2

*Option to substitute the pool swim with an OWSEnd of equivalent distance.

Olympic- to Half-Distance Training Plan

TRAINING CYCLE 4

	Week 13	Week 14	Week 15	Week 16
Coach cues	E: Save the best for last S: Open-water swimming B: Gearing R: Leg stiffness T: Fueling and hydrating	E: Navigating your taper weeks S: Open-water swimming B: Eating and drinking R: Hip position	S: Open-water swimming B: Cadence R: Cadence C: Write your race week plan	C: Visualization and pre-race nerves
Monday	OFF	OFF	OFF	OFF
Tuesday	L1: EndS2600.6 L2: TpS2800.7 L3: TpS3000.10	L1: EndS2400.3 L2: TpS2400.5 L3: TpS2800.8	L1: EndS2000.1 L2: TpS2000.2 L3: TpS2600.5	L1: RcWkS1500 L2: RcWkS1500 L3: RcWkS2000
	L1: ThB60.9 L2: TpB60.4 L3: TpB60.5	L1: EndB60 L2: TpB60.2 L3: TpB60.3	L1: ThB60.4 L2: ThB60.4 L3: ThB60.4	L1: EndB60 L2: RcWkB60 L3: RcWkB60
Wednesday	L1: EndR60 L2: ThR60.9 L3: ThR60.10	L1: ThR50.4 L2: ThR55.6 L3: ThR55.7	L1: EndR40 L2: ThR45.3 L3: ThR45.4	L1: EndR45 L2: RcWkR45 L3: RcWkR45
	Optional: BwSt.1 or St.3	Optional: BwSt.1 or St.1	Optional: BwSt.1 or St.3	Optional: Mob.1
Thursday	L1: ThSkS2400.4 L2: ThSkS2400.6 L3: ThSkS2400.10	L1: TpSkS2000.2 L2: ThSkS2000.4 L3: ThSkS2200.6	L1: TpSkS1600 L2: ThSkS1800 L3: ThSkS2000.3	ALL LEVELS: PreRcB45
	L1: SklB60 L2: SklB60 L3: EndB60	L1: SklB60 L2: SklB60 L3: EndB60	L1: SklB60 L2: SklB60 L3: EndB60	
Friday	L1: SklR60 L2: SklR60 L3: EndR60	L1: SklR40 L2: SklR50 L3: EndR50	L1: SklR30 L2: SklR40 L3: EndR40	ALL LEVELS: PreRcBrk30
	Optional: BwSt.2 or St.4	Optional: BwSt.2 or St.2	Optional: Mob.1	Optional: Mob.2
Saturday	ALL LEVELS: EndB210(56+)	L1: EndB150 L2: EndB150 L3: EndB180	ALL LEVELS: EndB90	ALL LEVELS: PreRcOWS15
	ALL LEVELS: EndRotb40	ALL LEVELS: EndRotb20		
Sunday	ALL LEVELS: EndR120	ALL LEVELS: EndR100	ALL LEVELS: EndR75	RACE DAY
	L1: IntroS1600* L2: IntroS1600* L3: IntroS1600 (optional)*	L1: IntroS1200* L2: IntroS1200* L3: IntroS1200 (optional)*		
	Optional: Mob.1	Optional: Mob.2	Optional: Mob.2	

*Option to substitute the pool swim with an OWSEnd of equivalent distance.

APPENDIX A

WORKOUT REFERENCE GUIDE

Workout terminology can feel like its own language. Effort levels, interval durations, warm-ups, and cool-downs may all read like gibberish at first. Take your time in the beginning, go through the workouts step by step, and you'll be fluent before you know it.

Understanding the Workout Titles and Descriptions

All workouts use the same naming convention: descriptor + sport + distance (swim and race simulation workouts) or descriptor + sport + duration (bike, run, and run off-the-bike workouts). For example, EndB60 is an endurance bike with a duration of 60 minutes. Some workout titles are followed by a number that indicates the progression number within a workout series. For example, ThR45.2 is a 45-minute run, progression 2 in the threshold-effort interval run series. Finally, select bike and run workout titles include both duration and distance: descriptor + sport + duration (distance). For example, EndR35(3) is a 35-minute endurance run with a 3-mile (4.8-km) minimum distance.

Each workout begins with a warm-up (except for run off-the-bike workouts, race simulation bikes, and race simulation runs). Some workouts transition from the warm-up to a steady-state effort level, while others will include segments such as one or more pre-sets, a transitional recovery, one or more main sets, and a cool-down. Each segment within each workout will be described with a distance or duration, an effort level, and a training zone. Chapter 8 explains the effort levels and training zones used within the plans. For workout steps described as "Race Effort," use the recommendations in the workout legend. For workouts with a Skill Focus segment or an overall session intention, use the Coach Cues for the recommended skill focus, or focus on an area of technique you know needs improvement.

Plan and Workout Legend

Workout Key

WU = Warm-up

CD = Cool-down

Plan Levels

L1 = Level 1

L2 = Level 2

L3 = Level 3

Coach Cues

E = Execution cues (chapter 11)

S = Swim cues (chapter 4)

B = Bike cues (chapter 5)

R = Run cues (chapter 6)

T = Triathlon cues (chapter 7)

C = Race cues (chapter 13)

Race Efforts

Use the following guidelines to determine the effort level for your race effort:

- *Sprint-Distance* – Level 1: moderate, zone 2; level 2: strong, zone 3; level 3: hard, zone 4
- *Olympic-Distance* – Level 1 or level 2: moderate, zone 2; level 3: strong, zone 3
- *Half-Distance* – All levels: moderate, zone 2

Swim Workouts

All swim workouts are defined by distance in yards or meters. (Use either yards or meters based on the length of your pool. There is no need to convert from yards to meters or vice versa.) The swim intervals within each workout set are defined by both the interval distance and the specified rest time after each swim interval; all interval distances are multiples of 25, where 25 represents one length of a 25-yard or 25-meter pool. Single-interval sets are written as: number of repetitions × [work interval; rest time after each interval]. Multi-interval sets are written as: number of repetitions × [interval 1; interval 2; interval 3; rest time after each interval within the set]. If no rest time is listed, rest as needed – typically 15 to 60 seconds. Unless specified, swim freestyle; where "choice of strokes" or "mixed strokes" is specified, incorporate backstroke, breaststroke, or both. Note the planned total distance for each workout, because the final step in most workouts will list "to finish" rather than a defined distance.

AnSkS: Anaerobic-Effort Interval, Skill Focus Swims

WU – 200 easy, zone 1, choice of strokes

Pre-Set #1 – 6 × [50 skill focus, easy to moderate, zone 1 to 2; rest as needed]

Pre-Set #2 – 4 × [25 fast, zone 5; 50 easy, zone 1; 10 seconds rest after each]

Recovery – 100 easy, zone 1, mixed strokes

Main Set

- *AnSkS2000.1* – 8 × [25 fast, zone 5; 15 seconds rest]
  200 easy, zone 1, mixed strokes
  8 × [25 fast, zone 5; 15 seconds rest]
  200 easy, zone 1, mixed strokes
  8 × [25 fast, zone 5; 15 seconds rest]
- *AnSkS2000.2* – 12 × [25 fast, zone 5; 15 seconds rest]
  300 easy, zone 1, mixed strokes
  12 × [25 fast, zone 5; 15 seconds rest]
- *AnkSkS2000.3* – 6 × [50 fast, zone 5; 15 seconds rest]
  300 easy, zone 1, mixed strokes
  12 × [25 fast, zone 5; 15 seconds rest]
- *AnSkS2000.4* – 6 × [50 fast, zone 5; 15 seconds rest]
  300 easy, zone 1, mixed strokes
  6 × [50 fast, zone 5; 15 seconds rest]

CD – easy, zone 1, mixed strokes to finish

EndS: Endurance-Effort Swims

WU – 200 easy, zone 1, choice of strokes

Pre-Set – 4 × [50 strong, zone 3; 50 easy, zone 1; 10 seconds rest after each]

Main Set

- *EndS1400* – 6 × [100 moderate with good form, zone 2; 10 seconds rest]
  2 × [50 strong, zone 3; 10 seconds rest]
- *EndS1600* – 2 × [150 moderate with good form, zone 2; 10 seconds rest]
  4 × [100 moderate with good form, zone 2; 10 seconds rest]
  4 × [50 strong, zone 3; 10 seconds rest]
- *EndS1800* – 4 × [150 moderate with good form, zone 2; 10 seconds rest]
  2 × [100 moderate with good form, zone 2; 10 seconds rest]
  6 × [50 strong, zone 3; 10 seconds rest]
- *EndS2000.1* – 6 × [150 moderate with good form, zone 2; 10 seconds rest]
  8 × [50 strong, zone 3; 10 seconds rest]
- *EndS2000.2* – 2 × [200 moderate with good form, zone 2; 10 seconds rest]
  4 × [150 moderate with good form, zone 2; 10 seconds rest]
  6 × [50 strong, zone 3; 10 seconds rest]
- *EndS2000.3* – 3 × [200 moderate with good form, zone 2; 10 seconds rest]
  3 × [150 moderate with good form, zone 2; 10 seconds rest]
  6 × [50 strong, zone 3; 10 seconds rest]
- *EndS2200.2* – 2 × [200 moderate with good form, zone 2; 10 seconds rest]
  4 × [150 moderate with good form, zone 2; 10 seconds rest]
  2 × [100 moderate with good form, zone 2; 10 seconds rest]
  6 × [50 strong, zone 3; 10 seconds rest]
- *EndS2200.3* – 3 × [200 moderate with good form, zone 2; 10 seconds rest]
  3 × [150 moderate with good form, zone 2; 10 seconds rest]
  2 × [100 moderate with good form, zone 2; 10 seconds rest]
  6 × [50 strong, zone 3; 10 seconds rest]
- *EndS2200.4* – 2 × [250 moderate with good form, zone 2; 15 seconds rest]
  2 × [200 moderate with good form, zone 2; 10 seconds rest]
  2 × [150 moderate with good form, zone 2; 10 seconds rest]
  6 × [50 strong, zone 3; 10 seconds rest]

- *EndS2200.5* – 2 × [300 moderate with good form, zone 2; 15 seconds rest]
  2 × [200 moderate with good form, zone 2; 10 seconds rest]
  2 × [100 moderate with good form, zone 2; 10 seconds rest]
  6 × [50 strong, zone 3; 10 seconds rest]
- *EndS2400.2* – 2 × [200 moderate with good form, zone 2; 10 seconds rest]
  4 × [150 moderate with good form, zone 2; 10 seconds rest]
  4 × [100 moderate with good form, zone 2; 10 seconds rest]
  6 × [50 strong, zone 3; 10 seconds rest]
- *EndS2400.3* – 3 × [200 moderate with good form, zone 2; 10 seconds rest]
  3 × [150 moderate with good form, zone 2; 10 seconds rest]
  4 × [100 moderate with good form, zone 2; 10 seconds rest]
  6 × [50 strong, zone 3; 10 seconds rest]
- *EndS2400.4* – 2 × [250 moderate with good form, zone 2; 15 seconds rest]
  3 × [200 moderate with good form, zone 2; 10 seconds rest]
  2 × [150 moderate with good form, zone 2; 10 seconds rest]
  6 × [50 strong, zone 3; 10 seconds rest]
- *EndS2600.5* – 2 × [300 moderate with good form, zone 2; 15 seconds rest]
  4 × [200 moderate with good form, zone 2; 10 seconds rest]
  2 × [100 moderate with good form, zone 2; 10 seconds rest]
  6 × [50 strong, zone 3; 10 seconds rest]
- *EndS2600.6* – 2 × [400 moderate with good form, zone 2; 20 seconds rest]
  2 × [300 moderate with good form, zone 2; 15 seconds rest]
  200 moderate with good form, zone 2; 10 seconds rest
  6 × [50 strong, zone 3; 10 seconds rest]

CD – easy, zone 1, mixed strokes to finish

EndSkS: Endurance-Effort, Skill Focus Swims

WU – 200 easy, zone 1, choice of strokes

Pre-Set #1 – 6 × [50 skill focus, easy to moderate, zone 1 to 2; rest as needed]

Pre-Set #2 – 4 × [50 strong, zone 3; 50 easy, zone 1; 10 seconds rest after each]

Main Set

- *EndSkS1400* – 4 × [100 moderate with good form, zone 2; 10 seconds rest]

- *EndSkS1600* – 4 × [100 moderate with good form, zone 2; 10 seconds rest]
  4 × [50 moderate with good form, zone 2; 10 seconds rest]
- *EndSkS1800* – 4 × [150 moderate with good form, zone 2; 10 seconds rest]
  2 × [100 moderate with good form, zone 2; 10 seconds rest]
- *EndSkS2000.1* – 2 × [200 moderate with good form, zone 2; 10 seconds rest]
  2 × [150 moderate with good form, zone 2; 10 seconds rest]
  3 × [100 moderate with good form, zone 2; 10 seconds rest]
- *EndSkS2000.2* – 3 × [200 moderate with good form, zone 2; 10 seconds rest]
  3 × [150 moderate with good form, zone 2; 10 seconds rest]

CD – easy, zone 1, mixed strokes to finish

IntroS: Introductory Swims

These swims are specifically designed to introduce you to fitness swimming for the first time or to reintroduce you to swimming after a hiatus from the pool.

IntroS500 Through IntroS700

Swim the specified distance at a comfortable effort level (easy to moderate, zone 1 to zone 2), focusing on a single form cue. Swim any combination of strokes you'd like and take breaks as needed.

IntroS800 Through IntroS1600

WU – 200 easy, zone 1, choice of strokes, taking breaks as needed

Pre-Set – 6 × [50 skill focus, easy to moderate, zone 1 to 2; rest as needed]

Main Set

- *IntroS800* – 4 × [50 moderate with good form, zone 2; 10 seconds rest]
- *IntroS900* – 3 × [100 moderate with good form, zone 2; 10 seconds rest]
- *IntroS1000* – 4 × [100 moderate with good form, zone 2; 10 seconds rest]
- *IntroS1100* – 5 × [100 moderate with good form, zone 2; 10 seconds rest]
- *IntroS1200* – 6 × [100 moderate with good form, zone 2; 10 seconds rest]
- *IntroS1300* – 2 × [150 moderate with good form, zone 2; 10 seconds rest]
  4 × [100 moderate with good form, zone 2; 10 seconds rest]
- *IntroS1400* – 4 × [150 moderate with good form, zone 2; 10 seconds rest]
  2 × [100 moderate with good form, zone 2; 10 seconds rest]
- *IntroS1600* – 4 × [150 moderate with good form, zone 2; 10 seconds rest]
  4 × [100 moderate with good form, zone 2; 10 seconds rest]

CD – 100 easy, zone 1, mixed strokes

OWS: Open Water Swims

These swims present an excellent opportunity to test out your wetsuit if you plan to use one during the triathlon. *Practice sighting (see chapter 4) throughout the swim, and use a range of strokes as you feel.*

OWSEnd: Open Water Swims at Endurance Effort

Swim continuously for 10 minutes at an easy, zone 1 effort level

Swim continuously for the remainder of the distance at a moderate, zone 2 effort level

OWSTh: Open Water Swims With Threshold-Effort Intervals

WU – Swim continuously for 10 minutes at an easy, zone 1 effort level

Swim the next 5 minutes at a moderate, zone 2 effort level

Main Set

- *OWSTh1800* – Swim for 12 to 15 minutes alternating 2 to 3 minutes at a hard effort, zone 4 and 1 minute at a moderate effort, zone 2
- *OWSTh2000* – Swim for 15 to 20 minutes alternating 2 to 3 minutes at a hard effort, zone 4 and 1 minute at a moderate effort, zone 2

CD – Swim continuously at a moderate, zone 2 effort level to finish

OWSTp: Open Water Swims With Tempo-Effort Intervals

WU – Swim continuously for 10 minutes at an easy, zone 1 effort level

Swim the next 5 minutes at a moderate, zone 2 effort level

Main Set

- *OWSTp1600* – Swim for 10 to 12 minutes alternating 2 to 3 minutes at a strong effort, zone 3 and 1 minute at a moderate effort, zone 2
- *OWSTp1800* – Swim for 12 to 15 minutes alternating 2 to 3 minutes at a strong effort, zone 3 and 1 minute at a moderate effort, zone 2
- *OWSTp2000* – Swim for 15 to 20 minutes alternating 2 to 3 minutes at a strong effort, zone 3 and 1 minute at a moderate effort, zone 2

CD – Swim continuously at a moderate, zone 2 effort level to finish

PreRcOWS: Pre-Race Open Water Swims

See Pre-Race Workouts

RcEffSimS and RcSimS: Race-Effort Simulation Swims and Race Simulation Swims

See Race Simulation Workouts

RcWkS: Race Week Swims

WU – 200 easy, zone 1, choice of strokes

Pre-Set #1 – 6 × [50 skill focus: open water swimming, easy to moderate, zone 1 to 2; rest as needed]

Pre-Set #2

- *RcWkS900* – none
- *RcWkS1200, RcWkS1500, RcWkS2000* – 4 × [25 hard, zone 4; 25 easy, zone 1; 10 seconds rest after each]

Recovery – 100 easy, zone 1, mixed strokes

Main Set

- *RcWkS900* – 4 × [50 moderate, zone 2; 15 seconds rest]
- *RcWkS1200* – 2 × [100 strong, zone 3; 50 moderate, zone 2; 15 seconds rest after each]
- *RcWkS1500* – 4 × [100 strong, zone 3; 50 moderate, zone 2; 15 seconds rest after each]
- *RcWkS2000* – 4 × [150 strong, zone 3; 100 moderate, zone 2; 15 seconds rest after each]

CD – easy, zone 1, mixed strokes to finish

ThS: Threshold-Effort Interval Swims

WU – 200 easy, zone 1, choice of strokes

Pre-Set – 4 × [50 hard, zone 4; 50 easy, zone 1; 10 seconds rest after each]

Recovery – 100 easy, zone 1, mixed strokes

Main Set

- *ThS2000.1* – 4 × [100 hard, zone 4; 100 strong, zone 3; 100 moderate, zone 2; 10 seconds rest after each]
- *ThS2200.2* – 4 × [150 hard, zone 4; 100 strong, zone 3; 100 moderate, zone 2; 10 seconds rest after each]
- *ThS2400.3* – 4 × [200 hard, zone 4; 100 strong, zone 3; 100 moderate, zone 2; 10 seconds rest after each]
- *ThS2400.4* – 4 × [200 hard, zone 4; 100 hard, zone 4; 100 moderate, zone 2; 10 seconds rest after each]

CD – 100 easy, zone 1, mixed strokes

ThSkS: Threshold-Effort Interval, Skill Focus Swims

WU – 200 easy, zone 1, choice of strokes

Pre-Set #1 – 6 × [50 skill focus, easy to moderate, zone 1 to 2; rest as needed]

Pre-Set #2 – 6 × [25 fast, zone 5; 25 easy, zone 1; 10 seconds rest after each]
Recovery – 100 easy, zone 1, mixed strokes

Main Set

- *ThSkS1800* – 6 × [50 hard, zone 4; 10 seconds rest]
  100 easy, zone 1, mixed strokes
  6 × [50 hard, zone 4; 10 seconds rest]
- *ThSkS2000.1* – 8 × [50 hard, zone 4; 10 seconds rest]
  100 easy, zone 1, mixed strokes
  8 × [50 hard, zone 4; 10 seconds rest]
- *ThSkS2000.3* – 6 × [75 hard, zone 4; 10 seconds rest]
  100 easy, zone 1, mixed strokes
  6 × [75 hard, zone 4; 10 seconds rest]
- *ThSkS2000.4* – 4 × [100 hard, zone 4; 10 seconds rest]
  100 easy, zone 1, mixed strokes
  6 × [75 hard, zone 4; 10 seconds rest]
- *ThSkS2000.5* – 4 × [100 hard, zone 4; 10 seconds rest]
  150 easy, zone 1, mixed strokes
  4 × [100 hard, zone 4; 10 seconds rest]
- *ThSkS2000.6* – 3 × [150 hard, zone 4; 10 seconds rest]
  150 easy, zone 1, mixed strokes
  4 × [100 hard, zone 4; 10 seconds rest]
- *ThSkS2200.2* – 8 × [75 hard, zone 4; 10 seconds rest]
  100 easy, zone 1, mixed strokes
  10 × [50 hard, zone 4; 10 seconds rest]
- *ThSkS2200.3* – 8 × [75 hard, zone 4; 10 seconds rest]
  100 easy, zone 1, mixed strokes
  6 × [75 hard, zone 4; 10 seconds rest]
- *ThSkS2200.4* – 6 × [100 hard, zone 4; 10 seconds rest]
  100 easy, zone 1, mixed strokes
  6 × [75 hard, zone 4; 10 seconds rest]
- *ThSkS2200.5* – 6 × [100 hard, zone 4; 10 seconds rest]
  200 easy, zone 1, mixed strokes
  4 × [100 hard, zone 4; 10 seconds rest]
- *ThSkS2200.6* – 4 × [150 hard, zone 4; 10 seconds rest]
  200 easy, zone 1, mixed strokes
  4 × [100 hard, zone 4; 10 seconds rest]
- *ThSkS2400.4* – 6 × [100 hard, zone 4; 10 seconds rest]
  150 easy, zone 1, mixed strokes
  8 × [75 hard, zone 4; 10 seconds rest]

- *ThSkS2400.6* – 4 × [150 hard, zone 4; 10 seconds rest]
  200 easy, zone 1, mixed strokes
  6 × [100 hard, zone 4; 10 seconds rest]
- *ThSkS2400.7* – 4 × [150 hard, zone 4; 100 hard, zone 4; 100 strong, zone 3; 10 seconds rest after each]
- *ThSkS2400.8* – 3 × [200 hard, zone 4; 150 hard, zone 4; 100 strong, zone 3; 10 seconds rest after each]
- *ThSkS2400.9* – 2 × [200 hard, zone 4; 150 hard, zone 4; 150 hard, zone 4; 150 strong, zone 3; 10 seconds rest after each]
- *ThSkS2400.10* – 2 × [200 hard, zone 4; 200 hard, zone 4; 150 hard, zone 4; 150 strong, zone 3; 10 seconds rest after each]

CD – easy, zone 1, mixed strokes to finish

TpS: Tempo-Effort Interval Swims

WU – 200 easy, zone 1, choice of stroke/s

Pre-Set – 4 × [50 hard, zone 4; 50 easy, zone 1; 10 seconds rest after each]

Recovery – 100 easy, zone 1, mixed strokes

Main Set

- *TpS1800* – 4 × [150 strong, zone 3; 100 moderate, zone 2; 10 seconds rest after each]
- *TpS2000.1* – 5 × [150 strong, zone 3; 100 moderate, zone 2; 10 seconds rest after each]
- *TpS2000.2* – 4 × [200 strong, zone 3; 100 moderate, zone 2; 10 seconds rest after each]
- *TpS2000.3* – 3 × [150 strong, zone 3; 100 strong, zone 3; 100 moderate, zone 2; 10 seconds rest after each]
  150 strong, zone 3
- *TpS2200.1* – 5 × [150 strong, zone 3; 100 moderate, zone 2; 10 seconds rest after each]
  150 strong, zone 3
- *TpS2200.2* – 4 × [200 strong, zone 3; 100 moderate, zone 2; 10 seconds rest after each]
  200 strong, zone 3
- *TpS2200.3* – 4 × [150 strong, zone 3; 100 strong, zone 3; 100 moderate, zone 2; 10 seconds rest after each]
- *TpS2200.4* – 4 × [150 strong, zone 3; 150 strong, zone 3; 50 moderate, zone 2; 10 seconds rest after each]

- *TpS2400.3* – 4 × [150 strong, zone 3; 100 strong, zone 3; 100 moderate, zone 2; 10 seconds rest after each]
  150 strong, zone 3
- *TpS2400.4* – 4 × [150 strong, zone 3; 150 strong, zone 3; 50 moderate, zone 2; 10 seconds rest after each]
  150 strong, zone 3
- *TpS2400.5* – 4 × [200 strong, zone 3; 150 strong, zone 3; 50 moderate, zone 2; 10 seconds rest after each]
- *TpS2600.5* – 4 × [200 strong, zone 3; 150 strong, zone 3; 50 moderate, zone 2; 10 seconds rest after each]
  200 strong, zone 3
- *TpS2600.6* – 4 × [250 strong, zone 3; 150 strong, zone 3; 50 moderate, zone 2; 10 seconds rest after each]
- *TpS2600.7* – 3 × [250 strong, zone 3; 200 strong, zone 3; 50 moderate, zone 2; 10 seconds rest after each]
  250 strong, zone 3
- *TpS2800.6* – 4 × [250 strong, zone 3; 150 strong, zone 3; 50 moderate, zone 2; 10 seconds rest after each]
  200 strong, zone 3
- *TpS2800.7* – 4 × [250 strong, zone 3; 200 strong, zone 3; 50 moderate, zone 2; 10 seconds rest after each]
- *TpS2800.8* – 4 × [300 strong, zone 3; 150 strong, zone 3; 50 moderate, zone 2; 10 seconds rest after each]
- *TpS3000.9* – 4 × [300 strong, zone 3; 200 strong, zone 3; 50 moderate, zone 2; 10 seconds rest after each]
- *TpS3000.10* – 3 × [400 strong, zone 3; 250 strong, zone 3; 100 moderate, zone 2; 10 seconds rest after each]

CD – easy, zone 1, mixed strokes to finish

TpSkS: Tempo-Effort Interval, Skill Focus Swims

WU – 200 easy, zone 1, choice of strokes

Pre-Set #1 – 6 × [50 skill focus, easy to moderate, zone 1 to 2; rest as needed]

Pre-Set #2 – 6 × [25 hard, zone 4; 25 easy, zone 1; 10 seconds rest after each]

Recovery – 100 easy, zone 1, mixed strokes

Main Set

- *TpSkS1400* – 4 × [100 strong, zone 3; 10 seconds rest]
- *TpSkS1600* – 6 × [100 strong, zone 3; 10 seconds rest]
- *TpSkS1800.1* – 4 × [50 hard, zone 4; 15 seconds rest]
  6 × [100 strong, zone 3; 10 seconds rest]

- *TpSkS1800.2* – 4 × [50 hard, zone 4; 15 seconds rest]
  2 × [150 strong, zone 3; 10 seconds rest]
  3 × [100 strong, zone 3; 10 seconds rest]
- *TpSkS2000.2* – 4 × [50 hard, zone 4; 15 seconds rest]
  2 × [150 strong, zone 3; 10 seconds rest]
  5 × [100 strong, zone 3; 10 seconds rest]
- *TpSkS2000.3* – 4 × [50 hard, zone 4; 15 seconds rest]
  4 × [150 strong, zone 3; 10 seconds rest]
  2 × [100 strong, zone 3; 10 seconds rest]
- *TpSkS2000.4* – 4 × [50 hard, zone 4; 15 seconds rest]
  3 × [200 strong, zone 3; 10 seconds rest]
  2 × [100 strong, zone 3; 10 seconds rest]
- *TpSkS2000.5* – 4 × [50 hard, zone 4; 15 seconds rest]
  2 × [200 strong, zone 3; 10 seconds rest]
  2 × [50 hard, zone 4; 15 seconds rest]
  3 × [100 strong, zone 3; 10 seconds rest]
- *TpSkS2000.6* – 4 × [50 hard, zone 4; 15 seconds rest]
  2 × [200 strong, zone 3; 10 seconds rest]
  4 × [50 hard, zone 4; 15 seconds rest]
  2 × [100 strong, zone 3; 10 seconds rest]
- *TpSkS2200.4* – 4 × [50 hard, zone 4; 15 seconds rest]
  3 × [200 strong, zone 3; 10 seconds rest]
  4 × [100 strong, zone 3; 10 seconds rest]
- *TpSkS2400.5* – 4 × [50 hard, zone 4; 15 seconds rest]
  3 × [200 strong, zone 3; 10 seconds rest]
  2 × [50 hard, zone 4; 15 seconds rest]
  5 × [100 strong, zone 3; 10 seconds rest]

CD – 100 easy, zone 1, mixed strokes

Bike Workouts

All bike workouts are defined by duration in minutes. Many include interval sets, which are written as: number of repetitions × [work interval; rest interval]. Note the planned total duration for each workout, as the final step in most workouts will list "to finish" rather than a defined duration.

AnB: Anaerobic-Effort Interval Bikes

WU – 15 minutes easy, zone 1

Pre-Set – 3 × [30 seconds fast, zone 5; 30 seconds easy, zone 1]

Recovery – 2 minutes easy, zone 1

Main Set #1

- *AnB50.1, AnB60.1* – 10 × [30 seconds fast, zone 5; 30 seconds easy, zone 1]
- *AnB60.2* – 8 × [45 seconds fast, zone 5; 45 seconds easy, zone 1]
- *AnB60.3* – 6 × [1 minute fast, zone 5; 1 minute easy, zone 1]
- *AnB60.4* – 4 × [90 seconds fast, zone 5; 90 seconds easy, zone 1]

Recovery – 5 minutes easy, zone 1

Main Set #2

- *AnB50.1, AnB60.1* – 10 × [30 seconds fast, zone 5; 30 seconds easy, zone 1]
- *AnB60.2* – 8 × [45 seconds fast, zone 5; 45 seconds easy, zone 1]
- *AnB60.3* – 6 × [1 minute fast, zone 5; 1 minute easy, zone 1]
- *AnB60.4* – 4 × [90 seconds fast, zone 5; 90 seconds easy, zone 1]

CD – easy, zone 1 to finish

EndB: Endurance Bikes

Select endurance bikes will be defined by both a duration and a distance target. If your workout has both targets, for example, EndB60(16), your "finish" is when both the specified duration and distance have been achieved; all endurance bike distance targets are defined in miles. *Be sure to practice your fueling and hydration plan during endurance bike workouts lasting more than 1 hour!*

WU – 10 to 15 minutes easy, zone 1

Moderate, zone 2 to finish

PreRcB: Pre-Race Bikes

See Pre-Race Workouts

RcEffB: Race-Effort Interval Bikes

WU – 15 minutes easy, zone 1

Main Set

- *RcEffB60.1, RcEffB75.1, RcEffB90.1* – 2 × [10 minutes moderate, zone 2; 10 minutes race effort]
- *RcEffB75.2, RcEffB90.2* – 15 minutes moderate, zone 2; 15 minutes race effort; 10 minutes moderate, zone 2; 10 minutes race effort
- *RcEffB90.3, RcEffB105.3, RcEffB120.3* – 2 × [15 minutes moderate, zone 2; 15 minutes race effort]
- *RcEffB120.4* – 2 × [20 minutes moderate, zone 2; 20 minutes race effort]
- *RcEffB120.5* – 3 × [15 minutes moderate, zone 2; 15 minutes race effort]

CD – moderate, zone 2 to finish

RcEffSimB and RcSimB: Race-Effort Simulation Bikes and Race Simulation Bikes

See Race Simulation Workouts

RcWkB: Race Week Bikes

WU – 10 minutes easy, zone 1

Pre-Set – 3 × [30 seconds hard, zone 4; 30 seconds easy, zone 1]

Recovery – 2 minutes easy, zone 1

Main Set

- *RcWkB45* – 3 × [3 minutes at race effort; 5 minutes easy, zone 1]
- *RcWkB60* – 4 × [3 minutes strong, zone 3; 3 minutes easy, zone 1]
  5 minutes easy, zone 1
  4 × [1 minute hard, zone 4; 2 minutes easy, zone 1]

CD – easy, zone 1 to finish

SklB: Skill Focus Bikes

WU – 10 minutes easy, zone 1

10 minutes skill focus, easy to moderate, zones 1 to 2

Moderate, zone 2 to finish

ThB: Threshold-Effort Interval Bikes

WU – 10 minutes easy, zone 1

Pre-Set – 3 × [30 seconds hard, zone 4; 30 seconds easy, zone 1]

Recovery – 2 minutes easy, zone 1

Main Set

- *ThB45.1* – 3 × [3 minutes hard, zone 4; 5 minutes easy, zone 1]
- *ThB50.2* – 4 × [3 minutes hard, zone 4; 5 minutes easy, zone 1]
- *ThB50.3, Th60.3* – 3 × [4 minutes hard, zone 4; 6 minutes easy, zone 1]
- *ThB60.4* – 5 × [3 minutes hard, zone 4; 5 minutes easy, zone 1]
- *ThB60.5* – 4 × [4 minutes hard, zone 4; 6 minutes easy, zone 1]
- *ThB60.6* – 6 × [3 minutes hard, zone 4; 4 minutes easy, zone 1]
- *ThB60.7* – 5 × [4 minutes hard, zone 4; 4 minutes easy, zone 1]
- *ThB60.8* – 4 × [5 minutes hard, zone 4; 5 minutes easy, zone 1]
- *ThB60.9* – 7 × [3 minutes hard, zone 4; 3 minutes easy, zone 1]

CD – easy, zone 1 to finish

TpB: Tempo-Effort Interval Bikes

WU – 10 minutes easy, zone 1

Pre-Set – 3 × [30 seconds hard, zone 4; 30 seconds easy, zone 1]

Recovery – 2 minutes easy, zone 1

Main Set

- *TpB60.1* – 4 × [5 minutes strong, zone 3; 4 minutes easy, zone 1]
- *TpB60.2* – 4 × [6 minutes strong, zone 3; 4 minutes easy, zone 1]
- *TpB60.3* – 3 × [8 minutes strong, zone 3; 4 minutes easy, zone 1]
- *TpB60.4* – 3 × [10 minutes strong, zone 3; 4 minutes easy, zone 1]
- *TpB60.5* – 2 × [15 minutes strong, zone 3; 5 minutes easy, zone 1]

CD – easy, zone 1 to finish

Run Workouts

All run workouts are defined by duration in minutes. Many include interval sets, which are written as: number of repetitions × [work interval; rest interval]. Note the planned total duration for each workout, as the final step in most workouts will list "to finish" rather than a defined duration.

Those using a run-walk approach can apply that strategy to all workouts within the plans. For interval workouts, if the work interval is longer than your run-walk-run interval, incorporate your run-walk strategy within it, adjusting the timing so that you begin each work interval with a run. If the work interval is shorter than your run-walk-run interval, then run the work interval and walk the rest interval.

EndR: Endurance Runs

Select endurance runs will be defined by both a duration and a distance target. If your workout has both targets, for example, EndR30(2.5), your "finish" is when both the specified duration and distance have been achieved; all endurance run distance targets are defined in miles. *Be sure to practice your fueling and hydration plan during endurance run workouts lasting more than 1 hour!*

WU

- *EndR15 through EndR30* – 10 minutes easy, zone 1
- *EndR35 through EndR120* – 15 minutes easy, zone 1

Moderate, zone 2 to finish

HillR: Hill Repeat Runs

WU – 15 minutes easy, zone 1

Main Set

- *HillR30.1, HillR40.1, HillR45.1* – 8 × [30 seconds strong uphill, zone 3; 45 seconds (or as long as it takes to return to the bottom of the hill) easy, zone 1]
- *HillR40.2* – 8 × [45 seconds strong uphill, zone 3; 75 seconds (or as long as it takes to return to the bottom of the hill) easy, zone 1]
- *HillR40.3, HillR45.3, HillR50.3* – 8 × [1 minute strong uphill, zone 3; 90 seconds (or as long as it takes to return to the bottom of the hill) easy, zone 1]
- *HillR45.4, HillR50.4* – 10 × [1 minute strong uphill, zone 3; 90 seconds (or as long as it takes to return to the bottom of the hill) easy, zone 1]
- *HillR50.5* – 8 × [90 seconds strong uphill, zone 3; 2 minutes 15 seconds (or as long as it takes to return to the bottom of the hill) easy, zone 1]

- *HillR55.6* – 6 × [2 minutes strong uphill, zone 3; 3 minutes (or as long as it takes to return to the bottom of the hill) easy, zone 1]

CD – easy, zone 1 to finish

HillThR: Hill Repeat and Threshold-Effort Interval Runs

WU – 15 minutes easy, zone 1

Main Set #1

- 6 × [1 minute strong uphill, zone 3; 90 seconds (or as long as it takes to return to the bottom of the hill) easy, zone 1]

Recovery – 2 minutes easy, zone 1

Main Set #2

- *HillThR50* – 2 × [5 minutes hard, zone 4; 3 minutes easy, zone 1]
- *HillThR60* – 3 × [5 minutes hard, zone 4; 3 minutes easy, zone 1]

CD – easy, zone 1 to finish

RcEffR: Race-Effort Interval Runs

WU – 15 minutes easy, zone 1

Main Set

- *RcEffR40.1, RcEffR50.1* – 3 × [3 minutes moderate, zone 2; 3 minutes race effort]
- *RcEffR45.2, RcEffR60.2* – 3 × [4 minutes moderate, zone 2; 4 minutes race effort]
- *RcEffR50.3, RcEffR70.3* – 3 × [5 minutes moderate, zone 2; 5 minutes race effort]
- *RcEffR75.4* – 4 × [5 minutes moderate, zone 2; 5 minutes race effort]

CD – moderate, zone 2 to finish

RcEffSimR and RcSimR: Race-Effort Simulation Runs and Race Simulation Runs

See Race Simulation Workouts

RcWkR: Race Week Runs

WU

- *RcWkR30* – 10 minutes easy, zone 1
- *RcWkR40, RcWkR45* – 15 minutes easy, zone 1

Pre-Set – 3 × [30 seconds hard, zone 4; 30 seconds easy, zone 1]

Recovery – 2 minutes easy, zone 1

Main Set

- *RcWkR30* – 2 × [2 minutes race effort; 3 minutes easy, zone 1]
- *RcWkR40* – 4 × [2 minutes race effort; 3 minutes easy, zone 1]
- *RcWkR45* – 3 × [2 minutes race effort; 3 minutes easy, zone 1] 3 × [1 minute hard, zone 4; 2 minutes easy, zone 1]

CD – easy, zone 1 to finish

SklR: Skill Focus Runs

Focus on a skill cue for the entire duration of the run.

WU

- *SklR15 through SklR30* – 10 minutes easy, zone 1
- *SklR35 through SklR60* – 15 minutes easy, zone 1

Moderate, zone 2 to finish

ThR: Threshold-Effort Interval Runs

WU

- *ThR30.1, ThR40.x* – 10 minutes easy, zone 1
- *ThR45.x, ThR50.x, ThR55.x, ThR60.x* – 15 minutes easy, zone 1

Pre-Set – 3 × [30 seconds hard, zone 4; 30 seconds easy, zone 1]

Recovery – 2 minutes easy, zone 1

Main Set

- *ThR30.1* – 5 × [1 minute hard, zone 4; 1 minute easy, zone 1]
- *ThR40.2, ThR45.2* – 8 × [1 minute hard, zone 4; 1 minute easy, zone 1]
- *ThR40.3, ThR45.3, ThR50.3* – 10 × [1 minute hard, zone 4; 1 minute easy, zone 1]
- *ThR40.4, ThR45.4, ThR50.4* – 6 × [2 minutes hard, zone 4; 2 minutes easy, zone 1]
- *ThR45.5, ThR50.5, ThR55.5* – 4 × [3 minutes hard, zone 4; 3 minutes easy, zone 1]
- *ThR50.6, ThR55.6* – 3 × [4 minutes hard, zone 4; 4 minutes easy, zone 1]
- *ThR50.7, ThR55.7, ThR60.7* – 3 × [5 minutes hard, zone 4; 5 minutes easy, zone 1]
- *ThR55.8, ThR60.8* – 3 × [6 minutes hard, zone 4; 5 minutes easy, zone 1]
- *ThR60.9* – 3 × [8 minutes hard, zone 4; 5 minutes easy, zone 1]
- *ThR60.10* – 3 × [10 minutes hard, zone 4; 5 minutes easy, zone 1]

CD – easy, zone 1 to finish

Run Off-the-Bike Workouts

All run off-the-bike workouts are defined by duration in minutes. Runs off-the-bike are executed immediately following the scheduled bike workout. Set up your run gear before starting your bike ride to make the transition as quick and seamless as possible.

EndRotb: Endurance Runs Off-the-Bike

Moderate, zone 2, run immediately following your bike workout

RcEffRotb: Race-Effort Runs Off-the-Bike

Immediately following your bike workout, complete the first half of the run at a moderate effort level, zone 2, and the second half at race effort

Race Simulation Workouts

All race simulation workouts are defined by distance in miles. Race simulation workouts allow you to practice every aspect of the race – or as many as are logistically feasible – before race day, almost like a dress rehearsal. Use the same gear you'll use on race day, wear the same clothing, eat the same breakfast, and follow your fueling and hydration plan.

RcEffSim: Race-Effort Simulation Workouts

- *RcEffSimS* – Swim the first half easy, zone 1, continuously and using any combination of strokes; complete the remaining distance at your race effort and using the strokes you intend to use on race day; if your race swim is in an open water venue and you have the opportunity to execute this swim in open water, please do so!
- *RcEffSimB* – On terrain similar to race day terrain, bike the first half at a moderate effort level, zone 2, and the remainder at race effort
- *RcEffSimR* – On terrain similar to race day terrain, run the first half at a moderate effort level, zone 2, and the remainder at race effort; be sure to cool down for 10 minutes – an easy walk works well! – after this run

RcSim: Race Simulation Workouts

- *RcSimS* – Swim 200 yd/m easy, zone 1, continuously and using any combination of strokes; complete the remaining distance at a moderate effort level, zone 2, and using the strokes you intend to use on race day; if your race swim is in open water and you have the opportunity to execute this swim in open water, please do so!
- *RcSimB* – Bike on terrain similar to race day terrain at a moderate effort level, zone 2
- *RcSimR* – Run on terrain similar to race day terrain at a moderate effort level, zone 2

Pre-Race Workouts

All pre-race workouts are defined by duration in minutes. Pre-race workouts provide an opportunity to do a final gear check and get some blood moving through your muscles before race day. Remember to keep the effort light and easy and save your energy for race day!

PreRcB: Pre-Race Bikes

Easy, high-cadence spin in zone 2; make sure the bike is in good working order

PreRcBrk: Pre-Race Bricks

Final check of the bike and race gear!

- *PreRcBrk15* – 10-minute easy, zone 1 bike immediately followed by a 5-minute easy, zone 1 run off-the-bike
- *PreRcBrk30* – 20-minute easy, zone 1 bike immediately followed by a 10-minute easy, zone 1 run off-the-bike

PreRcOWS: Pre-Race Open Water Swims

Easy, zone 1 practice swim at the race swim venue to preview the swim course; spend 5 minutes focusing on the open water swimming cue (see chapter 4)

Strength Training and Mobility Sessions

Optional strength training and mobility sessions are included in all training plans. If you are injury-prone or over 40 years old, please read "optional" as "recommended" and maybe even interpret that as "mandatory." A few notes on strength sessions:

- If you do not have experience with strength training, I recommend starting with the bodyweight strength sessions for 4 to 8 weeks before progressing to weighted strength sessions.
- Complete each upper- and lower-body strength exercise using a one-count when moving against gravity or resistance, and a two-count when moving with it.
- When performing a weighted strength session, choose a weight that yields a slight burn in your working muscles during the final few repetitions (reps) of each set – these are not meant to be heavy- or max-weight sessions.
- When the instructions ask you to perform a set of exercises "as a circuit," complete one set of each exercise listed, then repeat the entire list of exercises for the second round; otherwise, complete all sets of an exercise before moving on to the next one.
- Rest 45 to 90 seconds between each set of upper- and lower-body strength exercises.

See appendix B for all strength and mobility exercise instructions.

BwSt: Bodyweight Strength Training Sessions

Activation – Inchworm, 5 reps

Main Set

- *BwSt.1*
  - *2 sets each:* Bodyweight squat, 12 to 15 reps
    Single-leg deadlift, no weight, 12 to 15 reps on each side
    Push-up, 8 to 15 reps
  - *2 sets, as a circuit:* Bird dog, 12 to 15 reps on each side
    Dead bug, 12 to 15 reps on each side
    Sitting twist, 12 to 15 reps on each side
- *BwSt.2*
  - *2 sets each:* Lunge circuit*, 8 to 12 reps on each side
    Push-up, 8 to 15 reps
  - *2 sets, as a circuit:* Front plank with knee drive, 30 to 60 seconds
    Side plank, 20 to 30 seconds each side
    Glute bridge, 30 to 60 seconds

**One rep of the lunge circuit consists of 1 forward lunge, 1 side lunge, and 1 reverse lunge, all executed on the same side*

St: Weighted Strength Training Sessions

Activation

- Inchworm, 5 reps
- Walking lunge with rotation, 4 to 8 lb, 2 × 5 reps on each side

Main Set

- *St.1*
  - *2 sets each:* Goblet squat, 12 to 15 reps
    Single-leg deadlift, 12 to 15 reps on each side
    Lat pulldown (or dumbbell pullover), 12 to 15 reps
    Seated row (or bent-over row), 12 to 15 reps on each side
  - *2 sets, as a circuit:* Bird dog, 12 to 15 reps on each side
    Sitting twist, 10 to 12 lb, 12 to 15 reps on each side
    Dead bug, 12 to 15 reps on each side
    Side-lying hip abduction, 12 to 15 reps on each side
- *St.2*
  - *2 sets each:* Bulgarian split squat, 12 to 15 reps on each side
    Romanian deadlift, 12 to 15 reps
    Lat pulldown (or dumbbell pullover), 12 to 15 reps
    Seated row (or bent-over row), 12 to 15 reps on each side
  - *2 sets, as a circuit:* Front plank with knee drive, 30 to 60 seconds
    Side plank, 20 to 30 seconds each side
    Superman hold, 12 to 15 reps
    Glute bridge, 30 to 60 seconds
- *St.3*
  - *2 sets each:* Goblet squat, 12 to 15 reps
    Romanian deadlift, 12 to 15 reps on each side
    Lat pulldown (or dumbbell pullovers), 12 to 15 reps
    Seated row (or bent-over row), 12 to 15 reps on each side
  - *2 sets, as a circuit:* Bird dog, 12 to 15 reps on each side
    Sitting twist, 10 to 12 lb, 12 to 15 reps on each side
    Dead bug, 12 to 15 reps on each side
    Side-lying hip abduction, 12 to 15 reps on each side
- *St.4*
  - *2 sets each:* Lunge circuit*, 8 to 12 reps on each side
    Push-up, 10 to 15 reps
  - *2 sets, as a circuit:* Front plank with knee drive, 30 to 60 seconds
    Side plank, 20 to 30 seconds each side
    Superman hold, 12 to 15 reps
    Glute bridge, 30 to 60 seconds

**One rep of the lunge circuit consists of 1 forward lunge, 1 side lunge, and 1 reverse lunge, all executed on the same side*

Mob: Mobility Sessions

- *Mob.1* – 1 to 2 minutes each:
    - Thoracic spine rotations
    - Hip CARs
    - Half-kneeling hip opener with rotation
    - Wall slides
- *Mob.2* – 1 to 2 minutes each:
    - Cat-cow
    - Low lunge with rotation
    - 90/90 hip opener
    - Rocking frog

APPENDIX B

STRENGTH AND MOBILITY EXERCISE REFERENCE GUIDE

Strength and mobility are typically the most overlooked aspects of triathlon training. While they don't directly contribute to cardiorespiratory fitness, they support the work your body does during swimming, biking, and running, allowing your muscles to perform the movements you demand of them. Additionally, strength and mobility work support healthy, balanced movement patterns that help prevent overuse injuries caused by the repetitive movements of endurance exercise. Which is all a long way of saying: Do yourself a favor and make time for the strength and mobility sessions in your training plan. Your body will thank you.

Strength Exercises

The activation, upper- and lower-body, and core exercises described here are those included in the training plans' strength training workouts. These exercises develop the foundational strength and stability that support efficient, injury-resistant movement patterns. Specifically, the exercises develop posterior chain strength, single-sided strength, and core strength and stability while improving movement efficiency, enhancing movement quality, reducing injury risk, and increasing your athletic durability.

A few quick instructions for common positions and movements before we get started:

- *Tabletop position:* Kneel on the floor, then lower your upper body onto your hands with your wrists below your shoulders and your elbows slightly bent. Your hips should be directly over your knees; your toes can be either tucked under or flat on the floor. Hold your back flat and in a neutral position, with your head and neck aligned with your spine. (See the starting position for Bird Dog or Cat-Cow.)
- *High plank position:* From the tabletop position, extend your legs behind you and rest your weight on your toes, with your feet shoulder-width apart. Straighten your body, creating a straight line from your head through your shoulders and hips all the way to your heels. (See the starting position for Push-Up or Front Plank With Knee Drive.)
- *Hinge movement:* Flex at your hip joint while pushing your hips back with a neutral spine (used in Inchworm, Bent-Over Row, Bodyweight Squat, Goblet Squat, Romanian Deadlift, Side Lunge, and Single-Leg Deadlift).

Activation Exercises

Activation exercises prepare your body for the greater demands of strength training exercises, especially when using weights. They serve as a warm-up for the strength training session, turning on – activating – the muscles that will be stressed during the workout.

Upper- and Lower-Body Exercises

Upper- and lower-body exercises also incorporate your core. Start each exercise by engaging and stabilizing your core, and maintain core engagement throughout each repetition. Think of your midsection as a rigid cylinder, stiff and without movement during each exercise.

Core Exercises

Your core – your abdominals, obliques, glutes, and back – connects your upper and lower body, maintaining your posture and stability during exercises. To properly engage your core during core exercises, think of your stomach and back as two boards. Before starting the exercise, pull the boards together as closely as possible and hold them in this position for each repetition. Use slow and controlled movements to maximize the effectiveness of the exercises.

INCHWORM

MUSCLES TARGETED

Full-body activation exercise, with focus on shoulders, core, and hamstrings

EQUIPMENT

None

STARTING POSITION

Stand with your feet hip-width apart and bend forward, placing your hands on the floor in front of your feet.

MOVEMENT

Walk your hands forward, keeping your feet in place (figure *a*), until you are in a front plank position (figure *b*); hold for 1 second. Then hinge at your hips and walk your feet forward (figure *c*) to meet your hands. Begin the next rep from this position.

COACHING NOTES

Move slowly and with control. Keep your core engaged and your legs as straight as possible. If needed, use a slight bend in your knees to maintain good form.

a

b

c

WALKING LUNGE WITH ROTATION

MUSCLES TARGETED

Lower-body and core activation exercise, focusing on glutes, quads, and obliques

EQUIPMENT

Lightweight dumbbell or medicine ball (optional, max 10 pounds [5 kg])

STARTING POSITION

Stand with your feet hip-width apart and the dumbbell, medicine ball, or your hands held straight out in front of you (figure *a*).

a

MOVEMENT

Step forward and just slightly wide with your right foot, dropping your hips so that both knees are bent at 90 degrees and your left knee hovers just above the floor (figure *b*). Keeping your hips pointed forward and your arms outstretched, rotate your torso 90 degrees to the right or until your maximum range of motion is reached (figure *c*); hold for 1 second. Bring your arms back in front of you and step forward with your left foot to return to the starting position. Repeat on your left side, and continue in an alternating fashion.

b

c

COACHING NOTES

Step forward far enough that your forward knee is stacked above your ankle and you can feel your glutes engage.

BENT-OVER ROW

MUSCLES TARGETED

Latissimus dorsi, rhomboids, trapezius, posterior deltoids, biceps

EQUIPMENT

Weighted bar, barbell, dumbbells, or kettlebells

STARTING POSITION

Stand with your feet shoulder-width apart. Bend your knees slightly and hinge at the hips until your back is nearly parallel to the floor. Hold the barbell, kettlebells, or dumbbells with your arms extended straight toward the floor and held slightly wider than shoulder-width apart (figure *a*).

a

MOVEMENT

Squeeze your shoulder blades together and pull the weight straight up toward your torso, keeping your elbows at your side (figure *b*). Hold for 1 second, then return to the starting position.

b

COACHING NOTES

Focus on pulling your elbows back toward your hips, not straight up. Keep your neck in a neutral position and avoid rounding your back.

BODYWEIGHT SQUAT

MUSCLES TARGETED

Quadriceps, gluteus maximus, hamstrings

EQUIPMENT

None

STARTING POSITION

Stand with your feet shoulder-width apart and toes pointed forward or slightly turned out with both arms at your sides (figure *a*).

MOVEMENT

Keeping your chest up, your back straight, and your weight in your heels, hinge and lower your hips down and back, as if sitting into a chair, until your thighs are parallel to the floor – or even lower if you can do so with stability – while raising your arms in front of you until they are parallel to the floor (figure *b*). Hold for 1 second, then push through your heels to return to the starting position.

COACHING NOTES

Limit the forward movement of your knees while letting them track over your toes, ensuring they don't cave inward or fall too far out. Engage your core and keep your torso tall throughout.

BULGARIAN SPLIT SQUAT

MUSCLES TARGETED

Quadriceps, gluteus maximus, hamstrings, adductors

EQUIPMENT

Bench or a surface of equivalent height; dumbbells or kettlebells

STARTING POSITION

Stand one giant step in front of your bench (or equivalent) with the kettlebells or dumbbells held by your sides. Place the top of your right foot on the bench behind you. Keep your chest upright and your weight centered over your left (front) foot (figure *a*).

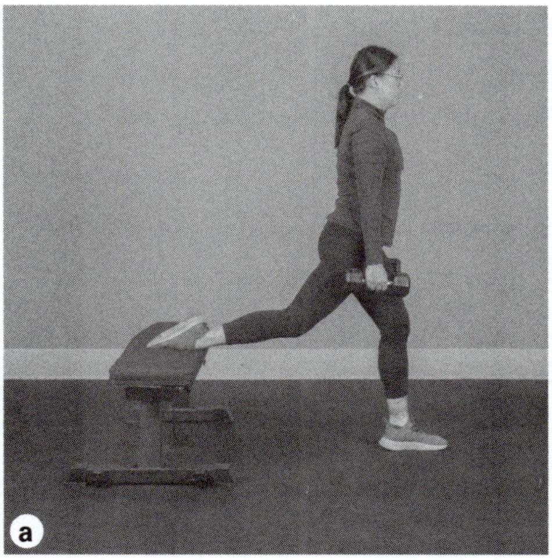

a

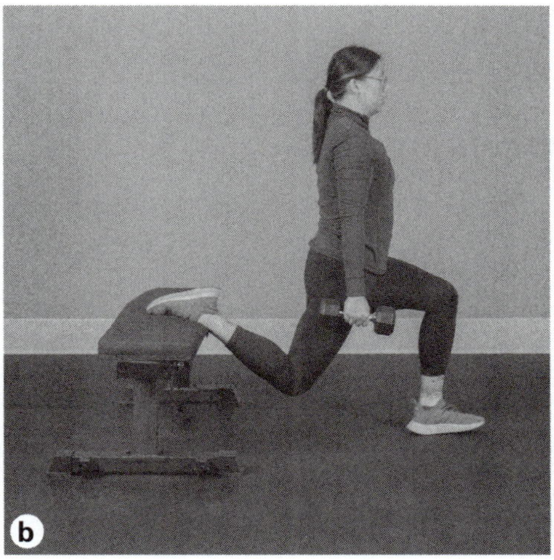

b

MOVEMENT

Keeping your weight in your left foot, lower your body into a lunge position (figure *b*). Hold for 1 second, then push through your heel to return to the starting position. Complete all reps on the left side, then repeat on the right.

COACHING NOTES

Keep your movement in the vertical plane only, without any horizontal (forward) shift. Make sure your front foot is positioned far enough forward so that your knee doesn't extend beyond your toes while in the lunge position. Additionally, watch to ensure your knee doesn't move laterally (side to side), but instead moves in line with your hip and toes.

DUMBBELL PULLOVER

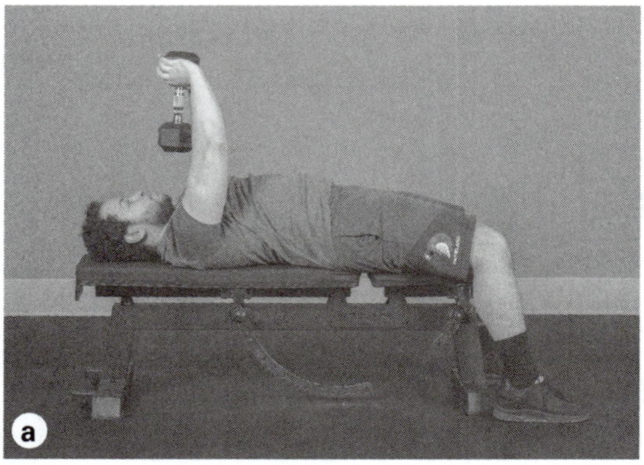

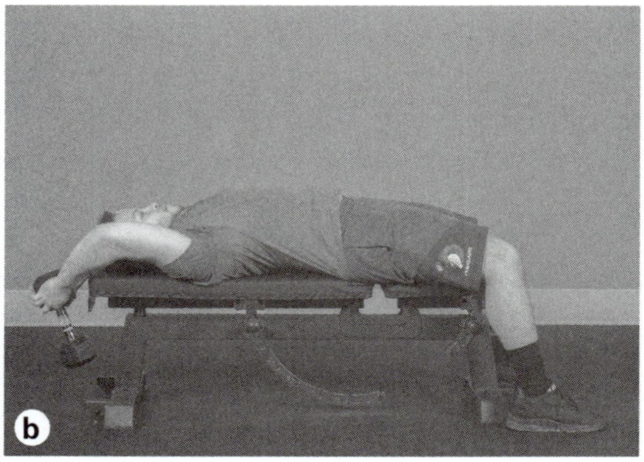

MUSCLES TARGETED

Latissimus dorsi, pectorals, triceps, rhomboids, posterior deltoids

EQUIPMENT

Bench; dumbbell or kettlebell

STARTING POSITION

Lie flat on your back on a bench with your head and hips supported and your feet planted on the floor. Hold a single dumbbell or kettlebell with both hands and your arms extended directly above your chest (figure *a*).

MOVEMENT

Slowly lower the weight back and over your head in a wide arc, keeping your elbows slightly bent, lowering the dumbbell or kettlebell nearly to the floor or until just before your maximum comfortable range of motion is reached (see figure *b*). Hold for 1 second, then return to the starting position.

COACHING NOTES

Keep your elbows slightly bent during the exercise, and avoid arching your back.

FORWARD LUNGE

MUSCLES TARGETED

Quadriceps, gluteus maximus, hamstrings

EQUIPMENT

Weighted bar, barbell, dumbbells, or kettlebells (optional)

STARTING POSITION

Stand with your feet hip-width apart, with the bar on your shoulders, the dumbbells or kettlebells by your sides, or your hands on your hips if using bodyweight only (see figure *a*).

MOVEMENT

Step forward with your right foot (see figure *b*), dropping your hips so that both knees are bent at 90 degrees and your left knee hovers just above the floor (see figure *c*). Hold for 1 second, then push off your right (front) foot to return to the starting position. Repeat on your left side, then continue in an alternating fashion.

COACHING NOTES

Make sure your front knee is aligned with your toes, and that your step is long enough to keep that knee stacked above your ankle. Keep your chest lifted and core engaged throughout the movement.

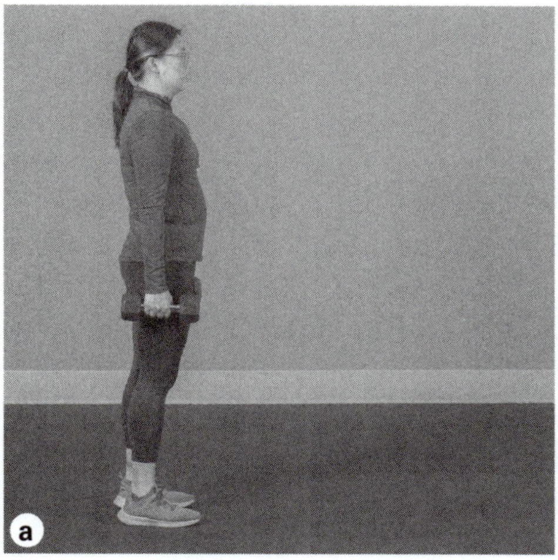

GOBLET SQUAT

MUSCLES TARGETED

Quadriceps, gluteus maximus, hamstrings

EQUIPMENT

Dumbbell or kettlebell

STARTING POSITION

Stand with your feet shoulder-width apart and toes pointed forward or slightly turned out, holding a single dumbbell or kettlebell close to your chest with both hands (see figure *a*).

a

MOVEMENT

Keeping your chest up, your back straight, and your weight in your heels, hinge and lower your hips down and back, as if sitting into a chair, until your thighs are parallel to the floor – or even lower if you can do so with stability (see figure *b*). Hold for 1 second, then push through your heels to return to the starting position.

b

COACHING NOTES

Keep the weight close to your chest to help maintain your balance. Limit the forward movement of your knees while letting them track over your toes, ensuring they don't cave inward or fall too far out. Engage your core and keep your torso tall throughout.

LAT PULLDOWN

MUSCLES TARGETED

Latissimus dorsi, biceps

EQUIPMENT

Lat pulldown machine or cable machine with bench and wide grip bar (if you don't have access to this equipment, substitute the dumbbell pullover)

STARTING POSITION

Sit on the bench and grip the bar with your hands just wider than shoulder-width apart (see figure *a*).

MOVEMENT

Pull the bar down to your chest, keeping your elbows pointed down and slightly back. As you pull, squeeze your shoulder blades together and down to engage your lats (see figure *b*). Hold for 1 second, and return to the starting position.

COACHING NOTES

Keep your feet in front of your knees and lean slightly back to maintain core engagement.

a

b

PUSH-UP

MUSCLES TARGETED

Deltoids, pectorals, triceps

EQUIPMENT

Exercise mat (optional)

STARTING POSITION

Begin in a high plank position. Your body should form a straight line from head to heels, with your core engaged and elbows pointing slightly back (see figure *a*).

MOVEMENT

Lower your chest toward the floor by bending your elbows, keeping your body straight and your elbows close to your sides. Stop when your chest is just above the floor (see figure *b*), hold for 1 second, then push through your hands to return to the starting position.

COACHING NOTES

You may start with push-ups from your knees if the plank position is challenging. In both positions, keep your body straight as a board – don't let your hips drop or float up in the air.

REVERSE LUNGE

MUSCLES TARGETED

Glutes, hamstrings, quadriceps

EQUIPMENT

Weighted bar, barbell, dumbbells, or kettlebells (optional)

STARTING POSITION

Stand with your feet hip-width apart, with the bar on your shoulders, the dumbbells or kettlebells by your sides, or your hands on your hips (figure *a*).

a

MOVEMENT

Step backward with your right foot (figure *b*), lowering your hips so that both knees are bent at 90 degrees and your right knee hovers just above the floor (figure *c*); hold for 1 second. Push through your left (front) foot to return to the starting position. Repeat on the left side, and continue in an alternating fashion.

b

COACHING NOTES

Adjust the length of the step backward to ensure that in the lunge position, your front thigh is parallel to the floor with your front knee aligned with your toes and stacked above your ankle. Keep your chest lifted and core engaged throughout the movement.

c

ROMANIAN DEADLIFT

MUSCLES TARGETED

Hamstrings, gluteus maximus, adductors

EQUIPMENT

Weighted bar, barbell, dumbbells, or kettlebells

STARTING POSITION

Stand with your feet hip-width apart and a slight bend in your knees. If using a bar or barbell, hold it with your hands slightly wider than shoulder-width apart. Hold the weight in front of your thighs, letting your arms hang straight down (figure *a*).

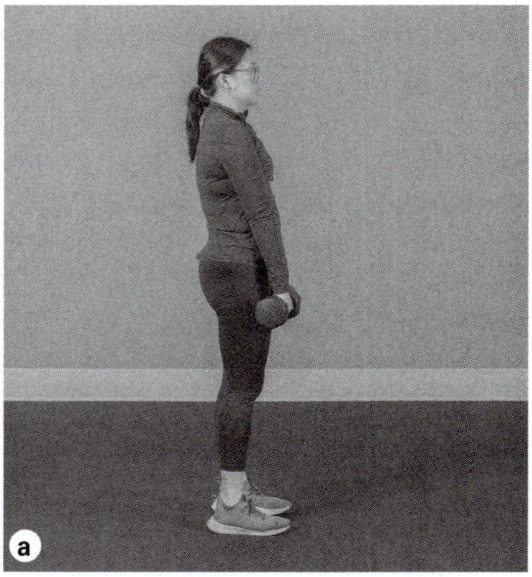

a

b

MOVEMENT

Hinge at your hips by pushing them straight back, lowering the weight straight down the front of your legs to your mid-shin or until you feel a strong stretch in your hamstrings (figure *b*). Hold for 1 second, then bring your hips forward to return to the starting position.

COACHING NOTES

Keep the movement slow and controlled and your weight in your heels, activating your glutes to ensure that your glutes and hamstrings do the work – not your back. The weights should stay close to your legs, and your spine should remain neutral throughout. Avoid rounding your back or bending too much at the knees.

SEATED ROW

MUSCLES TARGETED

Rhomboids, trapezius, latissimus dorsi, posterior deltoids

EQUIPMENT

Cable machine with bench and V-bar, open row attachment, or neutral grip handle, or a seated row machine (if you don't have access to this equipment, substitute the bent-over row)

STARTING POSITION

Sit tall on the bench with your feet on the footrest and your knees slightly bent. Hold the bar or handle with both hands, arms extended in front of you (figure *a*).

a

MOVEMENT

Maintain a slight backward lean and pull the handle toward your waist by squeezing your shoulder blades together (figure *b*). Keep your elbows close to your sides and your spine neutral. Hold for 1 second, then slowly extend your arms to return to the starting position.

b

COACHING NOTES

Lean slightly backward for the entire motion, but don't lean further backward during the motion. Focus on pulling from your back muscles, not just your arms.

SIDE LUNGE

MUSCLES TARGETED

Glutes, hamstrings, quadriceps

EQUIPMENT

Weighted bar, barbell, dumbbell, or kettlebell (optional)

STARTING POSITION

Stand with your feet hip-width apart, with the bar on your shoulders, the dumbbell or kettlebell held in front of your thighs, or your hands on your hips if using bodyweight only (figure *a*).

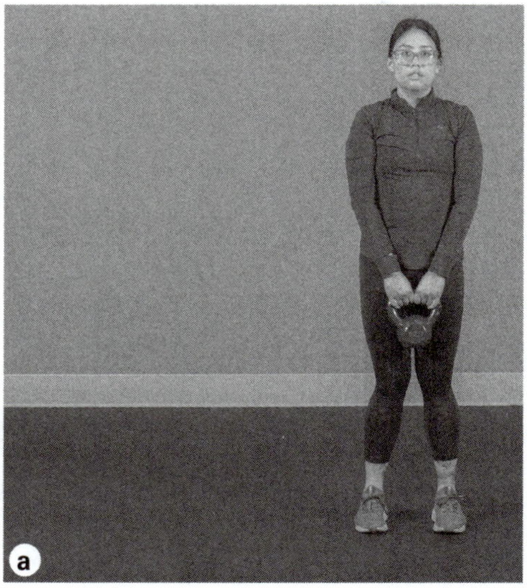

a

MOVEMENT

Take a wide step with your right foot directly to your right side, planting your weight on your right foot, pointing your toes outward, and bending your right knee while keeping your left leg straight. Hinge your hips back and down until your right thigh is parallel to the floor – or as close to that as you can get (figure *b*). Hold for 1 second, then push up off your right foot to return to the starting position. Repeat on the left side, and continue in an alternating fashion.

b

COACHING NOTES

Keep your chest lifted and core tight. Point your bent knee forward, allowing it to move forward slightly but tracking directly over your toes – not caving in or falling outward. Keep your opposite leg straight and grounded throughout the movement.

SINGLE-LEG DEADLIFT

MUSCLES TARGETED

Hamstrings, gluteus maximus, gluteus medius, gluteus minimus

EQUIPMENT

St workouts: dumbbells or kettlebells; BwSt workouts: none

STARTING POSITION

Stand on your left leg with a slight bend in your knee, and hold a single dumbbell or kettlebell in your left hand (or one in each hand) if you are using them (figure *a*).

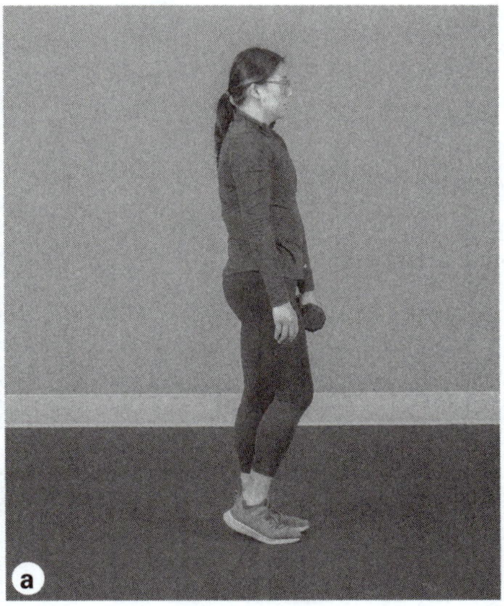
a

MOVEMENT

Hinge at your hips, reaching your right leg behind you and lowering the dumbbells or kettlebells toward the floor alongside your left foot (figure *b*). Hold for 1 second, and then return to the starting position. Complete all the reps on your left side, then repeat on your right side.

b

COACHING NOTES

Shift your weight into the ball of your foot to help maintain balance, and be sure to keep your hips square to the floor throughout the exercise.

BIRD DOG

MUSCLES TARGETED

Erector spinae, abdominals, gluteus maximus (extended leg), gluteus medius and minimus (supporting leg)

EQUIPMENT

Exercise mat (optional)

STARTING POSITION

Begin in the tabletop position (figure *a*).

MOVEMENT

Extend your left arm forward until it is straight and parallel to the floor while simultaneously extending your right leg backward until it is straight and parallel to the floor (figure *b*). Hold for 1 second, and return to the starting position. Repeat with your right arm and left leg, and continue in an alternating fashion.

a

b

COACHING NOTES

Keep your back flat and avoid shifting your weight side to side. Move with control, and focus on maintaining stability through your core and hips.

DEAD BUG

a

b

MUSCLES TARGETED

Abdominals, obliques, hip flexors

EQUIPMENT

Exercise mat (optional)

STARTING POSITION

Lie on your back with your arms and knees extended straight toward the ceiling, and your knees bent at 90 degrees, so that your shins are parallel to the floor (figure *a*). Press your lower back gently into the mat or floor.

MOVEMENT

Lower your left arm above your head so that it is straight and hovering an inch above the floor, while simultaneously lowering your right leg so that it is straight and hovering an inch above the floor (figure *b*). Keep your core tight, your back flat against the floor, and your right arm and left leg (the non-moving arm and leg) in the "dead bug" position. Hold for 1 second, and return to the starting position. Repeat with your right arm and left leg, and continue in an alternating fashion.

COACHING NOTES

Move slowly and with control. If your back starts to lift off the floor, reduce the range of motion for the exercise, only extending your arm and leg as low as you can while still keeping your back flat against the floor.

FRONT PLANK WITH KNEE DRIVE

MUSCLES TARGETED

Abdominals, obliques, hip flexors

EQUIPMENT

Exercise mat (optional)

STARTING POSITION

Begin in a high plank position, with your hands directly under your shoulders, arms straight, and your legs extended behind you, feet hip-width apart (figure *a*). Your body should form a straight line from head to heels.

MOVEMENT

Prioritizing control over speed, lift your right foot and drive your right knee toward your right elbow (figure *b*). Hold for 1 second, and return to the starting position. Repeat on your left side.

COACHING NOTES

Keep your hips level and your core tight – avoid letting your hips sag, twist, or lift during the movement.

GLUTE BRIDGE

MUSCLES TARGETED

Gluteus maximus, hamstrings, erector spinae

EQUIPMENT

Exercise mat (optional), dumbbell (optional)

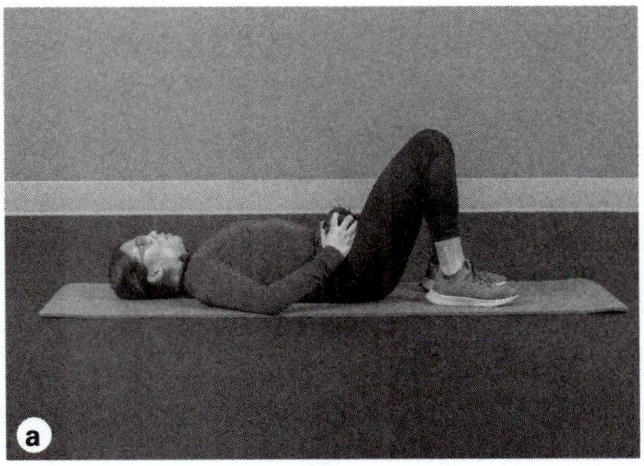

STARTING POSITION

Lie on your back with your knees bent and your feet flat on the floor, 4 to 6 inches (10-15 cm) from your buttocks. Hold the dumbbell horizontally across your hips or place your hands on the floor beside your hips, palms down (figure *a*).

MOVEMENT

Pressing through your heels and keeping your shoulders on the floor, lift your hips to the ceiling until your body forms a straight line from shoulders to knees (figure *b*). Squeeze your glutes and hold for 1 second, then return to the starting position.

COACHING NOTES

Initiate the movement with your glutes to emphasize those muscles over your hamstrings. Avoid arching your back at the top of the movement.

SIDE PLANK

MUSCLES TARGETED

Obliques, abdominals, gluteus medius and minimus

EQUIPMENT

Exercise mat (optional)

STARTING POSITION

Position yourself on your right side, placing your right elbow directly beneath your shoulder to lift your body off the floor. With your right hip on the floor, stack your feet on top of each other, or stagger them for more stability.

MOVEMENT

Put your weight into your right forearm and the edge of your right foot to lift your hips off the floor (figure *a*). Hold your body in a straight line, without letting your hips drop or twist, for the duration of the exercise. Repeat on the left side.

COACHING NOTES

If this position is challenging, drop your bottom knee and rest it on the floor, putting your weight there rather than on your bottom foot.

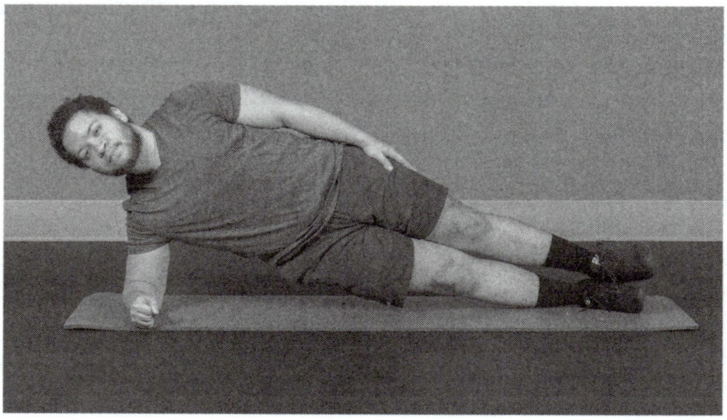

SIDE-LYING HIP ABDUCTION

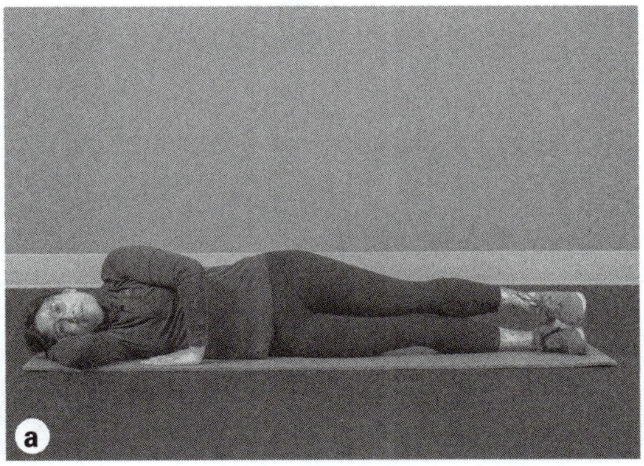

MUSCLES TARGETED

Gluteus medius

EQUIPMENT

Exercise mat (optional)

STARTING POSITION

Lie on your right side with your right arm supporting your head. Place your left hand on the floor in front of your torso (figure *a*).

MOVEMENT

Holding your left leg straight, lift the leg into the air as far as you can using a deliberate, controlled movement (figure *b*), and then slowly lower it back to the starting position. Complete all reps on the left side, then switch and repeat the exercise on the right side.

COACHING NOTES

Keep your upper leg in line with your upper body – don't let it drift forward of your torso. You can bend your lower leg, bringing your knee in front of your torso and keeping your foot behind it, to improve balance and range of motion.

SITTING TWIST

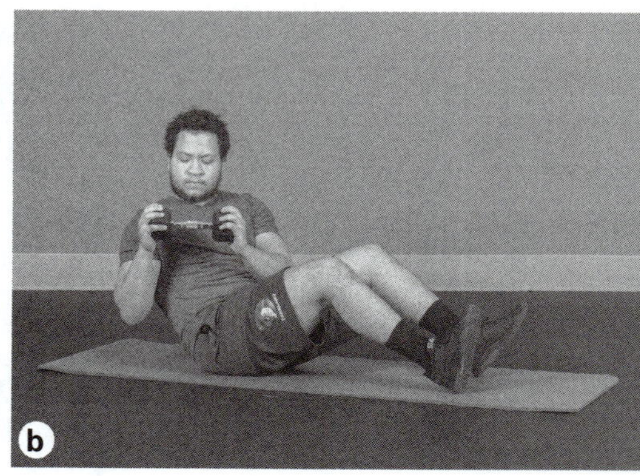

MUSCLES TARGETED

Obliques

EQUIPMENT

Exercise mat (optional); dumbbell or medicine ball (optional)

STARTING POSITION

Sit on the floor with your knees bent and your heels on the floor, holding your torso at or close to a 45-degree angle to the floor. With bent elbows, hold the dumbbell, medicine ball, or your hands in front of your chest (figure *a*).

MOVEMENT

Rotate your upper body to the right until your maximum range of motion is reached (figure *b*). Rotate back through the center and continue until you reach your maximum range of motion on the left. Repeat in an alternating fashion.

COACHING NOTES

Complete this exercise slowly, with controlled movement. Avoid using momentum or swinging the arms – let your torso do the work.

SUPERMAN HOLD

MUSCLES TARGETED

Erector spinae, gluteus maximus, hamstrings

EQUIPMENT

Exercise mat (optional)

STARTING POSITION

Lie face down on the floor, with your arms extended straight above you, shoulder-width apart, and your legs straight behind you, hip-width apart (figure *a*).

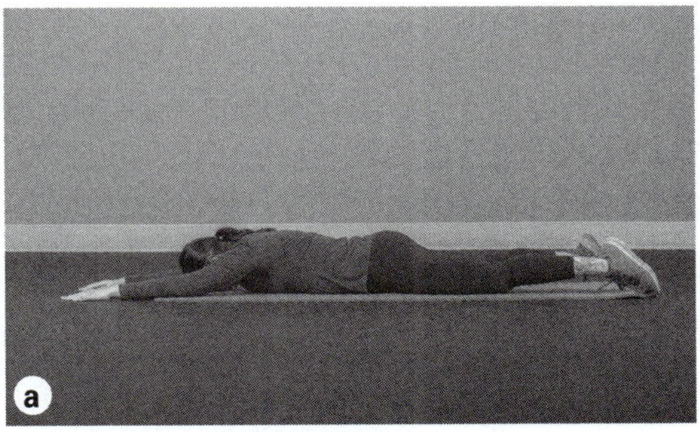

a

MOVEMENT

Lift your arms and legs 6 to 10 inches (15-25 cm) off the floor (figure *b*). Hold for 1 second, then return to the starting position.

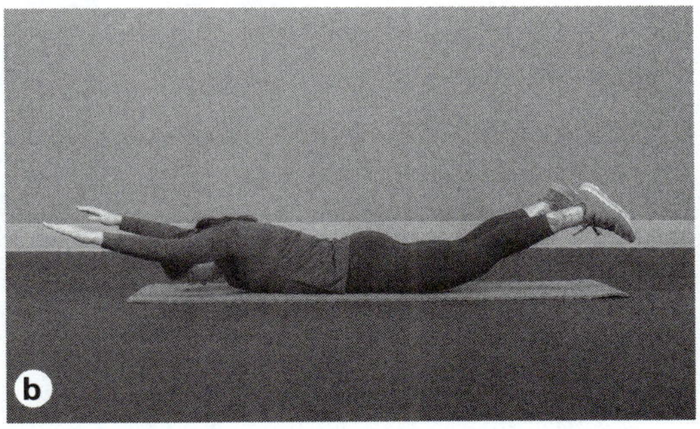

b

COACHING NOTES

Maintain a neutral neck position and avoid overextending your back. If this exercise is challenging, perform an alternating superman using the opposite arm and leg instead of both arms and legs, alternating for each rep.

Mobility Exercises

Mobility exercises are designed to improve your joint range of motion while also increasing joint stability. Use them as prescribed in the training plans – or every morning as you start your day; in the evening as you wind down; or before swims, bikes, or runs. Spending 5 to 10 minutes a day on mobility can do wonders to improve the quality of your movement, which helps your body stay healthy and injury-free.

90/90 HIP OPENER

MUSCLES TARGETED

Hip rotators and stabilizers (primarily gluteus medius, gluteus minimus, and deep hip muscles)

EQUIPMENT

Exercise mat (optional)

STARTING POSITION

Sit on the floor with both knees bent at 90 degrees, positioned to your right – your right thigh should point straight in front of you, and your left thigh should extend directly to your side. Keep your torso upright, your hips even, and place your right hand alongside your right hip and your left hand behind your left thigh for support (figure *a*).

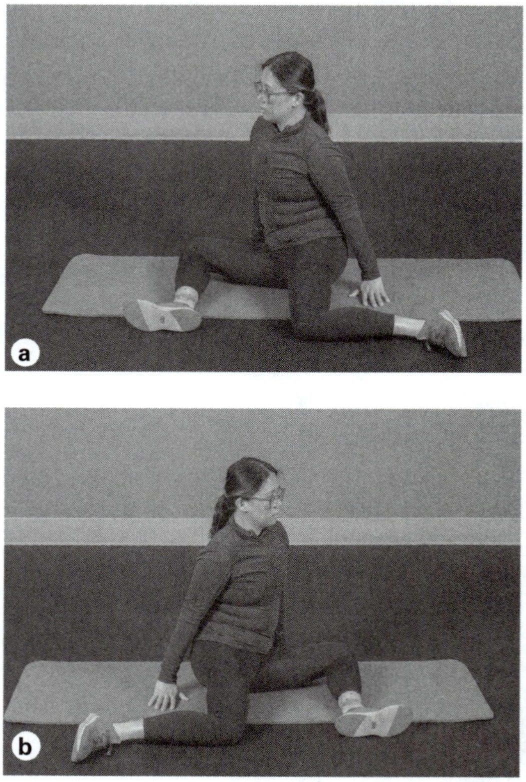

MOVEMENT

Put your weight in your hands for support and lift both knees while keeping your buttocks and feet in place on the floor. Sweep your knees over to your left side, with your left thigh pointing straight in front of you and your right thigh extending directly to your side (figure *b*). Hold for 1 second, then lift your knees to return to the starting position.

COACHING NOTES

Don't rush through the exercise, but instead focus on quality of movement.

CAT-COW

MUSCLES TARGETED

Spinal erectors, abdominals, and muscles involved in spinal mobility and posture

EQUIPMENT

Exercise mat (optional)

STARTING POSITION

Begin in the tabletop position (figure *a*).

MOVEMENT

Inhale, drop your belly to the floor, stick your tailbone up in the air, and lift your chest and chin upward to move into cow pose (figure *b*); hold for 1 second. Exhale, round your spine, point your tailbone to the floor, and tuck your chin to your chest to move into cat pose (figure *c*); hold for 1 second. Begin the next rep from this position.

COACHING NOTES

Match your breath to your movement. Move slowly and gently, focusing on spine mobility.

HALF-KNEELING HIP OPENER WITH ROTATION

MUSCLES TARGETED

Hip flexors, obliques, and spinal rotators

EQUIPMENT

Exercise mat (optional)

STARTING POSITION

Begin in a half-kneeling position, with your left knee on the floor and your right foot flat on the floor directly in front of you, your right knee bent at 90 degrees. Extend your arms straight in front of your body (figure *a*).

MOVEMENT

Shift your weight forward onto your right leg until you feel a stretch in the hip flexor of your back leg. As you do so, rotate 90 degrees to the right or until you reach your maximum range of motion (figure *b*). Hold for 1 second, and return to the starting position. Complete all the reps on your right side, then repeat on your left side.

COACHING NOTES

You should feel a stretch through the front of the hip on your back leg. To protect your lower back and deepen the stretch, squeeze the glute of your back leg as you move forward.

HIP CARS (CONTROLLED ARTICULAR ROTATIONS)

MUSCLES TARGETED

Deep hip stabilizers, glutes, and surrounding joint muscles

EQUIPMENT

Wall or stable surface for balance

STARTING POSITION

Stand with your left hand lightly resting on a wall or sturdy surface for balance, and put your weight in the heel of your left foot (figure *a*).

MOVEMENT

Raise your right knee in front of you, so that your thigh is parallel to the floor and your knee is bent at 90 degrees (flexion) (figure *b*). Holding the height and angle of your knee, move your right leg directly to your side (abduction) (figure *c*). Maintaining the height and angle of your knee as best you can, rotate your right thigh inward and point your foot behind you (rotation) (figure *d*). Keeping your foot behind you and your knee bent at 90 degrees, lower your right knee to meet your left (figure *e*). Reverse the movement, moving through rotation to abduction to flexion (*d* to *c* to *b*), to return to the starting position. Complete all reps on the right side, then repeat on your left side.

COACHING NOTES

Move slowly and stay in control the whole time. Keep your hips square – avoid leaning or twisting your torso. It's okay if your range of motion is small; focus on smooth, controlled movement.

a
b
c
d
e

LOW LUNGE WITH ROTATION

MUSCLES TARGETED

Hip flexors, gluteus maximus, quadriceps

EQUIPMENT

Exercise mat (optional)

STARTING POSITION

Begin in a high plank position.

MOVEMENT

Step your right foot forward into a low lunge position, with your right foot placed between your hands (figure *a*); hold for 1 second. Rotate your head, chest, and shoulders to the right, lifting your right hand to the sky and leaving your left hand on the floor by your right foot (figure *b*); hold for 1 second. Return your right hand to the floor and return to the starting position. Repeat on your left side, and continue in an alternating fashion.

COACHING NOTES

Keep your front knee stacked over your ankle, your hips square, and look to the sky to encourage full rotation.

ROCKING FROG

MUSCLES TARGETED

Adductors, hip flexors

EQUIPMENT

Exercise mat (optional)

STARTING POSITION

Begin in a tabletop position, then open your knees to the sides, sit down onto your heels, and extend your arms forward to lower your torso onto the mat or floor (figure *a*).

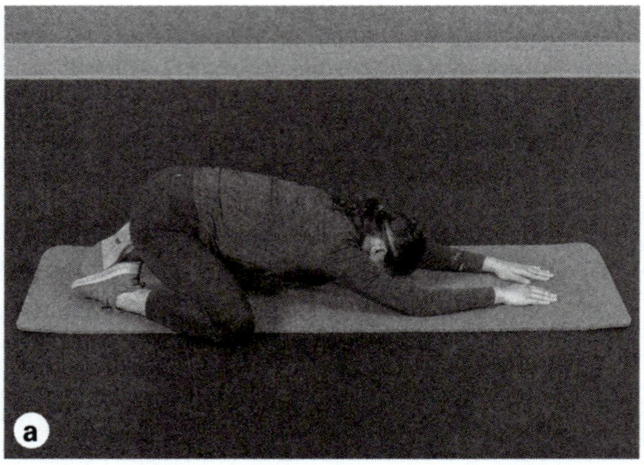

MOVEMENT

Lift your hips and rock forward, keeping your forearms on the mat or floor, shifting your hips in front of your knees and your shoulders in front of your elbows (figure *b*); hold for 1 second. Rock backward and drop your hips, returning to the starting position; hold for 1 second. Repeat.

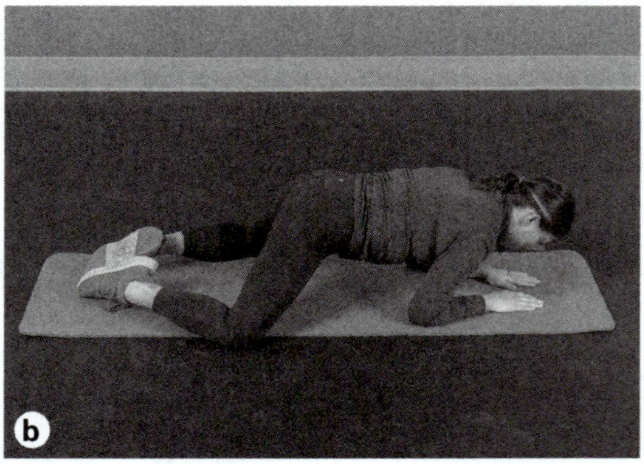

COACHING NOTES

Inhale as you rock forward, and exhale as you rock back.

THORACIC SPINE ROTATIONS

MUSCLES TARGETED

Thoracic erector spinae, obliques, rhomboids, and middle trapezius

EQUIPMENT

Exercise mat (optional)

STARTING POSITION

Begin in a tabletop position, then place your right hand behind your head and hold your right elbow out to the side.

a

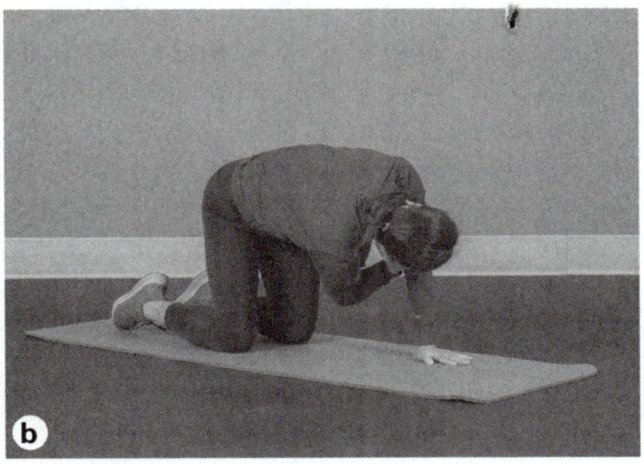
b

MOVEMENT

Keeping your hips square, rotate your torso to your right, extending your right elbow to the sky (figure *a*). Then rotate your torso to your left, bringing your right elbow to or past your left elbow (figure *b*); hold for 1 second. Begin the next rep from this position. Complete all the reps on the right side, then repeat on the left side.

COACHING NOTES

Follow your elbow with your eyes to encourage full rotation. Inhale as you rotate toward the ceiling, and exhale as you rotate toward your planted arm.

WALL SLIDES

MUSCLES TARGETED

Lower trapezius, rhomboids, deltoids, rotator cuff muscles

EQUIPMENT

A wall or similar flat, vertical surface

STARTING POSITION

Stand with your back flat against a wall, your head touching the wall, and your heels 6 to 10 inches (15-25 cm) away from the wall. Place your arms against the wall at shoulder height and bend your elbows to 90 degrees so that your arms make a "U" or goal-post shape (figure *a*).

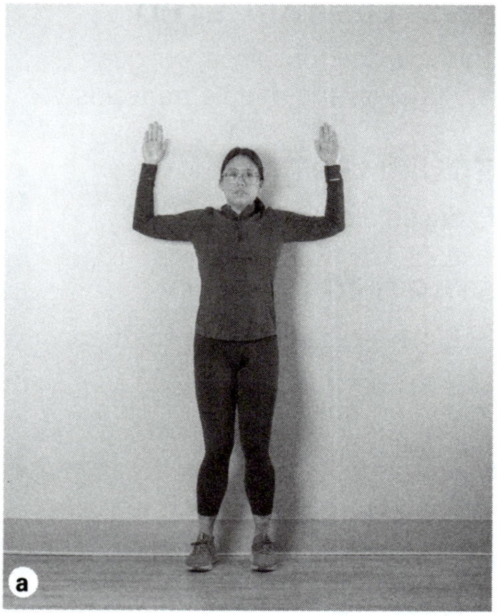

MOVEMENT

Slowly slide your arms upward, keeping your shoulders, elbows, and wrists in constant contact with the wall. Raise your arms as high as you can without losing contact with the wall (figure *b*). Hold for 1 second, then return to the starting position.

COACHING NOTES

Draw in your stomach to avoid arching your back.

REFERENCES

Bevis, Brittany. "How Long Is Ironman? A Look at How the Ironman Distance Came to Be." *Triathlete*, June 22, 2022. www.triathlete.com/training/how-long-is-ironman-a-look-at-how-the-ironman-distance-came-to-be/.

Burdick, Allie. "Functional Strength Training for Triathletes." *TrainingPeaks Blog*. www.trainingpeaks.com/blog/functional-training-how-to-strength-train-for-movement-not-muscle/.

The Editors of Encyclopedia Britannica. "Triathlon." *Encyclopedia Britannica*. www.britannica.com/sports/triathlon.

Fast Talk Labs. "Polarized Training Pathway." www.fasttalklabs.com/pathways/polarized-training/.

Frankl, Viktor E. *Man's Search for Meaning: An Introduction to Logotherapy*. 4th ed. Beacon Press, 1992.

Freeman, Alison. "How to Adjust Your Training Plan for Illness, Injuries, and Busy Days." *Triathlete*, July 19, 2023. www.triathlete.com/training/how-to-adapt-your-training-when-things-go-wrong/.

Freeman, Alison. "A Coach Explains How to Choose Your Next (or Any) Triathlon." *Triathlete*, August 1, 2024. www.triathlete.com/training/race-tips/choosing-the-right-triathlon__trashed/.

Freeman, Alison. "Yes, There Is a Technique to Pedaling a Bike." *Triathlete*, May 1, 2025. www.triathlete.com/training/yes-there-is-a-technique-to-pedaling-a-bike/.

Freeman, Alison. "The Ultimate Guide to Being the Best Race Support Crew for Your Triathlete." *Triathlete*, June 11, 2025. www.triathlete.com/training/race-tips/the-ultimate-triathlon-support-crew-guide/.

Freeman, Alison, and Susan Kitchen. "The Triathlete's Guide to Race Fueling for Every Distance." *Triathlete*, June 26, 2024. www.triathlete.com/nutrition/triathletes-guide-to-race-fueling/.

Gooden, Brett A. "Mechanism of the Human Diving Response." *Integrative Physiological and Behavioral Science* 29, no. 1 (1994): 6-16. https://doi.org/10.1007/BF02691277.

Hagerman, Patrick. *Strength Training for Triathletes*. 2nd ed. VeloPress, 2015.

Hanrahan, Jack. "5 Easy & Effective Hip Mobility Exercises." March 18, 2021. www.polar.com/blog/hip-mobility-exercises/.

The IRONMAN Group. "2025 Competition Rules: English." March 17, 2025. www.ironman.com/resources/rules-and-policies/competition-rules.

Marshall, Simon, and Lesley Paterson. *The Brave Athlete: Calm the F*ck Down and Rise to the Occasion*. VeloPress, 2017.

Miller, Ingrid Loos, and Jim Herkimer. *Functional Strength for Triathletes*. Meyer & Meyer Sport (UK) Ltd., 2012.

Schuldt, Woody. "Grounding Techniques." *Therapist Aid*. www.therapistaid.com/therapy-article/grounding-techniques-article.

Schultz, Mike. "The Primary Muscles Used in Cycling and How to Train Them." *TrainingPeaks Blog*. www.trainingpeaks.com/blog/the-primary-muscles-used-for-cycling-and-how-to-train-them/.

Thomas, D. Travis, Kelly Anne Erdman, and Louise M. Burke. "Position of the Academy of Nutrition and Dietetics, Dietitians of Canada, and the American College of Sports Medicine: Nutrition and Athletic Performance." *Journal of the Academy of Nutrition and Dietetics* 116, no. 3 (2016): 501-528. https://doi.org/10.1016/j.jand.2015.12.006.

TrainingPeaks. Accessed February 27, 2026. https://app.trainingpeaks.com.

USA Triathlon. "2025 USA Triathlon Multisport Rules." May 16, 2025. www.usatriathlon.org/multisport/rules.

Wassner Flynn, Sarah. "Recalled: The Origins of the Olympic-Distance Triathlon." *Triathlete*, September 21, 2023. www.triathlete.com/culture/recalled-the-origins-of-the-olympic-distance-triathlon/.

Wassner Flynn, Sarah. "Recalled: Julie Moss Gives Triathlon Its Breakthrough Moment." *Triathlete*, March 14, 2024. www.triathlete.com/culture/recalled-julie-moss-gives-triathlon-its-breakthrough-moment/.

ABOUT THE AUTHOR

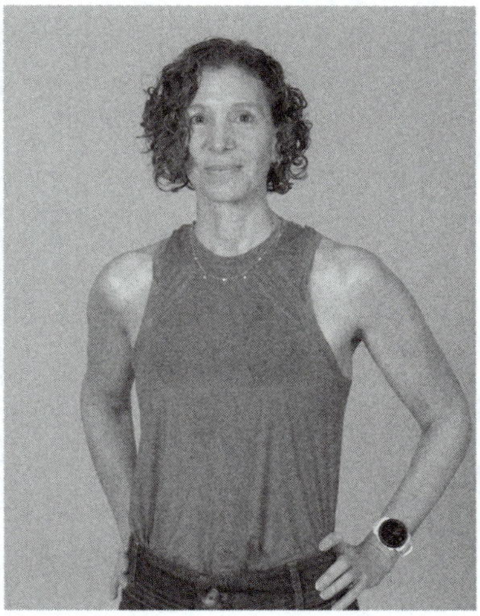

Alison Freeman is a triathlete, writer, and USA Triathlon Level III Coach, and she was named the 2025 USA Triathlon Coach Educator of the Year. Freeman specializes in guiding beginner and intermediate athletes through their first triathlon experiences. She has completed nearly 40 triathlons, including six Ironman events and 15 half-distance events, and has qualified for USA Triathlon Nationals five times. In 2021, she finished fourth in her age group at Ironman Texas.

As cofounder and principal coach at NYX Endurance, Freeman coaches athletes to their first finish lines at sprint-, Olympic-, half-, and full-distance races. She also leads beginner triathlon clinics in Boulder, Colorado, and developed an online course, *The Ultimate Guide to Your First Triathlon*, through NYX Endurance.

Outside of coaching, Freeman is a frequent contributor to Triathlete.com, where she has written over 50 articles on training, skill development, and the athlete mindset. Her articles emphasize clear and practical instruction, and her writing uses a supportive and accessible tone.

Freeman holds a BSE degree from Princeton University and an MBA degree from the University of California, Berkeley.